TO PLEDGE ALLEGIANCE

Reformation
to Colonization

Reformation
to Colonization

AMERICAN VISION

Gary DeMar

with *Fred Douglas Young and Gary L. Todd*

ATLANTA, GEORGIA

First Printing, December 1997

American Vision, Inc.
Post Office Box 724088
Atlanta, Georgia 31139

ISBN 0-915815-29-X

Printed in the United States of America

Cover painting:
N.C. Wyeth
The Mayflower Compact, 1940
Oil with tempera on panel
From the Collection of the University Museums,
Iowa State University
Cover design: James E. Talmage, JET Studio, Inc., Byron, Georgia

The Authors

Gary DeMar is president of American Vision, a Christian educational organization, and editor of *Biblical Worldview* magazine. He has published a number of books, including the three-volume *God and Government* series and *America's Christian History: The Untold Story*. Mr. DeMar received a B.A. from Western Michigan University and a M.DIV. from Reformed Theological Seminary, Jackson, Mississippi.

Dr. Gary L. Todd has eleven years of teaching experience at the college level, including at the University of Illinois, Southern Illinois University, the Illinois Department of Corrections Prison College Program, and the Sichuan College of Education in Chengdu, China. He has published articles on various historical topics. Dr. Todd received his PH.D. in American History from the University of Illinois at Urbana-Champaign.

Dr. Fred Young has taught history for over twenty years at the Westminster Schools in Atlanta, Georgia. His book, *Richard M. Weaver, 1910-1963: A Life of the Mind,* was published by University of Missouri Press in 1995. Dr. Young received his B.A. and his M.A. from Northeast Louisiana University and his PH.D. from Georgia State University.

Historical Consultants

Archie Jones, Ph.D.
Rocky Bayou Christian Academy, Niceville, Florida
Adjunct professor, Saint Leo College
Author of several titles on American history published by
Plymouth Rock Foundation

John McBride, Ph.D.
History Department,
The Baylor School, Chattanooga, Tennessee

Steven A. Samson, Ph.D.
Professor of political science and history,
University of Mary Hardin-Baylor, Belton, Texas

Roger Schultz, Ph.D.
Associate Professor of History,
Virginia Intermont College, Bristol, Virginia

John R. Struck
Twelve-year experience teaching history at the high school level,
Thomas Jefferson High School for Science and Technology,
Fairfax County, Virginia

Rev. Steve Wilkins
Pastor, Auburn Avenue Presbyterian Church in Monroe, Louisiana
Author of the audio tape series *America: The First 350 Years*

Additional Credits

Executive Editor:
Gary DeMar

Editor:
Jane M. Scott

Photo Research:
Gary DeMar, Carol DeMar

Colorization:
Elizabeth Hunt

Design:
James E. Talmage,
JET Studio, Inc.
Byron, Georgia

CONTENTS

PREFACE

REFORMATION TO COLONIZATION

Foundations

History matters because it is the fascinating story of God's dealing with His creation. In this volume of *To Pledge Allegiance,* we present the basic building blocks of history which are needed to serve as a foundation for understanding the awe-inspiring array of pivotal historical events. In some of our sidebars we have let the original historical documents speak for themselves. Think of these sidebars as a textual time machine, an opportunity to hear the makers of your history speak for themselves.

As you read, stop once in a while to think about how God worked the events and ideas together to accomplish His purposes. Then test your understanding with the questions at the end of each chapter. We believe that this textbook will stretch your understanding of how God reformed His church and then providentially led a part of this reformed church into the wilderness to establish new communities and lay the foundation for what would one day become a new nation.

A Word about Names and Dates

As you read through this text, remember that before spelling was standardized, the names of people and places were often spelled in a variety of ways. We have tried to be consistent with spelling, but you may read alternative spelling in other books.

In addition, the dates listed for people's life-spans are sometimes debatable, because records were not always so meticulously kept as they are today. We occasionally precede a set of dates with "c.," which stands for the Latin *circa* ("about" or "around").

Also, the dates in parentheses after the names of monarchs and emperors are the dates of their reigns, not their lifetimes.

From Reformation to Colonization

In 1492, when Christopher Columbus made his voyages of discovery in the western hemisphere, most western Europeans were Roman Catholic. Church councils and the pope claimed to have the final say over what Christians believed and how they behaved. The Roman Catholic Church said that no one could go directly to God, but that people must make all their petitions and praises to God by way of an intermediary, a priest. In order to encourage complete dependence upon Catholic interpretation, the church also prohibited people from reading God's Word for themselves. Therefore, the distribution of Bibles was discouraged, and Bibles which did exist were usually kept as property of the church. Not only were Bibles scarce and expensive, but also nearly all of them were written in Latin—a language generally unknown to the common man.

By the time Europeans began to colonize North America, however, the spiritual tenor of Europe had changed, especially northern Europe. Because of the work of the Reformation, the church embraced the Bible, not fallible men and councils, as the final authority in matters of faith and conduct. This ethical standard revolutionized the way people approached God, the way they approached government, and the way they approached each other. Believers took their petitions directly to God by prayer. They evaluated their governments and monarchs by the standard of Scripture. By the 1600s, the Bible was widely distributed among believers in their own languages. Many sought to create communities of like-minded believers who would put into practice the things they had learned in God's Word. The era of New World colonization had dawned.

CHAPTER

17

The DIVIDING of CHRISTENDOM

Charles v, Holy Roman Emperor

Medals of Charles v

In 1519, King Charles of Spain acquired the title of **Charles v,** Holy Roman Emperor. As emperor, Charles's rule extended far beyond the borders of Spain; it included parts of modern-day Austria, the Netherlands, Switzerland, Germany, Naples, Sicily, and Spanish possessions in the New World. No other European prince since Charlemagne, at the beginning of the ninth century, had possessed so vast a territory.

Charles hoped to reunite Christendom under his leadership and to use this unity to confront the Islamic Ottoman Turkish Empire which threatened Europe from the East. Charles, however, encountered several obstacles to realizing his dream. First of all, his efforts were not popular with other European princes who feared the centralization of political power and the loss of their sovereignty. In addition, the people of Europe identified more with their own nations and rulers than with an empire ruled by a foreign king. This devotion of people to their own nation **(nationalism)** weakened the political and religious unity of Europe and doomed any hope of a revived Roman Empire.

163

T H E   D I V I D I N G   O F   C H R I S T E N D O M

Martin Luther's 95 Theses	Henry viii Splits from Rome	Reign of Queen Elizabeth i Begins	Spanish Armada Destroyed	Signing of Mayflower Compact						
1517	1526	1534	1536	1558	1585	1588	1607	1620	1624
	Tyndale's English New Testament	Calvin's Institutes Published		First Roanoak Settlement		Jamestown, Virginia Founded		Dutch Found New Netherland	

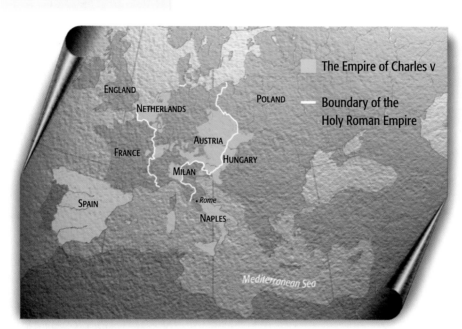

ENGLAND
NETHERLANDS
POLAND
FRANCE
AUSTRIA
HUNGARY
MILAN
• Rome
SPAIN
NAPLES
Mediterranean Sea

The Empire of Charles v

— Boundary of the Holy Roman Empire

The Holy Roman Empire in 1519

Francis i

One of Charles's main conflicts was with the king of France, **Francis i** The two kings were involved in a life-long feud over who should possess the title of Holy Roman Emperor. Charles gained the title through bribery, and Francis never forgave Charles for his deceit. The French king dedicated himself and his armies to the downfall of the empire.

Despite all these challenges, Charles forged ahead with his dream of creating a unified kingdom under the banner of the Roman Catholic Church. He was able to finance his empire-building efforts with the gold and silver that poured into the royal treasury from New Spain.

Changes in Catholic Europe

Spanish explorers and conquistadors who subdued lands and peoples for Spain also brought these territories into the orbit of the Holy Roman Empire and the Roman Catholic Church. But while Cortez and Pizarro were confronting the pagan religious

C H A P T E R   S E V E N T E E N

MASSACHUSETTS BAY FOUNDED	RHODE ISLAND FOUNDED		KING PHILIP'S WAR		GLORIOUS REVOLUTION		GEORGIA FOUNDED	
1629	1634	1636	1649	1675-6	1681	1688	1692	1733	1740-43
	MARYLAND FOUNDED		CHARLES I OF ENGLAND BEHEADED		PENNSYLVANIA FOUNDED		SALEM WITCH TRIALS		GREAT AWAKENING

practices of the Aztecs and Incas, the Roman Catholic Church was being challenged from within by its own religious reformers.

In sixteenth-century Europe, Christianity was defined in terms of Roman Catholic theology. The pope—the bishop of Rome and the self-professed "vicar of Christ"—was considered to be the official representative of Jesus Christ on earth. The pope, claiming the supreme religious authority in Christendom, issued commands binding every king and kingdom to pledge allegiance to his moral order. This resulted in *outward* religious unity.

This external unity could not hide the *inner* corruption that was weakening the church and her authority. Institutions which had been erected to protect the faith—monasteries, the clergy, and even the papacy—were filled with depravity that infected the

Hernando Cortez

Rome, the seat of papal authority

165

T H E   D I V I D I N G   O F   C H R I S T E N D O M

MARTIN LUTHER'S 95 THESES		HENRY VIII SPLITS FROM ROME		REIGN OF QUEEN ELIZABETH I BEGINS		SPANISH ARMADA DESTROYED		SIGNING OF MAYFLOWER COMPACT	
1517	1526	1534	1536	1558	1585	1588	1607	1620	1624
	TYNDALE'S ENGLISH NEW TESTAMENT		CALVIN'S *INSTITUTES* PUBLISHED		FIRST ROANOAK SETTLEMENT		JAMESTOWN, VIRGINIA FOUNDED		DUTCH FOUND NEW NETHERLAND

Rollicking Relics

Roman Catholic clergymen often claimed that they had remains of saints which had magical, holy qualities. Many people believed that if they could get close enough to these relics they could be healed of disease or granted special favors. Of course, they were usually charged a fee to sneak a peek. For a joke, Martin Luther once wrote an anonymous pamphlet which pretended to advertise a new collection of relics. In the pamphlet he described such wonders as half of the angel Gabriel's wing and a piece of the shout which brought down the walls of Jericho.

whole church. To make matters worse, many church leaders overlooked and often protected the offenders. Even Rome, the seat of papal authority and power, was not immune. In fact, it was said that the closer one got to Rome the more corruption one found.

The most serious problem with the church was its doctrinal error. The Bible teaches that the way of salvation is through Jesus Christ *alone.* There is "one mediator…between God and men, the man Christ Jesus" (1 TIMOTHY 2:5). But Rome taught that there were earthly *inter*-mediators that stood between sinners and Christ Jesus—the institutional Roman Catholic Church, its ecclesiastical officials (priests and bishops), and numerous religious ceremonies. A sinner seeking salvation through the church had to go through a priest and perform religious works outlined by him and approved by the church. Acts of penance, prayers to long-dead saints, good works, self-humiliation, fastings, indulgences, devotion to **relics,** vows of poverty, joining a monastic order, and going on holy pilgrimages were just a few of the church requirements. By teaching doctrines contrary to those of Scripture, the Roman Catholic Church erected barriers that kept sinners from experiencing the forgiveness and redemption that God makes available in the work of Jesus Christ.

Ignatius, second-century church father

The Holy Catholic Church

The word *catholic* comes from Latin and means "universal." As a theological term, it means all Christians who make up the church. The Apostles' Creed contains the phrase: "I believe in the Holy Catholic Church," that is, I believe that God's church is universal, incorporating Christians "from every tribe and tongue and people and nation" (Revelation 5:9). The universal or catholic church also encompasses those who have died and gone to be with the Lord. The "Holy Catholic Church" is not the same as the "Roman Catholic Church." The oldest document containing the term *catholic* is a letter by Ignatius from the early second century. He wrote, "Wherever Jesus Christ is, there is the catholic church."

Hocus Pocus and All That

The Roman Catholic Church conducted worship services in Latin, even though the common people could not understand a word of it. As a result, many people held to superstitious religious beliefs, especially about the ceremony of the Lord's Supper. They thought that the priest was something of a magician because he claimed to turn bread and wine into the body and blood of Christ. In fact, the Latin phrase *Hoc est meum corpum*, which means "This is my body," was soon used as a general magic formula and shortened to "Hocus Pocus."

I Beg Your Indulgence

Roman Catholic theologians taught that Jesus, the Virgin Mary, and the saints had accumulated extra good deeds (*works of supererogation*) that the church through the pope could draw on to forgive sins and reduce the amount of time a person would have to suffer in *purgatory.* The church sold these *indulgences* to raise money to purchase church positions (offices) and, in the time of Martin Luther, for constructing St. Peter's Basilica that still stands in Rome today. The origin of indulgences can be traced to the time of the Crusades when church members ventured to the Holy Land searching for ways to gain favor with God.

PURGATORY:
is derived from a Latin word meaning "to purge." The Roman Catholic Church teaches that the sufferings of purgatory are required of sinners before an individual can enter heaven. Nowhere does the Bible even suggest that there is a place called purgatory.

167

THE DIVIDING OF CHRISTENDOM

MARTIN LUTHER'S 95 THESES	HENRY VIII SPLITS FROM ROME	REIGN OF QUEEN ELIZABETH I BEGINS	SPANISH ARMADA DESTROYED	SIGNING OF MAYFLOWER COMPACT
1517	1526	1534	1536	1558	1585	1588	1607	1620	1624
TYNDALE'S ENGLISH NEW TESTAMENT	CALVIN'S *INSTITUTES* PUBLISHED	FIRST ROANOAK SETTLEMENT	JAMESTOWN, VIRGINIA FOUNDED	DUTCH FOUND NEW NETHERLAND

Martin Luther

IN SILENTIO FORTITVDO ET SPE ERIT VESTRA.

Singing for His Supper

Martin Luther was born at
Eisleben, Germany. His family was
so poor that he had to sing in the
streets begging for bread. The
Luthers' poverty did not keep
Martin from excelling at school.
His early educational training took
place at Latin schools where he
received a rigorous education. He
earned his Bachelor's degree in
1502 and his Master's degree in
1505. His father hoped that Martin
would choose a career in law.

A Monk's Monk

While the church had had vocal critics in the past, Wycliffe and
Hus being the most notable, it was an Augustinian monk named
Martin Luther (1483–1546) who took center stage in reform
efforts. Luther seemed an unlikely candidate to confront a
religious superpower when he entered an Augustinian monastery
in 1505. At that time, he had no understanding of the Bible's
central truths regarding forgiveness of sins and salvation by grace
through faith.

Luther entered the monastic life only after he was knocked from his horse by a bolt of lightning. In terror and helplessness, he cried out, "St. Anne, help me! I will become a monk."

Luther knew he was a sinner unworthy of God's love and forgiveness. No matter how long he prayed or fasted or how much penance he performed (and he performed a lot), he never felt that he could be forgiven by an all-holy God who demanded perfection. Even a trip to Rome where he visited the most sacred shrines in Christendom and attended a mass in the pope's own church, did nothing to remove the burden of unforgiven sin and guilt.

Luther's World

Martin Luther grew up in an era of great expectations. The headline news of the time included the following monumental events: Columbus had discovered a New World. Cortez had extended the kingdom of Spain with his exploits in Mexico. The Italian philosopher Niccolo Machiavelli (1469–1527) had written *The Prince* (1513) which emboldened kings to consolidate their political power. The Italian artist Michelangelo (1475–1564) added a new dimension to art with the deeply moving *Pieta,* the splendor of the gigantic *David,* and the sweeping frescoes decorating the Sistine Chapel in Rome. The Polish astronomer Copernicus (1473–1543) was the first to publish a book setting forth his belief that the earth and the other planets revolved around the sun.

Michelangelo

Luther in a thunderstorm

Copernicus

169

T H E   D I V I D I N G   O F   C H R I S T E N D O M

| MARTIN LUTHER'S 95 THESES | HENRY VIII SPLITS FROM ROME | REIGN OF QUEEN ELIZABETH I BEGINS | SPANISH ARMADA DESTROYED | SIGNING OF MAYFLOWER COMPACT |

1517   1526   1534   1536   1558   1585   1588   1607   1620   1624

| TYNDALE'S ENGLISH NEW TESTAMENT | CALVIN'S INSTITUTES PUBLISHED | FIRST ROANOAK SETTLEMENT | JAMESTOWN, VIRGINIA FOUNDED | DUTCH FOUND NEW NETHERLAND |

Savonarola

Bonfire of the Vanities

In 1498, an Italian friar by the name of *Savonarola* sparked a hotbed of debate. He started preaching against the immorality of the people and the corruptions of the church. He gained quite a following, even among state officials, and he eventually assumed power in Florence after his followers threw out the Medici establishment. He established a republic in Florence based on God's law and attempted to purge the society of its immorality. He even required citizens to renounce publicly their sinful lifestyles by throwing profane books, paintings and frivolities onto a bonfire, a "bonfire of vanities."

Rediscovery of Grace

After he returned from Rome to Germany, Luther was sent to study and teach in the little town of Wittenberg, in a part of Germany called Saxony. When he was given the assignment, he wondered how he could teach about the Christian religion when he did not know the answers himself. At Wittenberg, Luther met **Johann von Staupitz (1469?–1524)**, the dean of the theological faculty, who encouraged him to study the Bible in order to find the answers he searched for. Through daily meditation and examination of the Bible, Luther gradually came to realize a single truth that had previously escaped him. It was while studying Paul's letter to the Romans that Luther found the key that unlocked the redemptive story of the Bible. "The just shall live by faith," the apostle Paul wrote (ROMANS 1:17), not by penance, good works, absolution by priests, fasting, or devotion to relics.

For the first time in his life, Luther understood that the whole man has been corrupted by sin and needs God's forgiveness. People are not just guilty of particular sins that can be erased by church-ordained rituals, one by one. Redemption cannot be purchased through good works, penance, or indulgences. Only Jesus Christ can save the whole person, and only faith in Christ can justify the sinner before God. Luther's discovery of these basic biblical truths led him to write, "I felt myself to be reborn and to have gone through open doors to paradise. The whole of Scripture took on a new meaning, and whereas the 'justice of God' had filled me with hate, now it became to me inexpressibly sweet in greater love."

Although still devoted to the Roman Catholic Church, Luther's rediscovery of the grace of God set him on a road to challenge the core of Roman Catholic theology—the authority of the pope and his decrees.

Johann Tetzel

The Wages of Sin

The Catholic Church became so blatant in extorting money from its superstitious flock that roaming monks like Johann Tetzel promised eternal blessings to those who helped expand the treasury of Rome. A common sales jingle went, *"As soon as a coin in the coffer rings, a soul from purgatory springs."* Tetzel told his unsuspecting audiences that an indulgence made the sinner who made the purchase "cleaner than Adam before the fall." Martin Luther sharply criticized the sale of indulgences as "human folly."

Luther discussses the Bible with students of theology

171

T H E   D I V I D I N G   O F   C H R I S T E N D O M

MARTIN LUTHER'S 95 THESES	HENRY VIII SPLITS FROM ROME	REIGN OF QUEEN ELIZABETH I BEGINS	SPANISH ARMADA DESTROYED	SIGNING OF MAYFLOWER COMPACT
1517 1526 1534 1536 1558 1585 1588 1607 1620 1624

TYNDALE'S ENGLISH NEW TESTAMENT   CALVIN'S *INSTITUTES* PUBLISHED   FIRST ROANOAK SETTLEMENT   JAMESTOWN, VIRGINIA FOUNDED   DUTCH FOUND NEW NETHERLAND

Pope Leo x

Divide and Conquer?

"A wild boar has invaded thy vineyard," wrote Pope Leo x in 1520. Certainly the pope was threatened by Luther's challenge to the unbiblical practices which permitted medieval popes to live like kings. But the pope was also looking toward the east where the Ottoman Turks had already conquered the Balkans and were advancing into Europe. A divided Christendom, he feared, might give the Moslem empire just the opportunity it needed to overrun the rest of Europe. Luther could not be allowed to weaken Christian Europe in the face of the advancing Turks.

The Accidental Reformer

The indirect cause of the German Reformation was the papacy's attempt to finance a building project. **Pope Leo x (1475–1521)**, needed large sums of money to offset the costs of a war he was waging and to complete St. Peter's Basilica in Rome. To raise the necessary capital, Pope Leo permitted a Dominican friar **Johann Tetzel (1465?–1519)**, his official representative, to go through Germany selling certificates called **indulgences** that claimed to

Luther and his Ninety-five Theses

MASSACHUSETTS BAY FOUNDED	RHODE ISLAND FOUNDED		KING PHILIP'S WAR		GLORIOUS REVOLUTION		GEORGIA FOUNDED	
1629	1634	1636	1649	1675-6	1681	1688	1692	1733	1740-43
	MARYLAND FOUNDED		CHARLES I OF ENGLAND BEHEADED		PENNSYLVANIA FOUNDED		SALEM WITCH TRIALS		GREAT AWAKENING

pardon sins. A person who held such certificates was told that he could use them for himself or for friends and relatives either living or dead.

Luther found nothing within the Bible that resembled the teaching of the pope and Tetzel. Salvation is by grace through faith (EPHESIANS 2:8). There is no place for the sale of indulgences in God's plan of salvation.

Luther then began preaching against the sale of indulgences and wrote to the church hierarchy hoping to debate the subject. When he did not receive an answer, he posted his written objections in **Ninety-five Theses** (arguments) and nailed the document to the door of the castle church at Wittenberg on October 31, 1517. In this dramatic way, the Protestant Reformation began.

It was not Luther's intention to start a theological revolution. The Theses, he wrote to Pope Leo X, "were meant exclusively for our academic circle here." He admitted that he had no wish to publicize them.

Within two weeks, Luther's challenge to the church had spread throughout Germany. Unknown to Luther, his original Latin document had been translated and circulated to the working class by printers who saw a way to make money. Little did they realize that they were being used by God to spread the good news of the Gospel far and wide. No longer would theological debates be reserved for scholars who argued in theological Latin. Tens of thousands of copies of Luther's writings questioning the authority of the church and the pope to forgive sins were sold throughout Europe. This obscure monk was about to be drawn into an encounter that would change the world forever.

Gutenberg's invention helped spread the Reformation

THE DIVIDING OF CHRISTENDOM

MARTIN LUTHER'S 95 THESES	HENRY VIII SPLITS FROM ROME	REIGN OF QUEEN ELIZABETH I BEGINS	SPANISH ARMADA DESTROYED	SIGNING OF MAYFLOWER COMPACT
1517	1526	1534	1536	1558	1585	1588	1607	1620	1624
TYNDALE'S ENGLISH NEW TESTAMENT	CALVIN'S *INSTITUTES* PUBLISHED	FIRST ROANOAK SETTLEMENT	JAMESTOWN, VIRGINIA FOUNDED	DUTCH FOUND NEW NETHERLAND

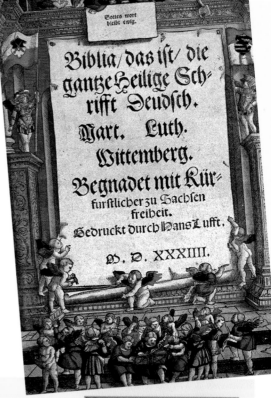

Luther's Able Associate

The Reformation was not a one-man show. Luther had a great deal of help. **Philip Melanchthon** (1497–1560), seated at Luther's left, directed the organizational, educational, and publishing aspects of the Reformation. He also helped Luther translate the Hebrew Old Testament into German.

Title page from Luther's translation of the Bible (1530)

Choosing His Words Carefully

Luther searched for ways to make his translation vivid and memorable as well as accurate. To learn the parts of animals used in sacrifices, he visited a slaughterhouse and watched a butcher kill several lambs. He studied thunderstorms so he could understand the mood of the psalmist when he wrote in PSALM 29:3 that "the God of glory thunders." To translate references in REVELATION 21 to specific precious stones, he asked a friend to "get permission from court to let us have the loan of some to see what they are like." In addition, Luther chose words used in everyday language over academic language used by scholars. As a result, Luther's German became the national language. During Luther's lifetime, more than 100,000 copies of his German New Testament were sold.

C H A P T E R   S E V E N T E E N

MASSACHUSETTS BAY FOUNDED		RHODE ISLAND FOUNDED		KING PHILIP'S WAR			GLORIOUS REVOLUTION		GEORGIA FOUNDED	
1629	1634	1636	1649	1675-6	1681	1688	1692	1733	1740-43
	MARYLAND FOUNDED		CHARLES I OF ENGLAND BEHEADED		PENNSYLVANIA FOUNDED		SALEM WITCH TRIALS		GREAT AWAKENING

Making Hebrew Writers Speak German

Martin Luther's main goal in translating the Bible into German was to make God's Word available in words that men and women use every day. He recognized that "God is in every syllable. No *iota* [the smallest Greek letter] is in vain." Because of Luther's translation, Germany was the first modern nation to adopt a single language over a cluster of regional dialects. Translating the New Testament was relatively easy for Luther. He only needed eleven weeks to complete his German version. The Old Testament, written in Hebrew and some Aramaic, was a different matter. Even with the help of friends, the task of translation took nine years! At one point he considered giving up the task. "How hard it is to make these Hebrew writers talk German," he complained. For example, sixteenth-century Germans had no knowledge of the chameleon. The closest Luther could come was the weasel. His complete German Bible, with a thoroughly revised New Testament translation, was completed in 1534. Before Luther's death in 1546, more than 750,000 copies of his various Bible translations were on the market.

Spouses Anyone?

Not only did Luther confront many Catholic doctrines as they related to salvation, but he also challenged the church's mandate that clergymen could not marry. Luther wrote that priests should be allowed to marry and quickly followed his own advice. In 1525, Luther married a former nun, **Katherina von Bora** (1499–1552), and found marriage most acceptable. Katherina was an excellent businesswoman, housekeeper, and wife, and was such a help to Luther that he sometimes called her "my lord Kate." Luther once said of his wife, "I would not give my Katie for France and Venice together." The Luthers had six children, four of whom survived to adulthood.

At first, Luther's challenge was dismissed by church authorities. The pope called Luther a "drunken German…who will think differently when he is sober." The church had dealt with theological attacks by upstart "reformers" before. Some were imprisoned and others died in the flames of an executioner's fire. But this time things were different. The printing press had changed everything. John Foxe, the sixteenth-century author of the famous *Book of Martyrs* (1563) wrote: "Although through might [the pope] stopped the mouth of John Huss, God hath appointed the Press to preach, whose voice the pope is never able to stop."

Thousands of Germans were now questioning official church doctrines, and the church was forced to respond in terms of reasonable and public debate.

Katherina von Bora

T H E   D I V I D I N G   O F   C H R I S T E N D O M

Martin Luther's 95 Theses		Henry VIII Splits from Rome		Reign of Queen Elizabeth I Begins		Spanish Armada Destroyed		Signing of Mayflower Compact	
1517	1526	1534	1536	1558	1585	1588	1607	1620	1624
	Tyndale's English New Testament		Calvin's *Institutes* Published		First Roanoak Settlement		Jamestown, Virginia Founded		Dutch Found New Netherland

The Peasants' Revolt

While most of Luther's teaching brought controversy that led to positive reform, some of his writings were interpreted in such a way that a revolution was started. Luther wrote that the poor in Germany were oppressed by "lords and princes" and "blind bishops and mad priests and monks." He went on to criticize the nobles for doing "nothing but flay and rob your subjects in order that you may lead a life of splendor and pride, until the poor common folk can bear it no longer." What was the response to these injustices and inequities? Many of the peasants, following the advice offered in the defiant sermons of Thomas Müntzer, called for a revolt. Acting on Müntzer's persuasive but extremist message, they pillaged churches, destroyed castles, demanded the common ownership of all property, and shook the very foundation of society. Luther responded by noting that rebellion is "contrary not only to Christian law and the gospel, but also to natural law and all equity….The fact that rulers are wicked and unjust does not excuse tumult and rebellion; to punish

Frederick the Wise, Martin Luther, and the Wittenberg Reformers stood firm against rebellion

wickedness does not belong to everybody, but to the worldly rulers who bear the sword," as ROMANS 13:4 and 1 PETER 2:13–17 clearly teach. Luther called on both sides—lords and peasants—to work out their grievances. No compromises were forthcoming from either side, however. The peasants revolted and committed atrocities against the populace. Luther was outraged and wrote a tract opposing them: *Against the Robbing and Murdering Peasants.* He counseled the rulers to "smite, slay, and stab, secretly or openly, remembering that nothing can be more poisonous, hurtful, or devilish than a rebel. It is just as when one must kill a mad dog; if you don't strike him, he will strike you, and the whole land with you." It has been estimated that in order to put down the uprising, between 70,000 and 100,000 peasants were killed in Germany in 1525. Clearly, the peasants needed to be freed from their oppressors, but was a bloody revolt the solution? Luther said no. He believed that such revolts lead to the breakdown and the eventual demise of civilized society. It was Luther's desire to "quiet the peasants and instruct the lords…. The peasants were unwilling, and now they have their reward. The lords, too, will not hear, and they shall have their reward also." In Luther's eyes, both sides were in the wrong.

Saying Nope to the Pope

The pope thought that Luther could be convinced that he was wrong, and as soon as he **recanted** his "heretical" beliefs, all would return to normal. The pope believed that Luther's doctrinal questions could be settled in a debate with one of the church's premier theologians, **Johann Maier Eck** (1486–1543), professor of theology at the University of Ingolstadt. Luther and Eck met in 1519 at the University of Leipzig. While Eck appealed to church tradition, church councils, and the infallibility of the pope in the development of church doctrine, Luther appealed to the Bible *alone*. He made it clear that it was possible for popes and church councils to be wrong but that the Bible is always right. Luther's arguments struck at the heart of the church's authority.

After the debate with Eck and subsequent meetings with church officials, Luther realized that the pope would not consider reform on the monk's terms. Luther turned to the state for help, but the Holy Roman Empire, led by Charles V, sided with the Holy Catholic Church. As a dedicated and sincere Catholic, Charles would do anything to prevent his kingdom from being

tainted by what he believed were heretical teachings. Luther then turned for support to the little German state of Saxony and the prince of Saxony, **Frederick the Wise** (1463–1525). He knew that he would need protection for what lay ahead.

Frederick the Wise

Professor Eck

Johann Eck (above) was the man most responsible for Martin Luthur's excommunication. Eck claimed that Luther was a heretic for refusing to recognize a council of church leaders as having the same authority as the Bible. Before he debated Eck, Luther still believed it was possible to reform the church from within. Hearing Eck convinced Luther that the church was too corrupt to be reformed.

THE   DIVIDING   OF   CHRISTENDOM

MARTIN LUTHER'S 95 THESES		HENRY VIII SPLITS FROM ROME		REIGN OF QUEEN ELIZABETH I BEGINS		SPANISH ARMADA DESTROYED		SIGNING OF MAYFLOWER COMPACT	
1517	1526	1534	1536	1558	1585	1588	1607	1620	1624
	TYNDALE'S ENGLISH NEW TESTAMENT		CALVIN'S *INSTITUTES* PUBLISHED		FIRST ROANOAK SETTLEMENT		JAMESTOWN, VIRGINIA FOUNDED		DUTCH FOUND NEW NETHERLAND

In 1521, the pope took more drastic measures and excommunicated Luther. This meant that Luther could no longer receive the sacraments of the church. His reply to the excommunication was to burn it. The pope took the confrontation a step further by calling on Charles v, as emperor of the Holy Roman Empire, to condemn Luther.

In April 1521, Luther stood before the princes of Germany and the Holy Roman Emperor Charles, the self-proclaimed successor of Charlemagne. Luther was shown a stack of his books on a table and asked to take back everything he had written in them. After given time to think about what would be a monumental decision, Luther responded:

Since Your Majesty and Your Lordships ask for a plain answer, I will give you one without either horns or teeth. Unless I am shown by the Bible or reason—I do not trust in Popes and councils since they have often made mistakes—unless I am shown out of the Bible, I neither can nor will take back anything. My conscience is a captive to the Bible, and I cannot go against conscience. God help me. Amen. Here I stand. I cannot do otherwise.

God's Outlaw

When attempts to negotiate broke down, Luther was condemned as a heretic and an enemy of the church. Even so, he was granted safe-conduct back to his home. Charles would later regret that he had not burned Luther at the stake.

As Luther and his traveling companions made their way back to Wittenberg through the Black Forest, armed horsemen appeared out of the shadows and kidnapped him. Frederick the Wise, anticipating an ambush by the king's forces had planned the abduction to keep Luther out of harm's way.

Luther was hidden in one of the king's castles in Wartburg. Because he was an outlaw, anyone could kill him with no fear of being arrested. To disguise himself, Luther let his beard grow and dressed like a knight, taking the title "Knight George." Luther's ministry did not end in retreat, however. He later returned to Wittenberg to continue to work for reforms.

When Martin Luther first challenged the pope on the subject of indulgences, he did not intend to start a new church but rather to reform the existing one. He had hoped to bring the Roman Catholic Church in line with sound biblical teaching. The pope and king refused to heed Luther's appeals.

Luther before the Emperor

179

THE   DIVIDING   OF   CHRISTENDOM

MARTIN LUTHER'S 95 THESES   HENRY VIII SPLITS FROM ROME   REIGN OF QUEEN ELIZABETH I BEGINS   SPANISH ARMADA DESTROYED   SIGNING OF MAYFLOWER COMPACT

1517   1526   1534   1536   1558   1585   1588   1607   1620   1624

TYNDALE'S ENGLISH NEW TESTAMENT   CALVIN'S *INSTITUTES* PUBLISHED   FIRST ROANOAK SETTLEMENT   JAMESTOWN, VIRGINIA FOUNDED   DUTCH FOUND NEW NETHERLAND

Luther at Wartburg Castle

A Mighty Fortress Is Our God

Martin Luther wrote both the words and music of the hymn of Christian

victory through Christ, *A Mighty Fortress Is Our God,* based on Psalm 46.

He wrote the hymn amidst a storm of doctrinal disputes, disease, and

depression. Through all his trials, Luther could ring out in praise that "We

will not fear, for God has willed His truth to triumph through us."

Martin Luther

Luther at home with his family

MASSACHUSETTS BAY FOUNDED	RHODE ISLAND FOUNDED		KING PHILIP'S WAR		GLORIOUS REVOLUTION		GEORGIA FOUNDED	
1629	1634	1636	1649	1675-6	1681	1688	1692	1733	1740-43
	MARYLAND FOUNDED		CHARLES I OF ENGLAND BEHEADED		PENNSYLVANIA FOUNDED		SALEM WITCH TRIALS		GREAT AWAKENING

FOR STUDY

CHAPTER 17:
The Dividing of Christendom

Terms

nationalism
relics
catholic
works of supererogation
purgatory
indulgences
Ninety-five Theses
recanted

People

Charles v
Francis i
Martin Luther
Savonarola
Johann von Staupitz
Pope Leo x
Johann Tetzel
Philip Melanchthon
Katherina von Bora
Johann Maier Eck
Frederick the Wise

When the sixteenth century began, most of the Christian world was united spiritually under the Roman Catholic pope. The Holy Roman Emperor hoped that he could unite it politically under his rule. In a few short years, a "wild boar"—Martin Luther—"invaded the vineyard," shattering forever the outward unity of the church and the hope of political unity. More importantly, Luther and the other reformers led a large segment of the church away from the rule of fallible men toward the rule of infallible Scripture.

Discussion Questions

1. Nationalism is regarded as both a negative and positive force in history. On which side would the leading figures in this chapter—Charles i of Spain, Francis i of France, Martin Luther—have lined up and why?
2. What were the reasons the Roman Catholic Church sold indulgences?
3. Explain how God used technology and capitalism to push Luther's views into the spotlight and help set the Reformation into motion.
4. How did Luther's arguments strike at the heart of the Roman Catholic Church's authority?

Optional Enrichment Projects

1. Read an encyclopedia article about the Ottoman Empire making note of its rise, its influence, and its eventual fall. How has its advance into Europe centuries ago affected the twentieth century?
2. Read several accounts of the Peasants' Revolt. Basing your reasoning on Scripture, support or refute Luther's opinion.
3. Read a biography of Martin Luther written from a Christian viewpoint and another from a secular one. What differences do you notice between them?

THE DIVIDING OF CHRISTENDOM

| MARTIN LUTHER'S 95 THESES | | HENRY VIII SPLITS FROM ROME | | REIGN OF QUEEN ELIZABETH I BEGINS | | SPANISH ARMADA DESTROYED | | SIGNING OF MAYFLOWER COMPACT |

1517 1526 1534 1536 1558 1585 1588 1607 1620 1624

TYNDALE'S ENGLISH NEW TESTAMENT CALVIN'S *INSTITUTES* PUBLISHED FIRST ROANOAK SETTLEMENT JAMESTOWN, VIRGINIA FOUNDED DUTCH FOUND NEW NETHERLAND

Perspectives

The Slogans of Grace

The Reformation was a rediscovery of vitally important biblical truths that swept through Europe and England in the sixteenth century and impacted the founding of America in the seventeenth century.

Sola gratia — *Salvation is by God's **grace alone**.*

Sola Christo — *Salvation does not come by way of the sinner's supposed righteousness, but by **Christ alone**.*

Sola fide — *Salvation is by **faith alone** whereby we receive Christ and his all-sufficient righteousness.*

Soli Deo gloria — *Saving faith takes all merit from the believer and gives all glory of saving the sinner to **God alone**.*

Sola scriptura — *The only source of special written revelation is found in **Scripture alone**, not in the traditions of the church.*

CHAPTER EIGHTEEN

MASSACHUSETTS BAY FOUNDED		RHODE ISLAND FOUNDED		KING PHILIP'S WAR		GLORIOUS REVOLUTION		GEORGIA FOUNDED	
1629	1634	1636	1649	1675-6	1681	1688	1692	1733	1740-43
	MARYLAND FOUNDED		CHARLES I OF ENGLAND BEHEADED		PENNSYLVANIA FOUNDED		SALEM WITCH TRIALS		GREAT AWAKENING

CHAPTER 18

Spreading and Challenging

The REFORMATION

Ulrich Zwingli

The Reformation, which was started by Luther's study of the Bible and his renewed focus on God's grace, was not confined to Germany. Just as Jesus promised that the gospel would spread "even to the remotest part of the earth" (ACTS 1:8), the Reformation expanded beyond the borders of Germany to the Scandinavian countries, Switzerland, France, England, and eventually to America. As we will see, Switzerland served as a stepping stone for dramatic changes in England and the New World.

Zwingli and the Swiss Reformation

Luther was not the only reform-minded churchman in Europe. While he provided the spark that kindled the Reformation, its flames were carried far and wide by others. Prior to the posting of the Ninety-Five Theses in 1517, **Ulrich Zwingli (1484–1531)** was laboring in Switzerland as a pastor. While he never lived as a monk in a monastery or struggled with the justice of God as deeply as Luther did, Zwingli saw similar problems with the Roman Catholic Church.

183

MARTIN LUTHER'S 95 THESES	HENRY VIII SPLITS FROM ROME	REIGN OF QUEEN ELIZABETH I BEGINS	SPANISH ARMADA DESTROYED	SIGNING OF MAYFLOWER COMPACT
1517	1526	1534	1536	1558	1585	1588	1607	1620	1624
TYNDALE'S ENGLISH NEW TESTAMENT	CALVIN'S *INSTITUTES* PUBLISHED	FIRST ROANOAK SETTLEMENT	JAMESTOWN, VIRGINIA FOUNDED	DUTCH FOUND NEW NETHERLAND

When the Going Gets Tough

In 1519, the plague struck Zurich, killing a third of the seven thousand townspeople in a six month period. Instead of escaping the disease-stricken city, Zwingli worked night and day among the sick. As a result, he was struck with the disease and nearly died. After recovering, he became one of the most popular and respected figures in Zurich. Zwingli's devotion to his calling and to the people of Zurich made many receptive to his Reformation message.

Scrambling Theological Eggs

It is said that the Renaissance scholar Desiderius Erasmus (*c.* 1467–1536) "laid the egg which Luther hatched" because he moved Catholicism towards reform. Erasmus was one of the most highly respected scholars of his day. He stressed going back to original sources when studying ancient writings—especially the Bible. In 1506, Erasmus began to lecture on Greek at Cambridge, England, laying the groundwork for the English translation of the New Testament by William Tyndale. His most important contribution to reform efforts was the publication of the Greek New Testament (the first ever published) in 1516—the year before the Reformation began. Luther used the Greek text to produce his German translation of the New Testament, and Zwingli studied Erasmus's works during his last years in Glarus (between 1513 and 1516). Even though Erasmus never left the Catholic Church, he was not opposed to criticizing the pope. His anonymous story *Julius Excluded* tells how the pope (Julius II) dies but cannot get into heaven—how embarrassing!

Like Luther, Zwingli did not start out as a reformer. Out of a desire to serve God, he had pursued a religious calling within the Roman Catholic Church. His study of the Bible, however, led him to some of the same conclusions as Luther—the Bible is the Christian's final authority, and salvation is by grace through faith. Unlike Luther, Zwingli had no formal theological training, although he had studied at the University of Basel where he had received his Master's degree in 1506. He was a self-taught theologian and was influenced by the Renaissance humanist scholar **Desiderius Erasmus** and his emphasis on Roman and Greek classical writers. In time, however, Zwingli moved steadily away from Erasmus's Renaissance positions, although he continued to appreciate and use his work in New Testament studies.

From Basel, Zwingli served as a pastor at Glarus, the chief town of the Swiss state of the same name. After ten years, he moved to Einsiedeln where he witnessed the superstitious worship of relics and saints by his parishioners. Like Luther, he objected to the sale of indulgences and to the unmarried state of priests and believed that these practices contradicted the clear teaching of the Bible.

In 1518, Zwingli was elected as the people's priest in Zurich, one of the leading towns of the Swiss confederation. It was in Zurich, in 1519, that he began to preach through the entire New Testament from the Greek text. The Catholic practice, which had been retained to some degree by Luther, was to read only certain parts of the Bible at worship services each Sunday. In six years, Zwingli had preached through the New Testament, except for the Book of Revelation. It was this emphasis on preaching the whole Word of God that began to spread the fires of reformation in Switzerland.

The Reformation Blues

As a young man, Zwingli displayed an aptitude for music and learned to play six musical instruments. He also composed a number of hymns, one of them about his ordeal with the plague called the "Plague Hymn." The first stanza reads:

Help me, O Lord,
*   My strength and rock:*
Lo, at the door
*   I hear death's knock*

Birthplace of Zwingli

MARTIN LUTHER'S 95 THESES		HENRY VIII SPLITS FROM ROME		REIGN OF QUEEN ELIZABETH I BEGINS		SPANISH ARMADA DESTROYED		SIGNING OF MAYFLOWER COMPACT		
1517	1526	1534	1536	1558	1585	1588	1607	1620	1624
	TYNDALE'S ENGLISH NEW TESTAMENT		CALVIN'S *INSTITUTES* PUBLISHED		FIRST ROANOAK SETTLEMENT		JAMESTOWN, VIRGINIA FOUNDED		DUTCH FOUND NEW NETHERLAND	

Have Sword–Will Travel

A **mercenary** Is a professional soldier hired for service by a foreign country. The word is derived from the Latin *merces,* meaning "reward." For a long time, Zurich's economy had been dependent on supplying these professional soldiers. While a young pastor in Glarus, Zwingli had served as a chaplain with mercenary troops in Italy. During the Italian campaign, Zwingli had witnessed the death of six thousand young Swiss mercenaries in service to the pope. He returned home convinced that "selling blood for gold" was demoralizing and corrupting the people. After preaching against the practice, he was forced to leave Glarus. The magistrates found his preaching against the mercenary trade "embarrassing." In Zurich, Zwingli continued to oppose it, and in 1521, the city officials suspended the practice, risking serious financial harm.

Zwingli Under Fire

Zurich was run by a council of representatives of the people. Unlike Germany, Switzerland was a part of the Holy Roman Empire in name only, and governmental control was maintained at the local level. Its thirteen cantons were united in a loose **confederacy,** each a self-governing mini-republic. Compared to the rest of Europe, Switzerland was the most politically free. Swiss soldiers were considered the best at their trade. Fierce and competent, they were hired as mercenaries by many European monarchs—most notably the king of France and the pope. Even

Swiss mercenaries pass their time at national games while waiting for the emperor's paymaster.

186

Zwingli's copy of Paul's Epistles

so, Zurich, like nearly all of Europe, was a Catholic stronghold, and civil rulers were members of the established church. That is why Roman Catholic religious leaders in the city called on the Zurich council to deal with Zwingli's novel reformational views.

In response, the Zurich City Council called a **disputation** in 1523 to discuss Zwingli's message. The Catholic leaders refused to debate the subject, charging that neither Zwingli nor the council had the right to change Christianity. With Bibles in Latin, Greek, and Hebrew before him, Zwingli defended his position that preaching the pure Gospel of Jesus Christ should continue. He pointed out that as a reformer he only wanted to go back to the Bible. The City Council agreed with his arguments, and Zurich entered the Reformation.

A Man of Greek Letters

Zwingli taught himself Greek and Hebrew so that he would have a better understanding of the Bible. He copied by hand the Apostle Paul's letters from Erasmus's Greek New Testament. He then memorized them in Greek!

187

MARTIN LUTHER'S 95 THESES		HENRY VIII SPLITS FROM ROME		REIGN OF QUEEN ELIZABETH I BEGINS		SPANISH ARMADA DESTROYED		SIGNING OF MAYFLOWER COMPACT	
1517	1526	1534	1536	1558	1585	1588	1607	1620	1624
	TYNDALE'S ENGLISH NEW TESTAMENT		CALVIN'S *INSTITUTES* PUBLISHED		FIRST ROANOAK SETTLEMENT		JAMESTOWN, VIRGINIA FOUNDED		DUTCH FOUND NEW NETHERLAND

Ulrich Zwingli

Not all of Switzerland followed Zurich's lead into the Reformation. Seven of the Swiss cantons remained Roman Catholic, while four embraced Protestantism. Some of the cantons made no decision, hesitating between the two opinions of Rome and the Reformation.

The Radical Reformers

Zwingli's efforts at reform and social stability were sidetracked when a group of disenchanted disciples believed that the Reformation in Zurich had not gone far enough, fast enough. These **radical reformers,** as they came to be known, separated themselves from Zwingli by denouncing the baptism of infants, an observance practiced by the church since the time of the apostles. They called for those who professed faith in Jesus Christ to undergo what they believed would be a "real" baptism. Their critics gave them the name of **Anabaptists** or "rebaptizers."

Throwing Out the Baby with the Baptismal Water

The Reformers believed that infant baptism was a duty for New Testament believers toward their children in the same way that circumcision was a duty for Old Testament believers toward their children (Colossians 2:11–12). Since infants were included in the covenant blessings under the old covenant, the Reformers reasoned, they should not be denied similar covenant blessings under the "better promises" of the new covenant (Hebrews 8:6). Water baptism in the New Testament replaced circumcision in the same way that the bread and wine of the Lord's Supper replaced the Passover lamb. The Anabaptists, however, did not agree. They did not believe in baptizing infants of believing parents and taught that if adult believers had been baptized as babies, they should be baptized again with a "real" baptism.

Zwingli (standing) carried on reform efforts started by Luther

"New Testament Only" Christianity

There was more to the Anabaptist argument than rebaptism, however. The Anabaptists set the stage for a monumental shift in the way society should operate and the role God's Word would play in reforming it. The Anabaptists developed a "New Testament only" theology, arguing that since believers had no impact politically or socially during the New Testament era, Christians today should follow their example and separate themselves from the world. Anabaptists restricted the application of the Bible to the individual believer, the family, and the church. Such a narrow view of the Christian life and a restricted view of the Bible were directly in conflict with reformational principles.

189

MARTIN LUTHER'S 95 THESES		HENRY VIII SPLITS FROM ROME		REIGN OF QUEEN ELIZABETH I BEGINS		SPANISH ARMADA DESTROYED		SIGNING OF MAYFLOWER COMPACT	
1517	1526	1534	1536	1558	1585	1588	1607	1620	1624
	TYNDALE'S ENGLISH NEW TESTAMENT		CALVIN'S *INSTITUTES* PUBLISHED		FIRST ROANOAK SETTLEMENT		JAMESTOWN, VIRGINIA FOUNDED		DUTCH FOUND NEW NETHERLAND	

Thomas Müntzer's Call to Arms

Thomas Müntzer (1489–1525), a radical Anabaptist and a one-time follower of Martin Luther, believed that the second coming of Christ was at hand and that the wicked must be destroyed to prepare the way for the Lord. He called on armed peasants to attack their upper class masters. "I tell you the time has come for bloodshed to fall upon this impenitent and unbelieving world….Why do you continue to let yourselves be led around by your noses? One knows full well and can prove it with Scripture that lords and princes as they now present themselves are not Christians. Your priests and monks pray to the devil and there are ever fewer true Christians. All your preachers have become hypocrites and worshippers of man. Why do you continue to place your hope in them?"

Thomas Müntzer

Reformers like Zwingli believed that even civil government was under obligation to reform itself according to the Word of God; therefore, Christians *must* be involved in politics—and everything else—to make such reforms possible. He wrote that "the secular power is confirmed by the teaching and example of Christ" (see LUKE 20:25; MATTHEW 22:21). The Reformers insisted that the Bible—the whole Bible—speaks to every area of life, to churchmen and statesmen, teachers and students, lawyers and judges, employers and employees. Anabaptists failed to consider that the reason why the first-century church was not politically active was that it operated under the repressive government of Rome. No occupied nation within the Roman Empire, Israel included, had any political role to play (see JOHN 18:28–32).

Later reformers hoped to avoid the two extremes of Roman Catholicism and Anabaptism. Roman Catholicism aspired to merge church and civil government, with the institutional church ruling the State, while Anabaptism taught the complete separation of church and State so that Christians had no role in serving in a civil capacity.

Anabaptist theology went off track because of its faulty view of Scripture. The Reformers criticized the Roman Catholic Church because it made tradition and church councils equal to the Bible as final authorities for the Christian life. In a similar way, the Reformers were critical of the Anabaptists because they also rejected the principle of *sola Scriptura* either by taking away from the Bible's full authority or by placing outside authorities over the Bible.

The Swiss Anabaptists insisted that the final authority for the Christian life and the order of the church was the New Testament alone. Some within this group recognized only the four Gospels as sacred and authoritative and only the words spoken by Jesus Himself, at that. Accordingly, they believed that the Old Testament had almost no role to play in the life of the believer. There were Anabaptists who believed that the "inner word" prompted by the "Spirit" was more authoritative than the Bible. Some within this group claimed they had received direct revelation from God through the Holy Spirit. Often these bits of new "revelation" contradicted the Bible. Still other Anabaptists believed that reason and not Scripture was the source of ultimate authority.

In this painting, Luther holds the Bible before the great men of history, showing them that they all must look to the Scriptures for wisdom in philosophy, theology, politics, science, literature, exploration, and the arts.

Martin Luther's 95 Theses		Henry VIII Splits from Rome		Reign of Queen Elizabeth I Begins		Spanish Armada Destroyed		Signing of Mayflower Compact		
1517	1526	1534	1536	1558	1585	1588	1607	1620	1624
	Tyndale's English New Testament		Calvin's *Institutes* Published		First Roanoak Settlement		Jamestown, Virginia Founded		Dutch Found New Netherland	

Preaching the Whole Counsel of God

Zwingli believed that there was a social dimension to God's Word and that it was the duty of ministers to preach it. He was concerned not just with personal religious reform but also with the reform of society. Heinrich Bullinger, his friend and successor, gives the following report on the content of Zwingli's preaching: "He praised God the Father, and taught men to trust only in the Son of God, Jesus Christ, as Saviour. He vehemently denounced all unbelief, superstition and hypocrisy. Eagerly he strove after repentance, improvement of life and Christian life and faith. He insisted that the government should maintain law and justice, and protect widows and orphans. That people should always seek to retain Swiss freedom."

Zwingli preaching in Zurich Cathedral

Impatient Radicals

To compound their errors, many Anabaptists believed that the world was about to come to an end as they expected Jesus to return in their day to set up an earthly kingdom. Because they believed that Jesus was soon to return to judge the world, they rejected the idea of working for gradual long-term societal reforms. Of course, as history has shown, they were wrong about the timing of Jesus' return.

Some of the more radical of their number believed that they were called on to speed up the judgment process. They formed "Christian" communes in an attempt to set up a truly pure church. Private property was denounced. Everyone was declared to be "equal." Of course, this meant that everyone got paid the same wage no matter how much work they did. Attempts to create a pure church soon turned ugly and violent. In 1534, the town of Münster in Westphalia, a small city-state in Germany near the Netherlands, became a focal point of Anabaptist coercion.

CHAPTER EIGHTEEN

MASSACHUSETTS BAY FOUNDED		RHODE ISLAND FOUNDED		KING PHILIP'S WAR		GLORIOUS REVOLUTION		GEORGIA FOUNDED	
1629	1634	1636	1649	1675-6	1681	1688	1692	1733	1740-43
MARYLAND FOUNDED		CHARLES I OF ENGLAND BEHEADED		PENNSYLVANIA FOUNDED		SALEM WITCH TRIALS		GREAT AWAKENING	

The city of Münster was ruled by a group of self-appointed "prophets." One of them, **Melchior Hoffmann** (1500–1543), claimed to be one of the two witnesses of Revelation 11:3. He urged Anabaptists to give up the principle of non-violence and to establish God's kingdom by force.

A disciple of Hoffmann, **Jan Matthys**, claimed that he was Enoch, sent to prepare the way for Christ's second coming. After the death of Matthys in 1534, **Jan van Leiden** (1509–1536) set himself up as "David," king of the "New Zion," and ruled Münster as an absolute despot. Claiming new revelations from God, he enforced a communistic lifestyle and introduced his own set of laws: all food and valuables were to be distributed by the new government, housing accommodations were based on need, polygamy was forced on women, and those who refused to participate were executed. While Jan van Leiden lived in splendor with his harem, the people of Münster starved. Something had to be done to end this reign of chaos, so Protestant nobles joined Catholic forces and besieged the city. After its fall, the Anabaptist radicals were killed, with "David" among the dead. Providentially, the Anabaptists did not succeed in maintaining control of the city of Münster or steering the direction of the Reformation.

Jan Matthys

Melchior Hoffmann

193

MARTIN LUTHER'S 95 THESES		HENRY VIII SPLITS FROM ROME		REIGN OF QUEEN ELIZABETH I BEGINS		SPANISH ARMADA DESTROYED		SIGNING OF MAYFLOWER COMPACT	
1517	1526	1534	1536	1558	1585	1588	1607	1620	1624
	TYNDALE'S ENGLISH NEW TESTAMENT		CALVIN'S *INSTITUTES* PUBLISHED		FIRST ROANOAK SETTLEMENT		JAMESTOWN, VIRGINIA FOUNDED		DUTCH FOUND NEW NETHERLAND

Jan van Leiden

After the disaster of the Münster episode, a group of peaceful Anabaptists began following the teachings of **Menno Simons** (*c.* 1496–1561), a former priest. The **Mennonites** placed a strong emphasis on pacifism and separation from the world, teaching that Christians cannot serve as magistrates. Unfortunately, this Anabaptist emphasis on separation made its way to America and continues to influence Christian thinking even today. Some of the socialistic and communistic elements of radical Anabaptism are also still with us.

The Mennonite Recovery

In reaction to the radical Anabaptists like Jan Mathys, Jan van Leiden, and Melchior Hoffmann, and their disaster at Münster, Menno Simons (right) opposed the militant nature of the movement. Menno Simons was a Catholic priest from the Netherlands who was attracted to reformational principles through reading Luther and other Reformers. Like many of the radical Reformers before him, he believed that Luther and Zwingli had not gone far enough with their reform efforts. Like Anabaptists in general, Simons stressed adult baptism, no marriage outside the community, withdrawal from the secular world, a distrust of learning, a refusal to take part in politics, and the speedy second coming of Christ. Because the Mennonites were less radical than their sixteenth-century counterparts, they survived efforts by others to suppress their movement. Today's Mennonites are still known for their pacifism.

Heinrich Bullinger

Zwingli's Successor

The Reformation did not stop with Zwingli's efforts. Even his untimely death in 1531 could not curtail the advance of this great movement of God. Although his work was surpassed by his successor at Zurich, **Heinrich Bullinger** (1504–1575), and by the great Genevan reformer, John Calvin, Zwingli remains an important Reformation figure.

From the Desk of Bullinger

After Zwingli's untimely death at age 47, Heinrich Bullinger was chosen to replace him as pastor in Zurich. Bullinger was a prolific writer and competent organizer. More than 12,000 of his letters, written to theological and political leaders throughout Europe, are still in existence. His correspondents included Henry VIII and Edward VI of England. While the center of the Swiss Reformation passed from Zurich to Geneva and John Calvin, Bullinger's influence continued for some forty years among those who followed Zwingli's version of the Reformation.

Drawn and Quartered

Zwingli died in 1531 in a battle between Protestant and Catholic states; fighting to preserve the freedom to preach the Gospel. Three times he was struck down in the heat of battle, but in each case he stood up again. On the fourth occasion, a spear reached his chin, and he fell to the ground. After the battle, when the Protestant forces had withdrawn, Catholic soldiers searched for his body. Upon finding him severely wounded, they asked Zwingli if he wanted a priest. He declined. They then appealed to him to "have the mother of God in his heart" to "call on the beloved saints to plead to God for grace on his behalf." Again he refused. At this, the Catholic soldiers grew impatient and cursed him as an "obstinate and cantankerous heretic" who should get what he deserved. His body was cut in four pieces and burned along with the entrails of pigs.

MARTIN LUTHER'S 95 THESES	HENRY VIII SPLITS FROM ROME	REIGN OF QUEEN ELIZABETH I BEGINS	SPANISH ARMADA DESTROYED	SIGNING OF MAYFLOWER COMPACT

1517	1526	1534	1536	1558	1585	1588	1607	1620	1624

TYNDALE'S ENGLISH NEW TESTAMENT	CALVIN'S *INSTITUTES* PUBLISHED	FIRST ROANOAK SETTLEMENT	JAMESTOWN, VIRGINIA FOUNDED	DUTCH FOUND NEW NETHERLAND

FOR STUDY

CHAPTER 18:
Spreading and Challenging the Reformation

Terms

mercenary
confederacy
disputation
Radical Reformers
Anabaptists
sola Scriptura
Mennonites

People

Ulrich Zwingli
Desiderius Erasmus
Thomas Müntzer
Melchior Hoffmann
Jan Matthys
Jan van Leiden
Menno Simons
Heinrich Bullinger

While Martin Luther was nurturing the Protestant Reformation in the northern German states, Ulrich Zwingli was doing much the same in some of the Swiss cantons. Both Reformers owed a great debt to the Renaissance scholar Erasmus who aided the reform movement greatly by his emphasis on going back to original sources when studying the Bible and by publishing the first Greek New Testament. But others rejected the Reformation principle of sola Scriptura and took their teachings to strange and dangerous extremes. Where wheat is sown, tares also grow.

Discussion Questions

1. What two activities did Zwingli begin in Zurich in 1519 that worked together to spread the Reformation in Switzerland? What might happen if Christians did these two activities regularly today?

2. List the characteristic beliefs of the Radical Reformers (Anabaptists). What effect did these beliefs have on the practices of the radicals? How did others respond to them? What effect do they have on the church and culture in America today?

3. Five important biblical truths formed the basis of the Reformation as it spread through Europe (see page 182). Memorize the Latin phrases and their meanings. Why were these phrases so revolutionary?

Optional Enrichment Projects

1. Use outside sources to trace the general history of the translation of the Bible up to the modern English versions. What important events were occurring in the world at each of these times of new translations?

2. Read more about Desiderius Erasmus's contributions to the Reformation. Why did he not join it?

3. In light of the actions of the Radical Reformers and the Roman Catholic Church, explain the necessity of *sola Scriptura*.

MASSACHUSETTS BAY FOUNDED	RHODE ISLAND FOUNDED	KING PHILIP'S WAR	GLORIOUS REVOLUTION	GEORGIA FOUNDED
1629	1634 1636	1649 1675-6 1681	1688 1692	1733 1740-43
MARYLAND FOUNDED	CHARLES I OF ENGLAND BEHEADED	PENNSYLVANIA FOUNDED	SALEM WITCH TRIALS	GREAT AWAKENING

CHAPTER 19

REUNITING CHRISTENDOM

*John Calvin,
the Genevan Reformer*

The Reformation took deepest root in Geneva, Switzerland, under the leadership of a Frenchman named **John Calvin** (1509–1564). **Calvinism** would prove to be the driving theological force behind New World development in colonial America. While Luther's work set the Reformation in motion, it was Calvin who gave it its fullest expression. The theological issues of justification by faith and *sola Scriptura* had already been settled by the time second generation Reformers like Calvin (right) came on the scene. But Calvin contributed to the advancing Reformation by systematizing reformational doctrines and developing the social and political implications of the Bible.

The French Connection

Calvin was born at Noyon in Picardy, France, on July 10, 1509. His father had planned for him to pursue a career in the church as a priest. At the age of fourteen, he was sent to study at the University of Paris.

197

REUNITING CHRISTENDOM

MARTIN LUTHER'S 95 THESES		HENRY VIII SPLITS FROM ROME		REIGN OF QUEEN ELIZABETH I BEGINS		SPANISH ARMADA DESTROYED		SIGNING OF MAYFLOWER COMPACT
1517	1526	1534	1536	1558	1585	1588	1607	1620	1624
	TYNDALE'S ENGLISH NEW TESTAMENT		CALVIN'S *INSTITUTES* PUBLISHED		FIRST ROANOAK SETTLEMENT		JAMESTOWN, VIRGINIA FOUNDED		DUTCH FOUND NEW NETHERLAND

The Bible Unrivaled

Calvin was a student of Greek and Roman classical literature. His first published work was a commentary on the work of the Roman philosopher Seneca (c. 4 B.C.–65 A.D.). But Calvin maintained that, when compared to the Bible, none of the classical writings could rival God's Word. "Read Demosthenes or Cicero, read Plato, Aristotle, or any others of that class; I grant you that you will be attracted, delighted, moved, and enraptured by them in a surprising manner; but if, after reading them, you turn to the perusal of the sacred volume, whether you are willing or unwilling, it will affect you so powerfully, it will so penetrate your heart, and impress itself so strongly on your mind, that, compared with its energetic influence, the beauties of rhetoricians and philosophers will almost entirely disappear; so that it is easy to perceive something divine in the sacred Scriptures, which surpasses the highest attainments and ornaments of human industry."

Demosthenes (c. 384–322 B.C.), the greatest of the Athenian orators: "Nothing is easier than self-deceit. For what each man wishes, that he also believes to be true."

Cicero (160–43 B.C.), a renowned orator during Rome's Golden Age. Later ages described eloquent rhetoric as Ciceronian. "The shifts of Fortune test the reliablity of friends."

Plato (428–347 B.C.), inspired by Socrates, became one of the world's greatest philosophers. "The life which is unexamined is not worth living."

After Calvin received a Master of Arts degree in 1528, his father redirected his son to pursue a career in law. In his father's opinion, "the legal profession commonly raised those who followed it to wealth." After receiving his doctorate in law in 1531, Calvin returned to Paris to become a classical scholar. His training in the classics prepared him for his later study of the Bible in the original languages.

Sometime between 1532 and 1534, Calvin became a Christian. While his conversion was not as dramatic as that of Luther, it had the same effect. After being "devoted to the superstitions of Popery," Calvin tells us, "God by a sudden conversion subdued and brought my mind to a teachable frame, which was more hardened in such matters than might have been expected from one at my early period of life."

The Lutheran Reformation had spread to France, and many, including Calvin, were influenced and persuaded by its arguments. In 1533, Calvin's friend Nicolas Cop gave an address calling for the church to purify itself and pursue Luther's call of salvation by grace through faith. As one might expect, the message caused alarm in Roman Catholic France. Because of his association with Cop, Calvin had to flee the authorities and remain in hiding for almost a year. Early in 1534, he was twice imprisoned for his faith. Though soon released, Calvin realized that France was too dangerous for him. Later in the year, King Francis I imprisoned hundreds of Protestants, burning thirty-five at the stake, including several close friends of Calvin.

Calvin's house in Noyon, France

Calvinism

Calvinism is the name theologians give to the system of doctrine taught by John Calvin. Calvinists emphasize the sovereignty of God, the authority of the Bible, predestination, and a presbyterian form of church government. Calvin never used the term "Calvinism" to describe his beliefs, preferring instead to think of his ideas as biblical Christianity.

R E U N I T I N G   C H R I S T E N D O M

| MARTIN LUTHER'S 95 THESES | HENRY VIII SPLITS FROM ROME | REIGN OF QUEEN ELIZABETH I BEGINS | SPANISH ARMADA DESTROYED | SIGNING OF MAYFLOWER COMPACT |

1517   1526   1534   1536   1558   1585   1588   1607   1620   1624

| TYNDALE'S ENGLISH NEW TESTAMENT | CALVIN'S *INSTITUTES* PUBLISHED | FIRST ROANOAK SETTLEMENT | JAMESTOWN, VIRGINIA FOUNDED | DUTCH FOUND NEW NETHERLAND |

The Christian's Calling

Calvin revived the dignity of work for everyone by preaching the biblical concept of the Christian's calling or vocation (from the Latin *vocare,* "to call"). Calvin believed that a Christian did not serve God by withdrawing from the world. In fact, true service in God's kingdom meant laboring in a useful occupation—whether minister or musician—with honesty and diligence. "Every individual's line of life," Calvin wrote in his *Institutes,* "is, as it were, a post assigned him by the Lord….There will be no employment so mean and sordid…as not to appear truly respectable, and be deemed highly important in the sight of God."

Mr. Calvin's Opus

After his departure from Paris in January 1535, Calvin went to Basel, Switzerland, to study Christian theology. It was while at Basel that he began working on what would be his most celebrated work, *Institutes of the Christian Religion*. He completed the first edition in 1535 when he was twenty-six, although it was not published until 1536. The *Institutes* was addressed to Francis I, "Most Christian King of France," as a defense of the Christian faith against the charge of "anarchy" and a call to end persecution of Protestants. Calvin wanted to distance his efforts and those of other Protestant Reformers from the Anabaptist movement that had embraced communal living and armed rebellion at Münster. He assured the king that the French Reformers were patriots who opposed economic and political revolution.

Beginning with a study of the knowledge of God and ending with instructions on civil government, the *Institutes* was Calvin's greatest work, his *magnum opus*. For nearly a quarter of a century, he revised, enlarged, and re-organized the material that would become the summation of Reformed theology for generations of Christians. The final edition, published in 1559, was four times the size of the original. It has been described as the most influential work to come out of the Reformation era.

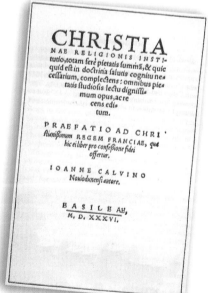

Title Page to Calvin's
Institutes of the Christian Religion

MASSACHUSETTS BAY FOUNDED		RHODE ISLAND FOUNDED		KING PHILIP'S WAR		GLORIOUS REVOLUTION		GEORGIA FOUNDED	
1629	1634	1636	1649	1675-6	1681	1688	1692	1733	1740-43
	MARYLAND FOUNDED		CHARLES I OF ENGLAND BEHEADED		PENNSYLVANIA FOUNDED		SALEM WITCH TRIALS		GREAT AWAKENING

God's Little Detour

From Basel, Calvin hoped to go to Strasbourg, a German free town, to pursue the quiet life of a scholar. However, because of hostilities between Francis I and Charles V and troop movements resulting in blocked roads, he detoured through Geneva, a city with a population of about 10,000 at the time. This providential redirection in July of 1536 changed the life of the young Reformer forever.

Calvin's reputation as author of the *Institutes* had preceded him to Geneva. When **William Farel** (1489–1565), another Reformation exile from France, learned that Calvin was in the city, he

Seal of Francis I

Liberty's Pioneer

At the beginning of the sixteenth century, individual freedom, either political or religious, was virtually unknown. Geneva was a good example. Before the city council had disestablished Roman Catholicism, the church ruled the state through the Roman Catholic bishop. Afterwards, the state ruled the church through the council. When Calvin (right) arrived at Geneva in August 1536, he was confronted with this unbiblical approach to government. Calvin's goal was to establish a church governmentally independent of the council while assuring that the council would not be independent of God's law as it pertained to its civil jurisdiction. His tool in accomplishing this difficult task was the Word of God. He preached and lectured from the Bible every day. He knew that when changes came they would come from the inside out—from the hearts of the people who desired a true Reformation without revolution. Calvin drew a clear line of distinction between the civil magistrate, whose authority was confined to civil matters, and the elders of churches, whose authority was confined to ecclesiastical matters. He established in Geneva the biblical idea of the jurisdictional separation between church and state. Contrary to popular opinion, Calvin did not set up a system of government in which the clergy dominated the city council. He appeared before the council only when he was called on to offer his opinions on theological issues. He never occupied a political or civil office in Geneva; in fact, Calvin did not even become a citizen of Geneva until 1559.

hoped to persuade him to remain and help in reform efforts. At first Calvin refused, informing Farel that he only desired to do the work of a scholar. Farel would not take no for an answer. The fiery Farel threatened Calvin with damnation if he did not dedicate himself to the work of the Lord in Geneva: "I speak in the name of Almighty God. You make the excuse of your studies. But if you refuse to give yourself with us to this work of the Lord, God will curse you, for you are seeking yourself rather than Christ." Calvin decided to stay in Geneva. "I was so terror-struck," Calvin wrote of Farel's ultimatum, "that I gave up the journey I had undertaken."

Farel exhorting Calvin to remain in Geneva

C H A P T E R   N I N E T E E N

MASSACHUSETTS BAY FOUNDED		RHODE ISLAND FOUNDED		KING PHILIP'S WAR		GLORIOUS REVOLUTION		GEORGIA FOUNDED	
1629	1634	1636	1649	1675-6	1681	1688	1692	1733	1740-43
	MARYLAND FOUNDED		CHARLES I OF ENGLAND BEHEADED		PENNSYLVANIA FOUNDED		SALEM WITCH TRIALS		GREAT AWAKENING

Prior to Calvin's arrival, the Geneva city council had officially broken with the Catholic Church, abolished the Sacrifice of the Mass, and called for the removal of all images and relics from the churches. Church properties had been converted to Protestant uses for religion, charity, and education. The council had committed the city to "live according to God's law and God's Word and to abandon idolatry."

"The Frenchman," as Calvin was called, was offered the position of "Professor of Sacred Scripture" by the council. He accepted the position and began a series of reform efforts. As part of his duties, he prepared a confession of faith to be accepted by everyone who wished to be a citizen of Geneva; he planned an educational program for the populace; and he insisted on the biblical doctrine of excommunication for those who broke God's law and refused to repent.

City of Geneva

The Academy of Geneva

Education was a major concern in Geneva. Calvin's most lasting educational achievement was the Academy of Geneva, founded in 1559. Students who entered the school began by learning to read and write French and Latin. They also studied Greek and Latin authors. On Saturdays, students reviewed the week's material and studied the catechism for Sunday instruction. Time set aside for prayer and the singing of psalms from the Bible had a fixed place in the teaching schedule. Those who distinguished themselves in the preparatory grades were permitted to advance to the academy level where they studied Hebrew and expanded their knowledge of Greek. Professors instructed the students in natural science, mathematics, public speaking, law, medicine, and divinity. In keeping with the his belief that all of life is under the jurisdiction of God's Word, students were, in Calvin's words, to prepare "for the ministry as well as for civil government." Students from all over Europe came to Geneva to see what John Knox of Scotland called "the most perfect school of Christ that ever was on earth since the days of the Apostles."

203

MARTIN LUTHER'S 95 THESES		HENRY VIII SPLITS FROM ROME		REIGN OF QUEEN ELIZABETH I BEGINS		SPANISH ARMADA DESTROYED		SIGNING OF MAYFLOWER COMPACT
1517	1526	1534	1536	1558	1585	1588	1607	1620	1624
	TYNDALE'S ENGLISH NEW TESTAMENT		CALVIN'S *INSTITUTES* PUBLISHED		FIRST ROANOAK SETTLEMENT		JAMESTOWN, VIRGINIA FOUNDED		DUTCH FOUND NEW NETHERLAND

Listen Up, Kings!

In Strasbourg, Calvin became friends with Martin Bucer who greatly influenced him theologically. Bucer was a reformer who rarely gets the same attention as Luther, Zwingli, or Calvin. Next to these men, he was the most influential of the Protestant Reformers. He debated the leading Anabaptists, corresponded with Erasmus, helped negotiate with Strasbourg magistrates and German princes, assisted Archbishop Thomas Cranmer with the English Reformation, and became a professor of divinity at Cambridge, England, in 1549. His last work, *De Regno Christi* (*On the Kingdom of Christ*), was dedicated to King Edward VI of England in 1550. In it Bucer stated: "Christian kings and princes, and all governors both can and should firmly restore for their peoples the blessed Kingdom of the Son of God, our only Redeemer, *i.e.*, renew, institute, and establish the administration not only of religion but also of all other parts of the common life according to the purpose of Christ our Savior and supreme King."

Martin Bucer

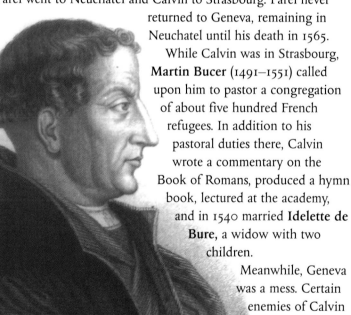

On the Road Again

It was over the issues of a strict moral code and church discipline that Calvin's efforts were opposed. The council believed that it, not the church, should have the authority and power to set the moral agenda and exercise discipline in the church. Calvin maintained that only the church and its government are given the authority to discipline church members.

In 1538, new officials were elected to the council. The **Libertines**, as Calvin described the new leadership, were now in control of the city. The new officers expelled Calvin and Farel. Farel went to Neuchatel and Calvin to Strasbourg. Farel never returned to Geneva, remaining in Neuchatel until his death in 1565.

While Calvin was in Strasbourg, **Martin Bucer** (1491–1551) called upon him to pastor a congregation of about five hundred French refugees. In addition to his pastoral duties there, Calvin wrote a commentary on the Book of Romans, produced a hymn book, lectured at the academy, and in 1540 married **Idelette de Bure,** a widow with two children.

Meanwhile, Geneva was a mess. Certain enemies of Calvin had threatened to return the city to the Roman Catholic Church. This threat, along

Calvin preached twice on Sunday and every morning during the week. Many of his sermons were transcribed and later published.

Calvin and the Lesser Magistrate

Calvin was neither unaware of nor indifferent to tyrannical rulers. He had experienced tyranny first-hand while living in France. While he did not preach the "right of revolution," he did support the belief that **lesser magistrates**—city or provincial governors—could lawfully resist a greater magistrate (*e.g.,* a prince or king) who was oppressing the people. Resistance to tyrants could not be accomplished by "private persons" or "individual citizens," as in the case of the Anabaptists, but rather by legal means and through duly ordained civil authority. This reformational view, developed by Calvin in his *Institutes,* would become the basis of America's struggle for independence with England in the eighteenth century.

with the change in the council leadership, a rise in immorality, the incompetency of the ministers who replaced Farel and Calvin, and pleas from the reform-minded in Geneva, led Calvin to visit the city once again.

205

R E U N I T I N G   C H R I S T E N D O M

MARTIN LUTHER'S 95 THESES	HENRY VIII SPLITS FROM ROME	REIGN OF QUEEN ELIZABETH I BEGINS	SPANISH ARMADA DESTROYED	SIGNING OF MAYFLOWER COMPACT
1517	1526	1534	1536	1558	1585	1588	1607	1620	1624
TYNDALE'S ENGLISH NEW TESTAMENT	CALVIN'S *INSTITUTES* PUBLISHED	FIRST ROANOAK SETTLEMENT	JAMESTOWN, VIRGINIA FOUNDED	DUTCH FOUND NEW NETHERLAND

Playing Cupid

While in Strasbourg serving as a pastor, Calvin began to look for a wife. He asked his friends William Farel and Martin Bucer to help him in his quest. He gave them a list of the desired qualities: "This only is the beauty which allures me—that she be chaste, not too fussy or fastidious, economical, patient, and careful for my health." God in His providence had placed Calvin's future wife in his congregation. Idelette de Bure, her husband Jean Stordeur, and their two children had come to Strasbourg as Anabaptists. After listening to Calvin's faithful exposition of God's Word, as well as having private discussions with Calvin, they embraced his Reformed views and had their youngest child baptized. In the spring of 1540, Jean Stordeur was stricken with the plague and died. A few months later, just as Calvin had almost given up any hope of finding a wife, Bucer asked him to consider Idelette. John and Idelette were married in August 1540. Life was not easy for the Calvins. Idelette was still in her thirties when disease, probably tuberculosis, began to affect her. In 1549, at the age of forty, she died. Calvin was grief-stricken. To a friend he wrote, "You know how tender, or rather, soft my heart is. If I did not have strong self-control I would not have been able to stand it this long. My grief is very heavy. My best life's companion has been taken from me." Calvin was only forty when Idelette died. He never remarried.

William Farel

Back in Geneva

Calvin knew that the job of reforming a city seemingly bent on self-destruction would not be easy. "There is no place in the world that I fear more," he confessed. Immorality was at an all-time high, with gambling, street brawls, drunkenness, adultery, and public indecency common everywhere. But not all was dark. When he arrived on September 13, 1541, a change had come over the city. The people actually wanted him to return. The city officials bestowed honors on him and apologized for the way he had been treated before. The council members assured Calvin that they would co-operate with him to restore the Gospel and moral order. The businessmen of the city were equally relieved to learn that Calvin might be returning. Calvin was overwhelmed by the outward display of affection and decided to remain in Geneva. On September 16th, he wrote to Farel, "Your wish is granted. I am held fast here. May God give His blessing."

Calvin's Contributions

Calvin continued his work of reformation, not by a heavy-handed use of the civil magistrate, but through the preaching of God's Word and the building of the church. Church government was lacking, not only in Geneva, but all over Protestant Europe. Calvin understood that only the church, not the state, could define orthodox theology and bring about true, long-term reform through the preaching of the Gospel. According to the Bible, the state and the church are *jurisdictionally separate.* Each has a God-ordained area of jurisdiction and authority—one civil (the state) and one ecclesiastical (the church). Even so, Calvin insisted, both church and state are ordained by God and obligated to follow His laws as they apply to their specific, appointed jurisdictions.

Calvin's view that God reigns everywhere and over all things led him to develop the biblical idea that man can serve God in every area of life—church, civil government, education, art, music, business, law, journalism. There was no need to be a priest, a monk, or a nun to get closer to God. God is glorified in everyday work and family life. Calvin's teaching led directly to what has become known as the "Protestant work ethic." Individual initiative leads to economic productivity as Christians work out their faith in their callings before God.

Calvin in his study

Persecution Breeds Success

Calvin's view of the relationship between church and state differed somewhat from the views of Luther and Zwingli. Luther and Zwingli tended to consider the state supreme, allowing the civil powers to determine where and how the Gospel would be preached. This often meant that if a certain magistrate was not converted, the city or canton over which he ruled would not receive Reformed preaching. As a result, the Reformation made little progress in areas where magistrates were *not* converted.

Calvin's view brought about different results. The jurisdictional separation of church and state meant that Christianity flourished even where opposition and persecution were most severe. The Reformation's success was not dependent upon a local ruler dictating the religion of his region. Calvinism succeeded in breaking through all national boundaries and making inroads throughout Europe. Finally, it became the driving religious and social force in the settlement and development of America.

Michael Servetus

The Servetus Affair

To this day, Calvin's enemies have used an episode in Geneva's history to discredit the Reformer's work there. This episode concerned a man named **Michael Servetus** (1511–1553), a Spanish scholar, student of medicine, and Anabaptist.

Servetus was a theological troublemaker who pressed his heretical views on the Trinity everywhere he went, comparing the Trinity to Cerebrus, the three-headed dog of Greek mythology. He denounced Trinitarians as heretics. Eventually, Roman Catholic authorities in Spain had ordered his arrest. To hide his identity and avoid the fires of the Inquisition, Servetus changed his name to Michael Villeneuve. Eventually, Servetus was captured,

MASSACHUSETTS BAY FOUNDED	RHODE ISLAND FOUNDED	KING PHILIP'S WAR	GLORIOUS REVOLUTION	GEORGIA FOUNDED	
1629	1634	1636	1649	1675-6	1681	1688	1692	1733	1740-43
	MARYLAND FOUNDED		CHARLES I OF ENGLAND BEHEADED	PENNSYLVANIA FOUNDED	SALEM WITCH TRIALS	GREAT AWAKENING

jailed, and interrogated by Roman Catholic authorities in Vienne, France. Servetus escaped and made his way to Geneva where he arrived on Sunday, August 13, 1553. He was promptly arrested.

Servetus not only denied the Trinity but went about calling for others to deny it as well. Reformers like Calvin believed that it was the duty of the state to establish true religion and to maintain that religion once it was in place. They believed that heretics who refused to repent must be punished. "Their sense of order was horrified by the thought of souls destroyed by false doctrine, of churches torn asunder into parties, of the vengeance of God displayed upon them in war, pestilence, famine." Servetus was asking Christians to worship a different god, in effect attempting to overthrow the existing social and civil order of Geneva and the rest of Europe.

Servetus had also come to Geneva to challenge Calvin's ecclesiastical authority. He most likely planned to work with the Libertines to overthrow Calvin's leadership authority.

The Libertines

Calvin's progress for reform in Geneva was often hampered by battles fought against numerous opponents. A group that gave him persistent trouble was the party of the **Libertines.** The word "libertine" was used to designate a religious sect, widespread in France and the Netherlands, which emphasized reliance on the "Spirit" and rejection of the law. In 1545, Calvin wrote the tract *Against the Fantastic and Raging Sect of the Libertines.* The word "libertine" is of Latin origin and means "to be made free." In the case of the Libertines in Geneva, they wanted to be free from the demands of God's law and the discipline that it requires.

Calvin forbids the Libertines to take the Lord's Supper

R E U N I T I N G   C H R I S T E N D O M

MARTIN LUTHER'S 95 THESES	HENRY VIII SPLITS FROM ROME	REIGN OF QUEEN ELIZABETH I BEGINS	SPANISH ARMADA DESTROYED	SIGNING OF MAYFLOWER COMPACT
1517	1526	1534	1536	1558	1585	1588	1607	1620	1624
TYNDALE'S ENGLISH NEW TESTAMENT	CALVIN'S INSTITUTES PUBLISHED	FIRST ROANOAK SETTLEMENT	JAMESTOWN, VIRGINIA FOUNDED	DUTCH FOUND NEW NETHERLAND

One Man's Opinion

The French historian Jules Michelet (1798–1874) offers a helpful perspective on the Servetus affair: "I went to Geneva myself to form an opinion. As a follower of freedom of thought I was inclined toward Servetus and his friends, the Libertines. However, research in the Geneva archives shows the matter in a different light from what I had conceived it to be through historical works. I gained the conviction from the Council meetings that the Libertines would have surrendered the city to France. This would have been an immeasurable misfortune for Europe."

By that time, Calvin's enemies had gained control of the city, and Servetus probably expected to benefit from the hostility the city council had towards the Reformer. Servetus's plans backfired. The city officials first used Servetus to stir up antagonism toward Calvin's teachings and then to show Calvin that they were in charge—not him.

Geneva had become a haven for hundreds of refugees, but those who came with theological or social revolution on their minds were not welcome. The Genevan authorities did not want the Servetus affair to flare up into a conflict like the siege of Münster (1534) or the failed Peasants' Revolt (1525). They believed that Servetus had to be brought to trial, and, if necessary, executed if he did not recant. Heretics and social revolutionaries were often put to death during that time, and not just in Geneva. In fact, executions were carried out after both the Münster rebellion and the Peasants' Revolt.

The city officials of Geneva were not the only ones hoping to stop Servetus. When Roman Catholic authorities learned that the escaped Servetus was in Geneva, they demanded that he be returned to their jurisdiction. The Geneva city council then offered Servetus a choice: he could either return to Vienne or remain in Geneva. Servetus chose to remain in Geneva and take his chances with Genevan justice. After his trial in Geneva, and after Servetus had consulted with many ministers and magistrates from Zurich, Bern, and Basel, the city council found him guilty of persistent heresy. Calvin asked the council to sentence him to a less painful death, but his request was denied. On the morning of October 27, 1553, Servetus was burned at the stake.

Calvin appeals to Servetus to recant

A Lasting Legacy

Stricken with tuberculosis, Calvin preached his last sermon on February 6, 1564. Although bedridden until his death on May 27, 1564, Calvin continued to work, extending his legacy through the lives of those who sat under his teaching ministry.

Thanks to Calvin's *Institutes of the Christian Religion,* his printed sermons, the Academy, his commentaries on nearly every book of the Bible (except the Song of Solomon and the Book of Revelation), and his pattern of church and civil government, Calvin dramatically influenced Christians around the world. The French Huguenots, members of the Dutch Reformed Church in Holland, the Presbyterians in Scotland, and English Puritans contributed the largest body of immigrants to America. Calvinism became the strongest single religious force in the thirteen colonies.

Calvin on his death bed

REUNITING CHRISTENDOM

| MARTIN LUTHER'S 95 THESES | HENRY VIII SPLITS FROM ROME | REIGN OF QUEEN ELIZABETH I BEGINS | SPANISH ARMADA DESTROYED | SIGNING OF MAYFLOWER COMPACT |

1517   1526   1534   1536   1558   1585   1588   1607   1620   1624

| TYNDALE'S ENGLISH NEW TESTAMENT | CALVIN'S INSTITUTES PUBLISHED | FIRST ROANOAK SETTLEMENT | JAMESTOWN, VIRGINIA FOUNDED | DUTCH FOUND NEW NETHERLAND |

The persecution many people suffered for the sake of the Reformation Gospel caused them to seek refuge in Geneva.

Haven on Earth

The English bishop John Bale, an exile from Protestant persecution under Mary Tudor in 1553, called Geneva "the wonderful miracle of the whole world." It seems that many others held a similar opinion since thousands flocked to the city seeking refuge from persecution. They came from France, England, Italy, Germany, Spain, and Scotland. From 1549 to 1559, more than 5,000 refugees were admitted to Geneva. In addition, after 1555 the Reformation principles taught by the pastors in Geneva began to take root in France, Scotland, and parts of Germany by those who returned to their native countries.

John Adams

The great American historian George Bancroft (1800–1891) stated, "He that will not honor the memory, and respect the influence of Calvin, knows but little of the origin of American liberty." The famous German historian, Leopold von Ranke (1795–1886), wrote, "John Calvin was the virtual founder of America." John Adams, second President of the United States, wrote, "Let not Geneva be forgotten or despised. Religious liberty owes it most respect."

FOR STUDY

CHAPTER 19:
Reuniting Christendom

Terms

Calvinism

*Institutes
of the Christian Religion*

De Regno Christi

Libertines

lesser magistrates

People

John Calvin

William Farel

Martin Bucer

Idelette de Bure

Michael Servetus

While Martin Luther started the Protestant Reformation, John Calvin organized and explained it in a way that had the greatest and most lasting impact. Calvin's preaching and writing took the Reformation to many countries in northern Europe and, through them, to America. He explained why all honest and moral work had value; why both the church and state had their own separate, God-ordained areas of jurisdiction and authority; and why a lesser magistrate, but not an individual, could lawfully resist the tyranny of a greater magistrate like a king. Calvin's ideas laid the foundation for the United States of America.

Discussion Questions

1. Explain the basic ideas of the "Protestant work ethic" as outlined by Calvin.
2. Describe the relation of church and state in Reformed theology.
3. What was the original purpose of Calvin's *Institutes of the Christian Religion?* What did it eventually become?
4. What Christian groups were heavily influenced by Calvin's writings and preaching? What is significant about these groups in relation to America?
5. What was Calvin's view of lawful resistance to tyranny, and how did that come into play in America's revolution of the 1770s?

Optional Enrichment Projects

1. Research the life and influence of one of the lesser-known reformers like Martin Bucer or William Farel.
2. Find another account of the Michael Servetus affair and compare it with the one in this text. How are the major players portrayed? How are the issues defined? Try to learn about the background and beliefs of the author and then explain how these beliefs influenced the way the writer told the story.
3. Look again at the quotations on page 212 from George Bancroft and Leopold von Ranke. Support or refute their contentions about Calvin's influence.

| MARTIN LUTHER'S 95 THESES | HENRY VIII SPLITS FROM ROME | REIGN OF QUEEN ELIZABETH I BEGINS | SPANISH ARMADA DESTROYED | SIGNING OF MAYFLOWER COMPACT |

1517   1526   1534   1536   1558   1585   1588   1607   1620   1624

| TYNDALE'S ENGLISH NEW TESTAMENT | CALVIN'S *INSTITUTES* PUBLISHED | FIRST ROANOAK SETTLEMENT | JAMESTOWN, VIRGINIA FOUNDED | DUTCH FOUND NEW NETHERLAND |

Perspectives

The Protestant Reformers left deep traces of Christian influence upon the political realm and the life of the State, and refused to shun current political affairs. While opposing the Roman Catholic union of Church and State, they did not refrain from action in political matters; they found no scriptural warrant for complete detachment from the political arena. Calvin, in fact, fought the Anabaptists, who contended that Jesus Christ has "nothing to do with civil authority" (*Institutes,* IV, xx, 2). Calvin not only dedicated to King Francis I of France his Institutes, in which he assigned a "most sacred" role to civil authorities (IV, xx, 4), but also extended his political counsel beyond Geneva to the Huguenots in France. Whatever problems may vex contemporary Protestantism in its battle over legitimate or illegitimate involvement in political affairs, a neglect of political duty by Christians is inexcusable.

Carl F. H. Henry

CHAPTER 20

ENGLAND Enters the REFORMATION

England had a head start on the Reformation because of the work of **John Wycliffe** (*c.* 1324–1384). It was Wycliffe who held that the Bible alone (*sola Scriptura*) set forth the definition of true Christianity. Wycliffe's efforts to translate the Bible into the language of the people prepared the way for a Reformation that would take England and the New World by storm.

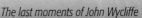
The last moments of John Wycliffe

215

E N G L A N D   E N T E R S   T H E   R E F O R M A T I O N

| MARTIN LUTHER'S 95 THESES | HENRY VIII SPLITS FROM ROME | REIGN OF QUEEN ELIZABETH I BEGINS | SPANISH ARMADA DESTROYED | SIGNING OF MAYFLOWER COMPACT |

1517   1526   1534   1536   1558   1585   1588   1607   1620   1624

| TYNDALE'S ENGLISH NEW TESTAMENT | CALVIN'S INSTITUTES PUBLISHED | FIRST ROANOKE SETTLEMENT | JAMESTOWN, VIRGINIA FOUNDED | DUTCH FOUND NEW NETHERLAND |

Like Luther, Zwingli, and Calvin, Wycliffe's reform efforts did not go unopposed. Thirty-one years after his death, the Council of Constance condemned Wycliffe on 260 different counts, ordered his writings to be burned, and directed that his bones be exhumed and buried in unconsecrated ground. In 1428, on orders from the pope, Wycliffe's remains were dug up and burned. His ashes were thrown into a nearby river. Wycliffe's followers, called **Lollards,** carried on his work under severe persecution from Thomas Arundel, Archbishop of Canterbury, under Henry IV (1399–1413) and Henry V (1413–1422).

Because of continued opposition from the crown and the outlawing of Bible reading in the English language, the Lollards worked in secret. By the late fifteenth century, the Lollards began to grow more bold in their faith. By 1520, it was difficult to distinguish the views of the Lollards from those of the new English Reformers.

Henry V

Little Germany
The earliest Reformation sermons in England that espoused the views of Martin Luther were preached at St. Edward's Church of Cambridge around 1521. Cambridge was a large university town with a prestigious faculty and distinguished student body. In the town, there was a pub

CHAPTER TWENTY

MASSACHUSETTS BAY FOUNDED		RHODE ISLAND FOUNDED		KING PHILIP'S WAR		GLORIOUS REVOLUTION		GEORGIA FOUNDED	
1629	1634	1636	1649	1675-6	1681	1688	1692	1733	1740-43
	MARYLAND FOUNDED		CHARLES I OF ENGLAND BEHEADED		PENNSYLVANIA FOUNDED		SALEM WITCH TRIALS		GREAT AWAKENING

Hugh Latimer (1485–1555) preaching before Edward VI

Luther's writings had a major impact on young English Reformers who met at the White Horse Inn.

called the White Horse Inn which served as a gathering place where intellectuals discussed the latest in Reformation thinking. Because of the popularity of Luther's work there, the pub was given the name "Little Germany."

A number of English Reformers were at Cambridge at this time: William Tyndale, Hugh Latimer, Thomas Cranmer, Nicholas Ridley, and Miles Coverdale. All these men played important roles in establishing the Reformation in England. But the person who had the greatest long-term impact on the developing English Reformation was William Tyndale, "the father of the English Bible."

E N G L A N D   E N T E R S   T H E   R E F O R M A T I O N

MARTIN LUTHER'S 95 THESES		HENRY VIII SPLITS FROM ROME		REIGN OF QUEEN ELIZABETH I BEGINS		SPANISH ARMADA DESTROYED		SIGNING OF MAYFLOWER COMPACT	
1517	1526	1534	1536	1558	1585	1588	1607	1620	1624
	TYNDALE'S ENGLISH NEW TESTAMENT		CALVIN'S *INSTITUTES* PUBLISHED		FIRST ROANOAK SETTLEMENT		JAMESTOWN, VIRGINIA FOUNDED		DUTCH FOUND NEW NETHERLAND

Tyndale's English Becomes the King's English

While only one copy of Tyndale's *original* edition exists intact today, more than forty *subsequent* editions were published, an astonishingly high number for the sixteenth century. Tyndale's translation shaped the development of the English language, which was far from standardized in his day. At the time, many considered the English language the guttural speech of barbarians. Latin remained the language of scholars. Tyndale's translation, however, took the English language and turned it into beautiful prose. He coined new terms like "scapegoat," "longsuffering," and "peacemaker" that remain in use today. Some literary historians claim that at least ninety percent of the King James Version (1611) was lifted directly from Tyndale's translation.

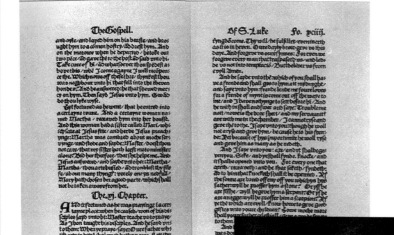

William Tyndale

Bible Smuggler

William Tyndale (*c.* 1494–1536), an Oxford teacher fluent in eight languages, was also an earnest preacher of the Reformed faith. When church officials tried to silence him, Tyndale resolved to translate the Bible into English so the people could read the truth for themselves. He grew convinced that "it was impossible to establish the lay people in any truth, except the Scripture were plainly laid before their eyes in their mother tongue." Tyndale soon learned that such an undertaking was not popular with the clergy or the crown. When a fellow priest advised him, saying, "It would be better to be without God's law than without the pope's law," Tyndale hotly replied to him: "If God spares my life, before many years pass I will make it possible for a boy behind the plow to know more Scripture than you do."

218

Like the Lollards before him, Tyndale had to work under cover. In 1408, a law had been passed against the Lollards forbidding any use of Scripture that was not in Latin. Tyndale's goal to circulate his translation among the people was an extremely dangerous proposition. Working on a translation in secret was one thing, but printing thousands of copies without the knowledge of the authorities was a different matter altogether. In 1524, Tyndale left England for Germany and the city of Hamburg. Sometime in the same year, he traveled to Wittenberg where he sought the help of Martin Luther.

After a number of close calls with officials, Tyndale finally finished his translation of the New Testament, and three thousand copies were printed in the German city of Worms, a city famous for its reformational vitality. The newly printed contraband was smuggled into England in bales of cotton and other merchandise beginning in the spring of 1526. While many of the New Testaments were burned by church and civil officials, other copies found their way into the hands of eager readers.

Tyndale's Judas

By 1535, several Englishmen were looking for Tyndale under orders from the king, Lord Chancellor Thomas More, or Bishop John Stokesley of London. Only one man succeeded in the search: Henry Phillips. His story is a wretched tale of greed, deceit, and betrayal. He had been entrusted with a large sum of money by his father to pay someone in London. Instead of delivering it, he gambled it away. Living the life of a fugitive and desperate for money, he came in contact with someone who wanted Tyndale. Phillips decided to set the trap. He registered as a student and soon gained the confidence of the English merchants, knowing that Tyndale often dined with them. In time, Phillips became acquainted with his prey. After gaining Tyndale's confidence, and even borrowing money from him, Phillips alerted the authorities, in effect handing his "friend" over to the executioners. After his betrayal of Tyndale, Phillips spent the next few years fleeing from the king's agents because of his earlier theft. In 1538, he arrived in Italy as a Swiss mercenary. He was eventually captured and imprisoned. Disowned by his family and country, he died in a filthy prison where John Foxe conjectures he was "consumed at last with lice."

The Lollards' prison

E N G L A N D   E N T E R S   T H E   R E F O R M A T I O N

MARTIN LUTHER'S 95 THESES	HENRY VIII SPLITS FROM ROME	REIGN OF QUEEN ELIZABETH I BEGINS	SPANISH ARMADA DESTROYED	SIGNING OF MAYFLOWER COMPACT
1517	1526	1534	1536	1558	1585	1588	1607	1620	1624
TYNDALE'S ENGLISH NEW TESTAMENT	CALVIN'S *INSTITUTES* PUBLISHED	FIRST ROANOAK SETTLEMENT	JAMESTOWN, VIRGINIA FOUNDED	DUTCH FOUND NEW NETHERLAND

Tyndale remained on the Continent, writing religious tracts and studying Hebrew in preparation for translating the Old Testament into English. Around 1534, he settled in Antwerp, Belgium, where he lived and worked in a house owned by English merchants. A price was then put on Tyndale's head. Bounty hunters, wearing disguises, paid for information that they hoped would lead them to the fugitive translator. In 1535, he was betrayed into the hands of local authorities and agents of Charles v by Henry Phillips, a down-and-out student who professed to be sympathetic to Tyndale's work. After his capture, Tyndale was imprisoned for more than a year at Vilvorde Castle near Brussels. Despite the deplorable conditions, he used his time to revise his New Testament and work on a translation of the books of Joshua through 2 Chronicles.

Henry viii

When Tyndale was brought to trial, he rejected the offer of counsel, knowing that the outcome had already been decided. On October 6, 1536, he was strangled and burned at the stake for heresy. When the executioner was attaching the wire around his throat, Tyndale made his last recorded appeal, a prayer: "Lord, open the king of England's eyes." Though only one intact copy of the first edition of his New Testament exists today, Tyndale's unfailing commitment inspired future translation efforts and greatly helped the Reformation to advance.

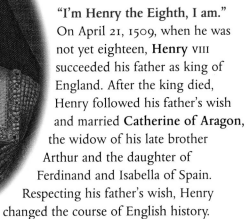

Catherine of Aragon, the first wife of Henry VIII

"I'm Henry the Eighth, I am." On April 21, 1509, when he was not yet eighteen, **Henry** VIII succeeded his father as king of England. After the king died, Henry followed his father's wish and married **Catherine of Aragon,** the widow of his late brother Arthur and the daughter of Ferdinand and Isabella of Spain. Respecting his father's wish, Henry changed the course of English history.

While Tyndale and others struggled with theological issues, Henry worried that he did not have a male heir to succeed him. Catherine had given birth to five children but only one, the Princess Mary, survived beyond infancy. In 1525, the queen was forty, and the prospects of her giving birth again seemed remote. In addition to wanting a male heir, Henry was also infatuated with a lady at court named **Anne Boleyn.**

Henry believed he could justify invalidating his marriage of eighteen years to Catherine by an appeal to the Bible. He took a command from the Book of Leviticus against adultery and applied it to his marital situation: "If there is a man who takes his brother's wife, it is abhorrent…They shall be childless" (20:21). Henry claimed that the reason God had not granted him a male heir was that he was under God's curse. But what he really wanted was a way to get out of his distasteful marriage. In 1527, Henry appealed to Pope Clement VII to invalidate his marriage to Catherine. He argued that Pope Pius II had been wrong to have given him a papal dispensation to marry Catherine in the first place.

Little Boy Blue

Thomas Wolsey (c. 1475–1530) was the son of an English butcher and inn-keeper who gained a string of impressive titles: chaplain to Henry VII and Henry VIII, bishop, Archbishop of York, and cardinal. He also became the pope's personal representative in England. Wolsey, however, had more interest in his own affairs than those of the church. His accumulation of property and wealth made him one of the richest men in England, second only to the king. His greed caused a great deal of resentment among many people. Satirists were quick to poke fun at the portly cardinal with biting lyrics that we recite today as nursery rhymes: "Little Boy Blue, come blow your horn" was written to remind the wealthy cleric of his humble origins, and "the sheep's in the meadow, the cow's in the corn" reminded Wolsey that he was only the son of a butcher.

MARTIN LUTHER'S 95 THESES		HENRY VIII SPLITS FROM ROME		REIGN OF QUEEN ELIZABETH I BEGINS		SPANISH ARMADA DESTROYED		SIGNING OF MAYFLOWER COMPACT	
1517	1526	1534	1536	1558	1585	1588	1607	1620	1624
	TYNDALE'S ENGLISH NEW TESTAMENT		CALVIN'S *INSTITUTES* PUBLISHED		FIRST ROANOAK SETTLEMENT		JAMESTOWN, VIRGINIA FOUNDED		DUTCH FOUND NEW NETHERLAND

Tyndale's Prayer is Answered

Tyndale's dying prayer was that God would "open the king of England's eyes" to accept an English translation of the Bible. A year after Tyndale's death, the king added the following to the title page of the "Matthew Bible": "Set forth with the king's most gracious license." This was the first officially licensed version of the English Bible. In 1538, the king ordered every church in England to display "one book of the whole Bible of the largest volume in English." He also urged the people to learn the Lord's Prayer and the Ten Commandments in English, a practice that sent seven people to the stake in 1519. Whether henry was motivated by spiritual conviction or political expediency (the latter being the most probable), from outward appearances it seemed that God had answered Tyndale's prayer in a dramatic way.

Pope Clement knew that if he submitted to Henry's demand for a divorce, he would offend Catherine's nephew, Emperor Charles V, who was more powerful than the English monarch and who could become a serious political threat. It did not help Henry's cause that the emperor's troops had sacked Rome, captured Pope Clement, and kept him confined. Under these conditions, it was unlikely that the pope would rule in Henry's favor.

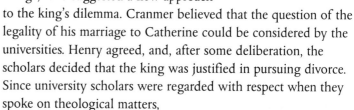

Thomas Cranmer

Henry Splits with Rome

In August 1529, King Henry happened to be visiting relatives in the town of Essex. While there, Henry was introduced to **Thomas Cranmer** (1489–1556), a lecturer in theology at Cambridge, who suggested a new approach to the king's dilemma. Cranmer believed that the question of the legality of his marriage to Catherine could be considered by the universities. Henry agreed, and, after some deliberation, the scholars decided that the king was justified in pursuing divorce. Since university scholars were regarded with respect when they spoke on theological matters, Henry hoped that their opinion would carry weight with the pope and the emperor. But the pope refused to give in. Henry was forbidden to remarry and threatened with excommunication if he did. Even so, Henry was not about to let a pope get in his way.

Thomas Cromwell (c. 1485–1540), a member of Parliament and an early

Thomas Cromwell

CHAPTER TWENTY

MASSACHUSETTS BAY FOUNDED	RHODE ISLAND FOUNDED	KING PHILIP'S WAR	GLORIOUS REVOLUTION	GEORGIA FOUNDED	
1629	1634	1636	1649	1675-6	1681	1688	1692	1733	1740-43
	MARYLAND FOUNDED	CHARLES I OF ENGLAND BEHEADED	PENNSYLVANIA FOUNDED	SALEM WITCH TRIALS	GREAT AWAKENING

supporter of Henry's policies, knew what to do next: disconnect England from papal jurisdiction and settle the issue in England. On January 25, 1533, in defiance of the pope's threat and with the favorable opinion of the universities in hand, Henry secretly married Anne Boleyn. To head off Catherine from making an appeal to Rome, Parliament enacted a **Restraint on Appeals** in March of the same year. The Restraint prohibited appeals to Rome in matrimonial cases. In May, Cranmer, now the newly installed **Archbishop of Canterbury** (the most important church official in England), pronounced the king's first marriage null and void. On June 1, 1533, Cranmer crowned Anne as queen, and shortly thereafter she gave birth, not to a male heir, but to Elizabeth, the future queen of England.

This title page from Gilbert Burnet's History of the Reformation of England *(1679) shows the principal architects of the English Reformation, Henry VIII and Thomas Cranmer*

Anglicana Ecclesia

The next step taken by the king was to proclaim the Church of England officially separate from the Roman Catholic Church and to name himself as its head. In 1534, the **Act of Supremacy** was enacted: "The king's majesty justly and rightly is and ought to be and shall be reputed the only supreme head in earth of the Church of England called *Anglicana Ecclesia,*" the Anglican Church. England now had a national church with Henry as its head.

Henry's marriage to Anne Boleyn was short-lived. On May 19, 1536, Anne was taken to the tower of London and beheaded on rumors that she had committed adultery. Ten days later Henry married **Jane Seymour.** The following year, on October 12, 1537, Jane Seymour gave birth to a son—the future King Edward VI.

ENGLAND ENTERS THE REFORMATION

Martin Luther's 95 Theses		Henry VIII Splits from Rome		Reign of Queen Elizabeth I Begins		Spanish Armada Destroyed		Signing of Mayflower Compact	
1517	1526	1534	1536	1558	1585	1588	1607	1620	1624
	Tyndale's English New Testament		Calvin's *Institutes* Published		First Roanoak Settlement		Jamestown, Virginia Founded		Dutch Found New Netherland

The Great Bible

Miles Coverdale (1488–1568), a frequent participant in discussions at the White Horse Inn, was the publisher of the first complete Bible in the English language. Coverdale (left) worked with Thomas Cromwell in the publication of **The Great Bible,** so named because of its size; its pages measured nine by fifteen inches. The format was so large that no printer in England had the equipment to print it. Coverdale sought out a Paris printer, but before the project could be completed, officials of the Roman Catholic Church interfered. Coverdale safely smuggled the printed sheets, presses, type, and even the printers to London to complete the project. The newly printed and officially sanctioned Bible appeared in 1539. It included this inscription: "Appointed to be read in Churches." The Great Bible never gained wide acceptance, however. It was too big and expensive for use in the home, and its black-letter type was difficult to read.

The More Things Change . . .

Henry's "divorce" from the Roman Catholic Church was a matter of convenience to him, not a matter of doctrinal differences. He had simply relocated all ecclesiastical authority to England while generally keeping the English Church the same theologically as the Roman Church. England had in effect proclaimed itself an empire—a sovereign state free from every foreign authority.

It would not be accurate to say that Henry was a Protestant. In fact, Pope Leo X had given him the title *Defensor Fidei,* "Defender of the Faith" (the Roman Catholic faith). Henry had been bestowed this grand title for criticizing Martin Luther in a pamphlet titled *Assertion of the Seven Sacraments against Martin Luther* (1521). In it, Henry had declared that no punishment could be too great for one who "will not obey the Chief Priest and Supreme Judge on earth," for "the whole Church is subject not only to Christ but . . . to Christ's only vicar, the pope of Rome." Henry's only real

C H A P T E R   T W E N T Y

MASSACHUSETTS BAY FOUNDED		RHODE ISLAND FOUNDED		KING PHILIP'S WAR		GLORIOUS REVOLUTION		GEORGIA FOUNDED	
1629	1634	1636	1649	1675-6	1681	1688	1692	1733	1740-43
	MARYLAND FOUNDED		CHARLES I OF ENGLAND BEHEADED		PENNSYLVANIA FOUNDED		SALEM WITCH TRIALS		GREAT AWAKENING

doctrinal change from when his pamphlet was written was that the last phrase was changed from "the pope" to "the king of England."

In addition to his title as Defender of the Roman Catholic Church, Henry continued to support Roman Catholic doctrines. In 1543, Henry supported the publication of *A Necessary Doctrine and Erudition for Any Christian Man.* This work explained that the English Church continued to support all seven Roman Catholic sacraments, affirmed transubstantiation, and described justification in Roman Catholic terms as a process "of attaining [one's own] justification." True reformation would have to wait until after Henry's death.

Thomas More

No Place to be Found

Thomas More (1478–1535), in addition to being the first layman to serve as lord chancellor to Henry VIII, was an accomplished scholar, writer, and social critic. More's most famous work was a fictional piece about a society he called Nusquarma (1515), "Nowhere." Someone changed the awkward title to the Greek equivalent **Utopia** (*ou* = no + *topos* = place). Today "utopia" refers to any idyllic society that people aspire to create but will never exist this side of heaven. More's fictional society was communistic—"all things being held in common"—and ruled by philosopher-kings patterned after Plato's *Republic*. Was *Utopia* More's view of an ideal society? Probably not. In fact, it looks as if More was actually criticizing communism. He wrote that a society that holds all things in common will never produce an abundance of goods because there will be no incentive to work. Some historians have tried to make the case that More patterned *Utopia* after the Maya civilization of Central America. The theory is possible because the existence of the Maya had been recorded by Columbus on his last voyage in 1502.

225

E N G L A N D   E N T E R S   T H E   R E F O R M A T I O N

MARTIN LUTHER'S 95 THESES	HENRY VIII SPLITS FROM ROME	REIGN OF QUEEN ELIZABETH I BEGINS	SPANISH ARMADA DESTROYED	SIGNING OF MAYFLOWER COMPACT
1517	1526	1534	1536	1558	1585	1588	1607	1620	1624
TYNDALE'S ENGLISH NEW TESTAMENT	CALVIN'S *INSTITUTES* PUBLISHED	FIRST ROANOAK SETTLEMENT	JAMESTOWN, VIRGINIA FOUNDED	DUTCH FOUND NEW NETHERLAND

The Second Josiah

It was actually during the reign of Henry's young son, **Edward** VI (1547–1553), that England made large strides toward Reformation principles. Protestant tutors were put in charge of Edward's education, and at an early age he became familiar with the works of John Calvin and those of the Strasbourg Reformer, Martin Bucer. At Edward's coronation, Cranmer referred to him as the second Josiah, as a king who would restore England to the true religion. (It was under King Josiah's reign in Judah that the "book of the law" was found in the temple—2 KINGS 22).

Under Edward's leadership, a number of important changes took place: religious services were conducted in English, the Catholic Mass was abolished, clergy were permitted to marry, and English Bibles were freely printed. Not everyone was happy with these changes, however. Henry's brand of Catholicism was still very popular, as future Reformers soon discovered.

Edward, sickly and frail from birth with chronic tuberculosis, reigned for only six years. On July 6, 1553, the young king died, praying, "My Lord and God, save this realm from popery, and maintain it in true religion." He was sixteen.

Edward VI, shown seated at right, uses the power of Scripture to crush the pope and the Catholic hierarchy. To the left of the young king hangs a painting depicting Reformers destroying church icons.

"The Nine-Day Queen"

Edward VI was determined to keep the Reformation moving forward in England. He agreed to a daring plan that would cast both of his half-sisters (Mary and Elizabeth) out of the line of succession on the grounds that they were illegitimate. The crown would then pass to **Lady Jane Grey** (1537–1554), the daughter of the Duke of Suffolk and a staunch Protestant. Henry had bequeathed the throne to the duke's heirs in the event that all his children died. Before Edward died on July 6, 1553, he named Lady Jane his successor. Jane was persuaded by her father, father-in-law, and husband to accept the throne, and she was declared queen four days later. However, Mary's support among the people was still strong. Jane's father-in-law, the Duke of Northumberland, mustered troops to face Mary's forces in order to secure the throne for Jane. The attempt failed. Northumberland was captured after his own troops deserted him. He was beheaded, and Jane and her husband were imprisoned. Jane had been declared queen on July 10, 1553, only to have the proclamation repudiated nine days later. Because they were viewed as threats to Mary, Jane and her husband were beheaded in 1554.

Home Sweet Rome

Princess Mary, the only surviving child of Henry VIII and Catherine of Aragon, was dedicated in her allegiance to the Catholic Church and Catholic Spain, the birthplace of her mother. After the death of Edward, Parliament annulled the divorce of Catherine, established Mary's legitimacy to claim the throne, and restored the church to what it had been at the end of Henry VIII's reign. England had gone back to the ways of Rome. On July 19, 1553, Mary was proclaimed Queen of England. Her brief reign (1553–1558) was one of intolerance to everything Protestant. Under Mary's direction, hundreds of Protestants were cruelly executed, which is why many people referred to her as **"Bloody Mary."** Providentially, Mary's attempts to restore Roman Catholicism in England were not successful. Mary died on November 17, 1558, leaving a legacy of bloodshed, but no heir.

Mary I

227

ENGLAND ENTERS THE REFORMATION

MARTIN LUTHER'S 95 THESES   HENRY VIII SPLITS FROM ROME   REIGN OF QUEEN ELIZABETH I BEGINS   SPANISH ARMADA DESTROYED   SIGNING OF MAYFLOWER COMPACT

1517   1526   1534   1536   1558   1585   1588   1607   1620   1624

TYNDALE'S ENGLISH NEW TESTAMENT   CALVIN'S *INSTITUTES* PUBLISHED   FIRST ROANOAK SETTLEMENT   JAMESTOWN, VIRGINIA FOUNDED   DUTCH FOUND NEW NETHERLAND

Nicholas Ridley

The burning of Ridley and Latimer

Hugh Latimer

The Book of Martyrs

John Foxe (1517–1587) was an English Protestant who just barely escaped from Mary I with his life. While he was in exile, Foxe began collecting accounts of martyrdom in England, many from eyewitnesses. Soon he expanded his research, compiling stories of Christian persecution over the centuries. The result of his research was the *Acts and Monuments* (1571), better known as the *Book of Martyrs*, which was one of the most popular books ever published in England. Foxe's emphasis on steadfast Christian faithfulness and the danger of tyranny later struck a responsive chord in America, where his book became one of the top five best-sellers during the colonial period.

Bloody Mary and the Fires of Reformation

History has come to know Mary as "Bloody Mary," a name given to her by John Foxe in his *Book of Martyrs*. More than 270 Protestants, men and women, were burned at the stake for heresy during Mary's short reign. In addition, nearly eight hundred Protestants fled the country and headed for cities sympathetic to the Reformation. Four of Queen Mary's early victims were Bishop John Hooper, John Rogers, Hugh Latimer, and Nicholas Ridley, all of whom were burned at the stake in 1555 for their Protestant beliefs. Hooper was executed for refusing to recant his faith. John Rogers was found guilty of editing the "Matthew Bible" eighteen years earlier. He was condemned at the same trial as Hooper and was burned to death at Smithfield. Latimer and Ridley were burned at the stake together for refusing to recant their Protestant beliefs. As the flames licked up around them, Latimer encouraged his companion with these words: "Be of good comfort, Master Ridley, and play the man. We shall this day light such a candle, by God's grace, in England, as I trust shall never be put out."

C H A P T E R   T W E N T Y

MASSACHUSETTS BAY FOUNDED	RHODE ISLAND FOUNDED	KING PHILIP'S WAR	GLORIOUS REVOLUTION	GEORGIA FOUNDED
1629	1634	1636	1649	1675-6	1681	1688	1692	1733	1740-43
	MARYLAND FOUNDED	CHARLES I OF ENGLAND BEHEADED	PENNSYLVANIA FOUNDED	SALEM WITCH TRIALS	GREAT AWAKENING

Queen Bess Sitting on the Fence

Mary was succeeded by **Elizabeth** I (1558–1603), the daughter of Henry VIII and Anne Boleyn. Elizabeth ruled England for the next forty-five years. During her administration, England was more sympathetic to Protestantism. Unlike Edward VI who chose Protestantism, and Mary, who hoped to return England to her Catholic roots, Elizabeth was a shrewd politician who compromised by choosing the "middle way" (*via media*) between Protestantism and Catholicism. Many Christians felt that the Church of England was not reformed enough and that it should be purified of Roman Catholic corruptions. These Puritans, as their critics called them, wanted a further reformation of the English Church. Ironically, Elizabeth's compromise actually encouraged further reform which would have a dramatic impact on the English colonization of America in the next century.

Elizabeth I

The Reformation in Scotland

The man most closely associated with the Reformation in Scotland is the preacher **John Knox** (1505–1572). Before Knox had made a spiritual impact on the land, however, Scotland was hardened against Protestantism. Patrick Hamilton, a student of Martin Luther who was the first to bring Reformed preaching to Scotland, was burned at the stake for his faith in 1529. After Hamilton's death, Scotland remained a Catholic stronghold for many years.

*John Knox
of Scotland*

One of the reasons why Scotland was so staunchly Roman Catholic was due to its monarchy. James V of Scotland (1513–1542) married a French princess, Mary of Guise. Because of this tie with Catholic France, any movement toward Reformation was firmly opposed.

This dangerous political climate did not stop John Knox from preaching the true doctrines of the faith, but he would pay dearly

229

MARTIN LUTHER'S 95 THESES	HENRY VIII SPLITS FROM ROME	REIGN OF QUEEN ELIZABETH I BEGINS	SPANISH ARMADA DESTROYED	SIGNING OF MAYFLOWER COMPACT
1517	1526	1534	1536	1558	1585	1588	1607	1620	1624
TYNDALE'S ENGLISH NEW TESTAMENT	CALVIN'S *INSTITUTES* PUBLISHED	FIRST ROANOAK SETTLEMENT	JAMESTOWN, VIRGINIA FOUNDED	DUTCH FOUND NEW NETHERLAND

Service as a Bodyguard

John Knox served as a bodyguard for a young preacher named George Wishart (c. 1513–1546). Armed with a two-edged sword (pictured at the far right of the above painting), Knox accompanied Wishart to protect him from Cardinal David Beaton, Archbishop of St. Andrews. In 1544, Beaton executed five Protestants and tried twice to have Wishart killed. Eventually Wishart was executed after he peacefully surrendered to authorities. Wishart was condemned as a heretic, strangled, and burned by order of Cardinal Beaton.

for his loyalty to the Bible. Because of his association with the Reformation movement, he was arrested and made a galley slave on a French vessel. He spent nineteen months chained to a bench and pulling oars. Released in an exchange of prisoners in 1549, Knox then went to England where he preached and eventually became chaplain to Edward VI. After Edward died and Mary I came to the English throne, Knox fled for his life and found refuge in Geneva.

In 1559, Knox returned to Scotland where he became the leader of the growing Reformation movement. He urged Scotland to renounce its French political alliance, embrace Protestantism, and join England under the Reformed banner. Before long, Knox's efforts were rewarded. In August of 1560, Parliament approved the First Scottish Confession and established the Church of Scotland.

But what about the Scottish monarchy? What were they doing while all this reformation was going on? By this time, **Mary Stuart,** the daughter of Mary of Guise, had become queen of the Scots. Although many strongly objected to Knox and his Reformation efforts, Mary's struggle to restore Romanism in Scotland had made her many enemies. Eventually, she was forced to abdicate her throne in 1567 in favor of her son, **James** VI (1567–

C H A P T E R   T W E N T Y

MASSACHUSETTS BAY FOUNDED		RHODE ISLAND FOUNDED		KING PHILIP'S WAR		GLORIOUS REVOLUTION		GEORGIA FOUNDED	
1629	1634	1636	1649	1675-6	1681	1688	1692	1733	1740-43
	MARYLAND FOUNDED		CHARLES I OF ENGLAND BEHEADED		PENNSYLVANIA FOUNDED		SALEM WITCH TRIALS		GREAT AWAKENING

1625), who later became James I of England. Mary fled to England and sought the protection of her cousin, Elizabeth I, but she soon made enemies in England as well. She was eventually imprisoned when several plots against Elizabeth were traced back to her. For this treason, she was beheaded in 1587.

Despite the Catholic leanings of their rulers, the Scottish people embraced the Reformation whole-heartedly. Knox's teaching won the day in Scotland when Protestantism was firmly established by the Scottish Parliament.

James VI of Scotland later became James I of England

Mary Queen of Scots being led to her execution

231

E N G L A N D   E N T E R S   T H E   R E F O R M A T I O N

| MARTIN LUTHER'S 95 THESES | | HENRY VIII SPLITS FROM ROME | | REIGN OF QUEEN ELIZABETH I BEGINS | | SPANISH ARMADA DESTROYED | | SIGNING OF MAYFLOWER COMPACT | |

1517   1526   1534   1536   1558   1585   1588   1607   1620   1624

TYNDALE'S ENGLISH NEW TESTAMENT   CALVIN'S *INSTITUTES* PUBLISHED   FIRST ROANOAK SETTLEMENT   JAMESTOWN, VIRGINIA FOUNDED   DUTCH FOUND NEW NETHERLAND

FOR STUDY

CHAPTER 20:
England Enters the Reformation

Terms
Lollards
Archbishop of Canterbury
Act of Supremacy
The Great Bible
Utopia
Book of Martyrs

People
John Wycliffe
William Tyndale
Henry VIII
Catherine of Aragon
Anne Boleyn
Thomas Wolsey
Thomas Cranmer
Thomas Cromwell
Jane Seymour
Miles Coverdale
Thomas More
Edward VI
Lady Jane Grey
Mary I ("Bloody Mary")
John Foxe
Elizabeth I
John Knox
Mary Stuart, Queen of Scots
James VI of Scotland
(James I of England)

The Reformation moved forward in England through the work of men such as Wycliffe and Tyndale, both of whom suffered great persecution for their stand. When England finally broke with Rome, however, it was not over theology but over a king's unhappy marriage. Although the Church of England rejected the Roman Catholic Church, it was never truly Reformed. This spirit of theological compromise within the Anglican Church provoked a group of reform-minded Christians, "Puritans," to call for the purification of the church. Unlike England, Scotland proved to be fertile ground for the spread of the Reformation, although not without its own bloody conflicts.

Discussion Questions

1. Compare and contrast the disagreement Martin Luther had with the Roman church and the disagreement Henry VIII had with Rome. What were the results?
2. Was Henry VIII a true Protestant? Support your answer.
3. Why did William Tyndale risk his life to translate the Bible into English?
4. Explain why Mary I of England has come down through history as "Bloody Mary."
5. What was unique about the progress of the Reformation in Scotland? What factors made this so?
6. Evaluate Henry VIII's Act of Supremacy (1534) in light of what the Bible states concerning the relationship of civil rulers and the church.

Optional Enrichment Projects

1. What were Rome's reasons for resisting the translation of the Bible into the language of the common man?
2. Read John Foxe's *Book of Martyrs* and write a short report on the life of one of the martyrs from this era.
3. Research the role that English translations of the Bible had in the development of the English language.

C H A P T E R 21

ENGLAND enters
the RACE for AMERICA

England: Tangled up in Roses

For many years, England had eyed the New World with eager interest. In the fifteenth century, King **Henry** VII (1485–1509) of England learned of Columbus's plan to reach the East by sailing across the Atlantic Ocean when the explorer's brother, Bartholomew, appealed to Henry for money to make the voyage. At the time, the king had problems of his own.

For about thirty years, there had been a constant struggle between the House of Lancaster (whose emblem was a red rose) and the House of York (whose emblem was a white rose) in what was called the **War of the Roses.** Both of these royal families wanted to rule the country. The conflict finally ended in 1485 when Henry, who was from the House of Lancaster, defeated the forces of King Richard III of the House of York. As soon as Henry was crowned king in Westminster Abbey, he announced that he was starting a new royal line, the Tudors, which would unite the houses of Lancaster and York. From that moment on, Henry VII was dedicated to two goals: building up the royal treasury and making his throne secure for his successor.

Henry VII

ENGLAND ENTERS THE RACE FOR AMERICA

| Martin Luther's 95 Theses | Henry VIII Splits from Rome | Reign of Queen Elizabeth I Begins | Spanish Armada Destroyed | Signing of Mayflower Compact |

1517 1526 1534 1536 1558 1585 1588 1607 1620 1624

Tyndale's English New Testament   Calvin's *Institutes* Published   First Roanoak Settlement   Jamestown, Virginia Founded   Dutch Found New Netherland

HENRY VII   HENRY VIII   EDWARD VI

Pushing off to the New World

Even though Henry VII had refused to support Columbus, he was interested in reports of the Admiral's voyages. When **John Cabot** (1450–1498), an Italian map-maker and navigator, told the king that he could find a passage around the New World to the Indies, Henry was intrigued. Faced with the lure of eastern wealth, Henry decided that sea exploration might be a wise investment.

When Cabot sailed into the Atlantic Ocean on May 20, 1497, he left without any financial support from Henry. True, the king had agreed to sponsor the voyage, but funding it was a different matter. Cabot left the English shores aboard one tiny vessel with a crew of only eighteen men, including

John Cabot in London

his three sons. The expedition was blessed with smooth sailing and reached the coast of North America on the morning of June 24, 1497.

Like Columbus, Cabot believed that he had sailed to the Indies. He named the place where he landed **Newfound-land** and claimed it for England. After briefly exploring its coast, he returned to England in record-breaking time for a small sailing ship—only fifteen days. The entire trip had taken only eleven weeks.

Henry VII was pleased with the results of Cabot's expedition, but he paid him a mere £10 for his efforts and sent him packing on a second expedition in 1498. This time, Cabot set out with five ships loaded with goods and instructions to start a trading post in Japan. One ship returned. Neither Cabot nor the four remaining ships were ever seen again.

Disappearing without a Trace . . . Almost

A few years after John Cabot disappeared into the unknown, another explorer made his way to the New World where he captured 57 Indians to take back to Europe. The captives had a couple of strange items in their possession: an Italian sword and a pair of earrings. It has been suggested that these items once belonged to Cabot. If so, the Genoese explorer probably experienced a nasty run-in with the natives.

MARTIN LUTHER'S 95 THESES		HENRY VIII SPLITS FROM ROME		REIGN OF QUEEN ELIZABETH I BEGINS		SPANISH ARMADA DESTROYED		SIGNING OF MAYFLOWER COMPACT	
1517	1526	1534	1536	1558	1585	1588	1607	1620	1624
	TYNDALE'S ENGLISH NEW TESTAMENT		CALVIN'S *INSTITUTES* PUBLISHED		FIRST ROANOAK SETTLEMENT		JAMESTOWN, VIRGINIA FOUNDED		DUTCH FOUND NEW NETHERLAND

Henry VIII

A Spanish Claim on England

During the mid-1550s, Philip II was married to Queen Mary I of England, the daughter of King Henry VIII and his first wife Catherine of Aragon. On that basis, Philip believed that he was the rightful heir to the English throne when Mary died.

When Henry VII died in 1509, he was succeeded by his second son, Henry VIII. Henry's attention was so focused on his series of wives and producing a male heir that he gave little notice to overseas exploration. After the death of Henry, his daughter Mary I took the throne. During her reign, she focused on bringing England back to the Roman Catholic Church. She attempted to form an alliance with Catholic Spain by marrying **Philip II** (1556–1598), son of the Holy Roman Emperor Charles V. With these concerns and a war with France occupying her time, overseas expeditions were far from her mind.

Good Queen Bess

It was under Henry other daughter, Elizabeth I, that England entered the race for a new world empire. When Mary died in 1558, Elizabeth became queen. She was twenty-five years old. Elizabeth's reign was a long and prosperous one for England; it was a golden age for industry, art, literature, and exploration. Her nation, and in particular the members of her court, admired the strength of their shrewd female monarch, whom they called the **Virgin Queen** because she never married. She said of herself: "I know I have the body of a weak and feeble woman, but I have the heart . . . of a king." The common people affectionately called her "Good Queen Bess."

Elizabeth's father and grandfather had left her a full treasury and a secure throne, and England was now strong enough to look beyond her shores.

Philip II of Spain

236

Frobisher's departure

Under Elizabeth, England became the most powerful Protestant country in Europe. Daring and venturesome men such as **Sir Francis Drake** (*c.* 1542–1596), **John Hawkins** (1532–1595), and **Martin Frobisher** (1535–1595) became known as the **Elizabethan Sea Dogs.** These men owned private fleets and regularly looted Spanish ships laden with gold and silver, faithfully giving Elizabeth a portion of the plunder. Drake even raided Spanish colonies in America, a leading source of Spanish wealth. On one expedition in 1572, his plunder included thirty tons of silver seized from a Spanish mule train on the Isthmus of Panama. The queen encouraged Drake to disrupt Spanish dominance of the South American coast. The Spanish ambassador protested that it was wicked for the queen to participate in such theft. Elizabeth angrily denied that she was accountable for the actions of the Sea Dogs. After all, they were not English naval officers, but private citizens!

Mirror, Mirror on the Wall

Queen Elizabeth surrounded herself with flattering courtiers, although she never married. She was an extremely vain woman, clothing herself in the most magnificent, extravagant garments. She dyed her hair red, plucked her eyebrows, and painted her face white. Despite all this pampering, she did not grow old gracefully. For one thing, her excessive indulgence in candies like comfits and marchpane eventually blackened her teeth. As she aged, she banned all mirrors from her court.

Don't Bank on It

English explorers were just as convinced as the Spanish and French that they could find a Northwest Passage through the New World to the Orient. Martin Frobisher, who served under Hawkins and Drake in several expeditions, was commissioned by Sir Humphrey Gilbert, an English soldier, navigator, and pioneer colonist in America, to explore the islands and mainland of North America in search of a route to China. After traveling through what later became known as Hudson Strait, Frobisher was certain that he had found his passage—and his fortune. He returned to England with two hundred tons of "gold ore" that turned out to be nothing more than worthless rock.

ENGLAND ENTERS THE RACE FOR AMERICA

MARTIN LUTHER'S 95 THESES		HENRY VIII SPLITS FROM ROME		REIGN OF QUEEN ELIZABETH I BEGINS		SPANISH ARMADA DESTROYED		SIGNING OF MAYFLOWER COMPACT	
1517	1526	1534	1536	1558	1585	1588	1607	1620	1624
	TYNDALE'S ENGLISH NEW TESTAMENT		CALVIN'S *INSTITUTES* PUBLISHED		FIRST ROANOAK SETTLEMENT		JAMESTOWN, VIRGINIA FOUNDED		DUTCH FOUND NEW NETHERLAND

Yes, Sir-ee Francis

The English "Sea Dog" Francis Drake was the first sea captain to survive a voyage around the world. During his voyage, Drake came to the New World, possibly anchoring in the San Francisco Bay. He claimed the new land for England, naming it "New Albion." Queen Elizabeth was so thrilled with Drake's navigational success (and the riches he brought back with him) that she went aboard his ship to meet him upon his arrival. She knighted him on the spot, thus making him *Sir* Francis Drake.

Sir Francis Drake

Sea Dogs Bark, and the Armada Has No Bite

Tension between England and Spain had been growing for some time. The Spanish king, Philip II, argued that he had a right to the English throne since he had been married to Queen Mary I when she was ruling England. He knew that a successful invasion of England would not only end the pesky raids of the English Sea Dogs, but would also widely extend his kingdom, restore England to Roman Catholicism, and give Protestantism a crushing blow.

Philip began using huge resources of gold and silver from the New World to build an invasion fleet. This project, however, suffered a major setback when Sir Francis Drake sailed boldly into the main Spanish harbor of Cadiz and set the fleet on fire, boasting that he had singed the king of Spain's beard! Of course, this gesture only made Philip more determined, and by 1588 his fleet, the **Spanish Armada**, was ready to sail for England. It was the largest invasion fleet that Europe had ever seen, one hundred

MASSACHUSETTS BAY FOUNDED		RHODE ISLAND FOUNDED		KING PHILIP'S WAR		GLORIOUS REVOLUTION		GEORGIA FOUNDED	
1629	1634	1636	1649	1675-6	1681	1688	1692	1733	1740-43
	MARYLAND FOUNDED		CHARLES I OF ENGLAND BEHEADED		PENNSYLVANIA FOUNDED		SALEM WITCH TRIALS		GREAT AWAKENING

and thirty ships. So sure was Philip of its success that he called it the Invincible Armada.

The Armada proved to be not so invincible after all. In a victory which England believed came about because of God's direct intervention, the Armada was destroyed. Smaller English ships outmaneuvered the huge Spanish war vessels and launched fire ships which consumed part of the fleet. Because the English ships had longer range guns, they could avoid close fighting. In addition, an immense storm arose which sent the Armada into the North Sea, forcing the ships to sail around the British Isles. Only half of the Spanish fleet limped back home. The defeat of the Spanish Armada in 1588 was one of the most important naval battles in all of history. From that time on, Spanish naval power waned as England's increased. As a result, English prosperity soared.

From Sea Dog to Knight

John Hawkins (above) was the cousin of Sir Francis Drake and one of Queen Bess's Sea Dogs. He was the first Englishman to traffic in slaves. During 1562–1567, he made three voyages to Africa and carried his slaves to the Spanish colonies in the New World. This was a risky venture since Spain did not permit foreigners to engage in trade with her colonies. On his third voyage, Hawkins was ambushed by Spanish ships off Mexico's coast and barely escaped. After his Sea Dog days, Hawkins was elected to the British House of Commons in 1572. He was knighted in 1588 after serving as rear admiral against the Spanish Armada. Hawkins remained a man of the sea to the end. He died off the coast of Puerto Rico while on an campaign against Spain.

239

ENGLAND ENTERS THE RACE FOR AMERICA

MARTIN LUTHER'S 95 THESES		HENRY VIII SPLITS FROM ROME		REIGN OF QUEEN ELIZABETH I BEGINS		SPANISH ARMADA DESTROYED		SIGNING OF MAYFLOWER COMPACT	
1517	1526	1534	1536	1558	1585	1588	1607	1620	1624
	TYNDALE'S ENGLISH NEW TESTAMENT		CALVIN'S INSTITUTES PUBLISHED		FIRST ROANOAK SETTLEMENT		JAMESTOWN, VIRGINIA FOUNDED		DUTCH FOUND NEW NETHERLAND

Nearer Than He Thought

On his return home from the New World, the fleet of Sir Humphrey Gilbert (above) sailed right into a torrential storm. Gilbert himself was in one of his smallest ships, the *Squirrel*. The ship was quickly swamped and sank with no survivors, but Gilbert remained calm under pressure. Even in the face of disaster, he did not appear frightened, though he knew his death could be imminent. Just before the accident, Gilbert was seen reading a book on deck. He shouted over to another of his ships, "We are as near to heaven by sea as by land."

The Pathfinders

Ten years before the defeat of the Armada, **Sir Humphrey Gilbert** (*c.* 1539–1583) secured a six-year patent from Elizabeth authorizing him to discover, occupy, and take possession of "any remote barbarous and heathen lands not possessed of any Christian prince or people." His first try in 1578 failed. Then, in June of 1583, he made a second voyage, sailing with five ships to an area north of Newfoundland. He was not able to find a suitable place for a colony, so he decided to return to England and try again the following year. On his way back to America, Gilbert's ship was "devoured and swallowed up by the sea." Although he failed to establish a colony in the new world, Humphrey Gilbert was an able pathfinder for England.

Sir Walter Raleigh

MASSACHUSETTS BAY FOUNDED		RHODE ISLAND FOUNDED		KING PHILIP'S WAR		GLORIOUS REVOLUTION		GEORGIA FOUNDED	
1629	1634	1636	1649	1675-6	1681	1688	1692	1733	1740-43
	MARYLAND FOUNDED		CHARLES I OF ENGLAND BEHEADED		PENNSYLVANIA FOUNDED		SALEM WITCH TRIALS		GREAT AWAKENING

In 1584, Gilbert's half-brother, **Sir Walter Raleigh** (*c.* 1552–1618) took up where Gilbert had left off by persuading Elizabeth to revive his half-brother's charter to start a settlement in America. His patent gave him and his heirs the **proprietary right** over all territory they occupied. In return, Raleigh was required to pay to the crown one fifth of all the gold and silver he found. He sent out an expedition led by two of his captains on a voyage of exploration. Philip Amadas and Arthur Barlowe sailed by the Canary Islands to Florida and followed the coast of North America to present-day North Carolina. Sailing back to England, Raleigh's men gave him an encouraging report about friendly Indians and rich soil.

Persuading the Queen

Raleigh then turned to his friend **Richard Hakluyt** (*c.* 1552–1616) and asked him to write a pamphlet to persuade Elizabeth to establish a royal colony in the New World. Hakluyt was an Anglican minister with a passion for spreading the Gospel of Christ and a thorough fascination with geography. It was a perfect combination of interests because cartography (map-making) and the art of navigation were essential for the spread of the Gospel to foreign shores. Hakluyt's pamphlet, *A Discourse of Western Planting,* appealed to national pride, arguing that as the leading Protestant nation of Europe, England should present the "true and sincere religion" to the Indians.

Hakluyt argued that the English should settle the New World quite differently than the Spanish did. Spain had established what were essentially frontier outposts, manned by a few people with little sense of permanence. Hakluyt urged the English to establish permanent settlements in the New World in order to provide more security from Indian attacks and to provide a more solid base for mission work. By living in permanent colonies, missionaries could live peaceably among the Indians,

The Queen's Courtier

Sir Walter Raleigh was a soldier, sailor, explorer, poet, and courtier, a true "Renaissance man." He was a dashing courtier; in fact, it is said that once when Queen Elizabeth had to cross a muddy patch of ground, Raleigh threw down his rich cloak for his queen to step upon. He was promptly rewarded and won the constant favor of a doting queen. But this bold and gallant man was also a scholar of amazing intellect. He never left home without taking with him a trunk full of books. Later, when James I imprisoned him for thirteen years in the Tower of London, Raleigh conducted scientific experiments, composed poetry, and wrote a *History of the World.*

Queen Elizabeth I

MARTIN LUTHER'S 95 THESES	HENRY VIII SPLITS FROM ROME	REIGN OF QUEEN ELIZABETH I BEGINS	SPANISH ARMADA DESTROYED	SIGNING OF MAYFLOWER COMPACT
1517 1526	1534 1536	1558 1585	1588 1607	1620 1624
TYNDALE'S ENGLISH NEW TESTAMENT	CALVIN'S INSTITUTES PUBLISHED	FIRST ROANOAK SETTLEMENT	JAMESTOWN, VIRGINIA FOUNDED	DUTCH FOUND NEW NETHERLAND

learn their language and customs, and convince them of their friendly intentions in order to "distill into their purged minds the sweet and lively liquor of the gospel."

As it turned out, Elizabeth was not interested in spending her money on such a risky venture, but she did agree to let Raleigh name the region Virginia in honor of herself, the "Virgin Queen." At this time, the area called Virginia was a huge territory, stretching from today's South Carolina all the way to Maine.

Samuel Purchas, another Anglican clergyman, echoed the message of English expansion preached by Hakluyt. In two widely-read books, *Purchas His Pilgrimage* and *Hakluytus Posthumous,* Purchas carried on the vision of English colonies for national honor, defense, profits, population growth, and scientific discovery. But for Purchas one theme served as the foundation for all the others: If England is to colonize, she must do so first and foremost "to the glory of God."

Up in Smoke

Sir Walter Raleigh (above with his eldest son) loved a good smoke. In fact, he was instrumental in popularizing tobacco use in England, even though Europe had already been introduced to tobacco (Spanish and French explorers had picked up the habit from pipe-smoking Indians). Legend goes that when Raleigh's servant first saw him puffing away, he thought that Raleigh was on fire and doused him thoroughly with water. Raleigh's name went down in history not only as the name of a city in North Carolina but as the name of a pipe tobacco.

Purchas the Archeologist

Samuel Purchas was not only a devout Christian and an Anglican clergyman, he was a scientist and historian as well. He had a special interest in pre-Columbian civilizations in America. Once while serving as chaplain of the English embassy in Paris, Purchas acquired an ancient Mayan manuscript from the captain of a French cruiser who had captured it on the high seas. He copied this manuscript and published it, thereby adding to our understanding of an ancient Mexican civilization.

MASSACHUSETTS BAY FOUNDED		RHODE ISLAND FOUNDED		KING PHILIP'S WAR		GLORIOUS REVOLUTION		GEORGIA FOUNDED	
1629	1634	1636	1649	1675-6	1681	1688	1692	1733	1740-43
	MARYLAND FOUNDED		CHARLES I OF ENGLAND BEHEADED		PENNSYLVANIA FOUNDED		SALEM WITCH TRIALS		GREAT AWAKENING

FOR STUDY

CHAPTER 21:
England Enters the Race for America

Terms

War of the Roses

Newfoundland

Virgin Queen

Elizabethan Sea Dogs

Spanish Armada

proprietary right

People

Henry VII

John Cabot

Philip II

Sir Francis Drake

John Hawkins

Martin Frobisher

Sir Humphrey Gilbert

Sir Walter Raleigh

Richard Hakluyt

Samuel Purchas

Internal strife, and especially the threat of mighty Spain, kept England from the American shores for nearly a century. Except for the voyages of John Cabot under Henry VII's reign, England had very little contact with the New World until the reign of Elizabeth I. Only a handful of English adventurers, backed secretly by a queen with a vision for the growth of English power, dared challenge Spanish supremacy in the New World. The providential destruction of the Invincible Armada ended Spanish dominance on the high seas and opened the way for English colonization of North America by explorers such as Gilbert and Raleigh.

Discussion Questions

1. Explain why the English could not pay serious attention to the New World until the reign of Elizabeth I.
2. Discuss Hakluyt's and Purchas's statements on the purpose and procedure of English expansion into the New World. Compare and contrast the purposes and practices of the English with those of the Spanish.
3. Who were the Sea Dogs and how did they contribute to the rise of England to a European super-power?

Optional Enrichment Projects

1. One reason the English Sea Dogs were so successful had to do with the influence of ship design on tactics and strategy. Research ship design as practiced by Spain and England during that time. How did the differences affect the outcome of battle?
2. Sir Walter Raleigh was a preeminent man of his age. Read a biography and, if possible, a modern edition of one of his works.
3. The defeat of the Spanish Armada was a defining moment in English and naval history. Read the account by Winston Churchill in his *History of the English Speaking People.* How did this defeat change the course of history?

ENGLAND ENTERS THE RACE FOR AMERICA

MARTIN LUTHER'S 95 THESES	HENRY VIII SPLITS FROM ROME	REIGN OF QUEEN ELIZABETH I BEGINS	SPANISH ARMADA DESTROYED	SIGNING OF MAYFLOWER COMPACT

1517 1526 1534 1536 1558 1585 1588 1607 1620 1624

TYNDALE'S ENGLISH NEW TESTAMENT	CALVIN'S *INSTITUTES* PUBLISHED	FIRST ROANOAK SETTLEMENT	JAMESTOWN, VIRGINIA FOUNDED	DUTCH FOUND NEW NETHERLAND

Perspectives

It remains to be thoroughly weighed and considered by what means and by whom this most godly and Christian work may be performed of enlarging the glorious gospel of Christ, and reducing [leading] of infinite multitudes of these simple people that are in error into the right and perfect way of their salvation. The blessed apostle Paul, converter of the Gentiles, writes in this manner: "Whosoever shall call on the name of the Lord shall be saved. But how shall they call on him in whom they have not believed? and how shall they believe in him of whom they have not heard? and how shall they hear without a preacher? and how shall they preach except they be sent?" (ROMANS 10:10–11) Then it is necessary, for the salvation of those poor people who have sat so long in darkness and in the shadow of death, that preachers should be sent unto them. But by whom should these preachers be sent? By them no doubt who have taken upon them the protection and defense of the Christian faith. Now the Kings and Queens of England have the name of Defenders of the Faith. By which title I think they are not only charged to maintain and patronize the faith of Christ, but also to enlarge and advance the same.

Richard Hakluyt

244

CHAPTER

VIRGINIA LEADS the WAY

Roanoke—Founded and Lost

Despite the fact that Elizabeth I could not be persuaded to invest her wealth in risky New World investments, Sir Walter Raleigh would not give up his dream of establishing a colony, even if he had to pay for it himself. In 1585, Raleigh sent out an expedition of colonists to Virginia to settle on Roanoke Island in Pamlico Sound, in what would someday be North Carolina. After a horrible winter, these settlers abandoned the colony and sailed back to England, catching a ride with Sir Francis Drake, who had been in the area raiding Spanish ships.

Raleigh, furious that these colonists had not stayed, was determined to try again. Since he had spent nearly all of his own money, he had to finance this second try through a **joint stock company:** Investors would buy shares in a company and "share" either the profits if the colony did well or the losses if it did poorly. If the venture failed, no one investor would be saddled with the entire loss. In just one year, Raleigh had established the stock company and had organized another expedition to Virginia.

Sir Walter Raleigh sent out his own expedition of colonists to Virginia

245

V I R G I N I A   L E A D S   T H E   W A Y

MARTIN LUTHER'S 95 THESES	HENRY VIII SPLITS FROM ROME	REIGN OF QUEEN ELIZABETH I BEGINS	SPANISH ARMADA DESTROYED	SIGNING OF MAYFLOWER COMPACT
1517	1526	1534	1536	1558	1585	1588	1607	1620	1624
TYNDALE'S ENGLISH NEW TESTAMENT	CALVIN'S *INSTITUTES* PUBLISHED	FIRST ROANOAK SETTLEMENT	JAMESTOWN, VIRGINIA FOUNDED	DUTCH FOUND NEW NETHERLAND

The word **PLANTATION** originally meant a cutting taken from a parent plant and placed in new ground—what we would call a *transplant.* The word developed to mean a settlement in a new country, and today is used mainly to describe an estate which is cultivated by resident labor.

A Family Affair

John White, who had spent a year in the colony in 1585, headed this new expedition in 1587, leading several families to Roanoke Island. It was an innovative approach to send families to the New World instead of individual adventurers and explorers. The hope was that by establishing a **plantation**, transplanting entire English families, the settlement would have a better chance of surviving and thriving.

The second settling at Roanoke began with high hopes for the future. Shortly after the colonists arrived in America, John White's daughter, Ellinor Dare, gave birth to the first child of English parents in the New World. The baby was named **Virginia Dare.**

After just a month at Roanoke, Governor White sailed back to England for supplies. Raleigh and his company soon got seven ships ready for White to return to Roanoke. Unforeseen events, however, delayed the return because at that very time England was expecting to be invaded by Spain, and it was too risky to let this small group of ships sail. For two years, the supply ships were delayed; it was not until 1590 that the expedition finally made its way back to Roanoke. Upon arrival, the travelers were greeted by the melancholy sight of an abandoned island. This is why the second Roanoke settlement became known as the **Lost Colony.** The only clue as to what might have happened to the settlers was the word **CROATAN** carved on a post and the letters **CRO** on a tree (left). We may never know for sure what happened to these settlers, but descendants of the Croatan Indians say they joined their tribe and over forty names of the Roanoke colonists may be found among them.

246

The Forgotten Translation

John Knox

During the reign of "Bloody Mary," hundreds of English scholars fled the country. A number of them fled to Geneva: Miles Coverdale, Thomas Sampson, William Whittingham, John Foxe, and John Knox. With the protection of the Genevan civil authorities and the support of John Calvin and the Scottish Reformer John Knox, these scholars collaborated to produce an English Bible with notes to explain the meaning of certain texts. In 1560, a complete Bible was published, "translated according to the Hebrew and Greek, and conferred with the best translations in divers [many] languages." The **Geneva Bible** was born. While other English translations failed to capture the hearts of the reading public, the Geneva Bible was instantly popular. Between 1560 and 1644, at least 144 editions appeared. King James I did not like the Geneva Bible because of its strong Reformed theology. He especially disliked the way it condemned ungodly rulers. A marginal note for Exodus 1:19 (below right) stated that the Hebrew midwives were correct in disobeying the Egyptian king's orders to kill the Hebrew babies. A note on 2 Chronicles 15:16 (below left) said that King Asa should have had his mother executed and not merely deposed for the crime of worshipping an idol. The king considered these notes to be a political threat to his kingdom. "I profess," he said, "I could never yet see a Bible well translated in English; but I think that, of all, that of Geneva is the worst." Because of his distaste for the Geneva Bible, King James arranged for a new translation without Calvinistic notes. The new translation became known as the **King James Version** (1611).

V I R G I N I A   L E A D S   T H E   W A Y

MARTIN LUTHER'S 95 THESES	HENRY VIII SPLITS FROM ROME	REIGN OF QUEEN ELIZABETH I BEGINS	SPANISH ARMADA DESTROYED	SIGNING OF MAYFLOWER COMPACT
1517 **1526**	**1534** **1536**	**1558** **1585**	**1588** **1607**	**1620** **1624**
TYNDALE'S ENGLISH NEW TESTAMENT	CALVIN'S *INSTITUTES* PUBLISHED	FIRST ROANOAK SETTLEMENT	JAMESTOWN, VIRGINIA FOUNDED	DUTCH FOUND NEW NETHERLAND

James I

James Pitches into the New World

When Queen Elizabeth died in 1603 after a long reign of forty-five years, she was succeeded by her cousin, James VI of Scotland, who became **James** I (1603–1625) of England. Thus began the reign of the Stuart line of kings. James had visions of extending England's domain in the New World, so in 1606 he granted a charter to a joint stock company, the **Virginia Company** of London. The Virginia Company included two groups of investors who planned to plant colonies in America: the **London Group,** which wanted to settle the southern part of Virginia, and the **Plymouth Group,** which had an eye on northern Virginia.

The charter created the London and Plymouth companies and gave the owners distinct regional jurisdictions. Impatient to get their colonies planted, both companies moved quickly. The Plymouth group arrived first, starting a colony in 1607 at the mouth of the Kennebec River in Maine (of course it was still called Virginia, not Maine, back then). The colony lasted only one winter; poor crops and deaths shut the group down. Shortly afterwards, the London group sponsored an expedition to southern Virginia. In 1607, a group of 104 men commanded by Captain Christopher Newport set sail in three ships, the *Susan Constant,* the *Godspeed,* and the *Discovery.* After three months of rough seas, the ships sailed into Chesapeake Bay and up a wide river which they named the **James** in honor of their king. They chose a place for their settlement, which they named **Jamestown.** This was the first permanent English settlement in North America.

Landing at Jamestown

248

The Gunpowder Plot

Two years before the settlement of Jamestown, a group of Catholic conspirators (above) plotted to assassinate King James I and members of Parliament by blowing up the House of Lords and the House of Commons. By destroying the government, they hoped to recapture the crown and return the country to Roman Catholicism. The conspirators rented a house immediately adjoining Parliament. Thirty-six barrels of gun powder were placed in a cellar under the House of Lords, where King James was to address Parliament on November 5, 1605. Iron bars and huge stones were placed over the mound of powder to increase the destructive force of the blast. The volatile concoction was then hidden under coal and wood. When the fateful day arrived, nothing happened. An anonymous letter had been sent to the parliamentary leader warning him not to attend the forthcoming session of Parliament, and the plot was exposed. **Guy Fawkes,** one of the conspirators, was arrested as he entered the cellar before the planned explosion. Fawkes and seven others were eventually tried and executed. To this day, every year on November 5, England celebrates Guy Fawkes Day by setting off fireworks and burning Fawkes in effigy. Would America's history have taken a different path if Fawkes had been successful in carrying out his plan to kill the king and members of Parliament?

Trial of Guy Fawkes

249

Martin Luther's 95 Theses	Henry viii Splits from Rome	Reign of Queen Elizabeth i Begins	Spanish Armada Destroyed	Signing of Mayflower Compact
1517	1526	1534	1536	1558	1585	1588	1607	1620	1624
Tyndale's English New Testament	Calvin's *Institutes* Published	First Roanoak Settlement	Jamestown, Virginia Founded	Dutch Found New Netherland

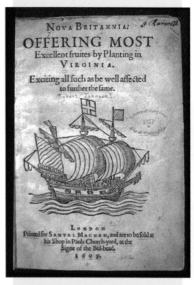

Colonists bowling while there was work to do

False Advertising?

Despite the hardships of life in Jamestown, the Virginia Company continued to advertise the colony to get more people to settle there. Their marketing ploy was to highlight opportunities for "excelling fruits by planting" and to downplay the struggles and starvation that came with settlement.

GENTRY:
Social rank of an individual born into a prominent family.

Calamity Jamestown

Although Jamestown was blessed with some godly leaders, the rank and file settlers were single men who had come to the New World primarily to make their fortune and seek adventure. They were generally more interested in self-advancement than in either establishing a Christian commonwealth or carrying the Gospel to the Indians.

The Jamestown settlers soon discovered that they would have more to contend with than how to get rich quick. Not only was the land plagued by mosquitoes and unfriendly Indians, but the seven-man council appointed by the king to govern Jamestown spent much of its time arguing. In addition, many of the settlers were unwilling to do the plowing, planting, and building that were necessary to insure the success of the colony. Some settlers were of the **gentry** class who thought themselves too good for common labor. Others were lazy or simply wanted to spend their time looking for gold.

C H A P T E R T W E N T Y T W O

MASSACHUSETTS BAY FOUNDED		RHODE ISLAND FOUNDED		KING PHILIP'S WAR		GLORIOUS REVOLUTION		GEORGIA FOUNDED	
1629	1634	1636	1649	1675-6	1681	1688	1692	1733	1740-43
	MARYLAND FOUNDED		CHARLES I OF ENGLAND BEHEADED		PENNSYLVANIA FOUNDED		SALEM WITCH TRIALS		GREAT AWAKENING

Another factor that caused great conflict in the colony was a requirement that each colonist put whatever he produced into a **common storehouse**. The settlers then received food from the storehouse as they needed it. This arrangement encouraged laziness and made the community poorer, because the hardest workers were not rewarded for their labor by getting a larger portion of goods. Those who did little work received a share of goods equal to that of the most industrious. Of course, the worst thing about Jamestown-style communism was that it undermined biblical values of private property and individual responsibility. By the spring of 1608, starvation and sickness had halved their numbers.

The First Charter of Virginia (April 10, 1606), drawn up by the chief legal officers of England, stated that the purpose of all colonization in the New World was to spread the Christian religion. It reads in part: "We, greatly commending and graciously accepting of, their Desires for the Furtherance of so noble a Work, which may, by the Providence of Almighty God, hereafter tend to the Glory of His Divine Majesty, in propagating … [the] Christian Religion to such People, as yet live in Darkness and miserable Ignorance of the true Knowledge and Worship of God, and may in time bring the Infidels and Savages, living in those parts, to human Civility and to a settled and quiet Government: DO, by these our Letters Patents, graciously accept of, and agree to, their humble and well-intentioned Desires."

251

V I R G I N I A   L E A D S   T H E   W A Y

| MARTIN LUTHER'S 95 THESES | HENRY VIII SPLITS FROM ROME | REIGN OF QUEEN ELIZABETH I BEGINS | SPANISH ARMADA DESTROYED | SIGNING OF MAYFLOWER COMPACT |

1517   1526   1534   1536   1558   1585   1588   1607   1620   1624

TYNDALE'S ENGLISH NEW TESTAMENT   CALVIN'S *INSTITUTES* PUBLISHED   FIRST ROANOAK SETTLEMENT   JAMESTOWN, VIRGINIA FOUNDED   DUTCH FOUND NEW NETHERLAND

Globetrotting Hero

John Smith (right) accomplished a great deal in his life and liked to brag about it. According to him, he had done everything and been everywhere. He had run away to go to sea. He had fought as a mercenary for Hungary against the Muslim Turks, and he had cut the heads off three Turkish noblemen in one day. For this, he had been granted a coat of arms that pictured three Turkish heads on a shield (above). After that, Smith was captured and sold as a slave. As Smith tells it, he could not be held captive for long. He escaped and went to Russia, Poland, Germany, and North Africa where he encountered pirates. All this happened before the age of 28. Then he came to Jamestown where he whipped the colonists into shape. Smith wrote a book about all his adventures and illustrated it with flattering sketches of his heroism.

Smith to the Rescue

The sickness, strife, and starvation continued until a remarkable young soldier, Captain **John Smith** (1580–1631), took control. Smith was a soldier of fortune who had fought with the Dutch against Spain and with the Holy Roman Empire against the Turks. Before coming to America, he had fought in battles in Europe, Asia, and Africa. The Hungarians honored him as a hero for defeating a powerful Turkish nobleman in "single combat." Shortly afterward he was wounded, imprisoned, and enslaved by the Turks. The year before he died, he would inspire the world with tales of his daring exploits in *The True Travels, Adventures, and Observations of Captain John Smith*.

When he was twenty-seven years old, Smith traveled to the New World with other adventurers to establish the Jamestown colony. Smith

Pocahontas

was bold and brash but had relatively little authority in the colony at first. Before long, he started arguing that he knew the best way to organize the colony. Few listened to him. Even so, he soon began to organize trading expeditions which persuaded neighboring Indians to deliver—sometimes at gunpoint—life-saving stores of corn. This immediately changed the other colonists' opinion of Captain Smith, whom they promptly elected president of the Jamestown council.

Protesting Smith's Work Ethic

Smith put some strong but necessary restrictions on the colony, including the biblical rule that if you do not work you will not eat (2 THESSALONIANS 3:10). According to Smith, "4 hours each day was spent in worke, the rest in pastimes and merry exercise." Even though the gentlemen settlers chafed at doing even a half day's work, Smith's call for a longer work day did get a fort built and crops planted. Gradually, the colonists learned to respect Smith for his strong leadership and courageous contacts with the Indians. They especially appreciated the trade relations Smith established which allowed the colonists to barter for food.

A modern rendition of the fort at Jamestown

Hollywood-style History

The events surrounding Pocahontas have often been garbled, with no help from recent animated versions of "Pocahontas." For one thing, when the settlers came to Jamestown, the Indian princess was only eleven or twelve years old, not seventeen or eighteen. In addition, there is no evidence of any romantic connection be-tween Pocahontas and John Smith. Instead, her vivacious per-sonality captivated the heart of John Rolfe, whom she eventually married. Rolfe wrote that she "entangled and enthralled [me] in so intricate a labyrinth that I was even awearied to unwind myself thereout."

253

V I R G I N I A   L E A D S   T H E   W A Y

Martin Luther's 95 Theses	Henry VIII Splits from Rome	Reign of Queen Elizabeth I Begins	Spanish Armada Destroyed	Signing of Mayflower Compact

1517 1526 1534 1536 1558 1585 1588 1607 1620 1624

Tyndale's English New Testament	Calvin's *Institutes* Published	First Roanoak Settlement	Jamestown, Virginia Founded	Dutch Found New Netherland

This artistic interpretation of the baptism of Pocahontas hangs in the Rotunda of the United States Capitol

Smith's bravery even earned him the admiration of the Indians. He wrote that on one occasion he got into a quarrel with the powerful **Chief Powhatan** and found his head on the chopping block. Smith claimed that the chief's daughter, **Pocahontas** (*c.* 1595–1617), saved his life by throwing herself between Smith and the executioner's hatchet.

Pocahontas was later converted to Christianity and baptized by Reverend Whitaker after he had instructed her in the Christian faith. Eventually, the Indian princess married one of the settlers, **John Rolfe** (1585–1622).

A Royal Visit

Jamestown's governor decided to encourage interest in the New World by sending one of its "queens"—Pocahontas—to meet the king of England. By the time Pocahontas arrived in England, she was already a celebrity. Pocahontas was likewise fascinated by the English, copying their clothing styles and mannerisms. King James was so captivated by her that he asked whether her son would inherit the throne of the Americas. Unfortunately, the princess did not live to enjoy her success for long. She fell ill in England and died of smallpox while preparing to return to America. She was buried in an unmarked grave.

"Little Mischief"

Pocahontas's real name was actually Matoaka. (Pocahontas was her nickname–it meant "Little Mischief.") However, after she converted to Christianity and was married, she took a new name to show her new faith and her new family: Rebecca Rolfe. Like Pocahontas, the biblical Rebecca left her home for a new life.

Presentation of Pocahontas at court in England

255

VIRGINIA LEADS THE WAY

| MARTIN LUTHER'S 95 THESES | HENRY VIII SPLITS FROM ROME | REIGN OF QUEEN ELIZABETH I BEGINS | SPANISH ARMADA DESTROYED | SIGNING OF MAYFLOWER COMPACT |

1517　1526　1534　1536　1558　1585　1588　1607　1620　1624

| TYNDALE'S ENGLISH NEW TESTAMENT | CALVIN'S *INSTITUTES* PUBLISHED | FIRST ROANOAK SETTLEMENT | JAMESTOWN, VIRGINIA FOUNDED | DUTCH FOUND NEW NETHERLAND |

A series of engravings from Captain John Smith's Generall Historie

Slave or Servant?

An **indentured servant** is a person who owes a debt but is unable to repay it and sells himself and his labor for a specified period of time in order to satisfy the obligation. Most laborers in early Virginia, whether white or black, were indentured servants. This kind of servitude is biblical, as opposed to **chattel slavery** (man-owning) which we usually associate with slavery.

In 1619, a Dutch ship arrived in Jamestown harbor carrying a group of about twenty black laborers from Africa. Though they were recorded as "indentured servants," they had no specific term of service listed after their names like the white servants did. Moreover, unlike the white servants, they only had their first names recorded. Many historians believe that these were the first slaves in the English colonies.

The Starving Time

In 1609, Smith was so severely burned in a gunpowder explosion that he had to return to England. Left without a strong leader, Jamestown took a serious down-turn. The remaining settlers did not have the courage to buy supplies from the Indians. Some were so indifferent to work that they would not cut firewood. The winter of 1609–1610 was the low point for the colony. Starvation weakened the colonists, and the severe winter brought illness and death almost every day. Some colonists literally burned their houses down around them as they used the boards for fuel. They ate dogs, cats, rats and mice, as well as snakes. There were even a few instances of cannibalism. Of the more than five hundred settlers who were in Jamestown in October when John Smith left for London, only sixty were alive the following spring.

Since Jamestown desperately needed a leader to structure the community, the London Company appointed **Thomas West** (1577–1618), whose title was **Lord De la Warr**, to be governor of the colony. De la Warr was unable to leave England right away, so the Company sent **Sir Thomas Gates** to serve as the acting governor. Unfortunately, Gates's expedition was caught in a violent storm just off the coast of Bermuda and shipwrecked.

C H A P T E R   T W E N T Y   T W O

MASSACHUSETTS BAY FOUNDED		RHODE ISLAND FOUNDED		KING PHILIP'S WAR		GLORIOUS REVOLUTION		GEORGIA FOUNDED	
1629	1634	1636	1649	1675-6	1681	1688	1692	1733	1740-43
	MARYLAND FOUNDED		CHARLES I OF ENGLAND BEHEADED		PENNSYLVANIA FOUNDED		SALEM WITCH TRIALS		GREAT AWAKENING

When Gates finally arrived at Jamestown in the spring of 1610, he found the colony in ruins. The survivors of Jamestown pleaded with him to take them back to England. Gates looked at the desolation of the colony, saw the hunger and illness of the remaining settlers, and agreed. They boarded his two ships, but just as they were on their way down the James River, they met an expedition of additional settlers and supplies led by the new governor, Lord De la Warr. De la Warr was not about to let them give up, so he ordered them back to Jamestown where he and Gates did their best to reshape the colony.

The settlers' aversion to work was still evident in May of 1611 when a new governor arrived, seeing them at "their daily and usuall workes, bowling in the streetes."

De la Warr arriving at Jamestown

257

| MARTIN LUTHER'S 95 THESES | HENRY VIII SPLITS FROM ROME | REIGN OF QUEEN ELIZABETH I BEGINS | SPANISH ARMADA DESTROYED | SIGNING OF MAYFLOWER COMPACT |

1517   1526   1534   1536   1558   1585   1588   1607   1620   1624

TYNDALE'S ENGLISH NEW TESTAMENT   CALVIN'S *INSTITUTES* PUBLISHED   FIRST ROANOAK SETTLEMENT   JAMESTOWN, VIRGINIA FOUNDED   DUTCH FOUND NEW NETHERLAND

The Gate to Shakespeare

The nine ships that Thomas Gates navigated to the New World were devastated by a violent storm off the coast of Bermuda. His own flagship, *Sea Adventure*, was destroyed in the tempest. Although everyone survived the wreck, the trauma was well-known in Europe. In fact, this shipwreck may have inspired William Shakespeare to write his play *The Tempest*. In the play, Shakespeare tells about a hideous monster, Caliban. This deformed creature was perhaps based on rumors that the New World was filled with horrible dog-headed monsters.

The cultivation, curing, and drying of tobacco

Jamestown's "Lucky Strike"

The colony struggled on for the next few years and in 1612 came to a turning point when several colonists tried their hand at the tobacco trade. The Indians had already introduced the practice of smoking dried tobacco leaves in clay pipes. Because the colonists did not like the local variety, they began to import tobacco seeds from South America and the Caribbean. Rolfe was the first colonist to have any real success. His West Indian tobacco became a raging success in England, and Jamestown finally had a profitable crop. Even the streets were planted in tobacco for a time. In 1617, the colony shipped 20,000 pounds of it to England.

A thriving tobacco industry was not the only reason for Jamestown's prosperity. Just as important was the termination of the common storehouse system. The abandonment of this communal program required each man to work hard to provide for his own needs and the needs of his family.

Some Indian villages consisted of a cluster of houses surrounded by fields of corn, tobacco, pumpkins and forests.

Hybrid Smokes

John Rolfe (the man who married Pocahontas) is called one of the heroes of Jamestown for turning Jamestown's economy around. Following the pattern of Indian agriculture where tobacco and corn were planted side by side, Rolfe turned tobacco into a cash crop. He imported some tobacco seeds from the West Indies and crossed them with local tobacco. The result was a mild smoke that soon became all the rage in England. Before long, the Jamestown colonists were selling pounds of the stuff at a great profit. King James emphatically denounced smoking as "a custom loathsome to the eye, hateful to the Nose, harmful to the brain, dangerous to the Lungs, and in the black stinking fume thereof, nearest resembling the horrible Stygian smoke of the pit that is bottomless."

V I R G I N I A   L E A D S   T H E   W A Y

Martin Luther's 95 Theses		Henry VIII Splits from Rome		Reign of Queen Elizabeth I Begins		Spanish Armada Destroyed		Signing of Mayflower Compact	
1517	1526	1534	1536	1558	1585	1588	1607	1620	1624
	Tyndale's English New Testament		Calvin's *Institutes* Published		First Roanoak Settlement		Jamestown, Virginia Founded		Dutch Found New Netherland

The First American Legislature

Control of the London Company changed hands in 1618, and along with the change of authority came a new direction for the colony. **Sir Edwin Sandys** (pronounced **Sands**) (1561–1629), an English parliamentary leader and a chief promoter of the London Company, instituted a number of governmental reforms. He called for the establishment of a popular assembly which would be the governing body that passed the laws for the colony. The colonial governor agreed that he needed help to run the colony. By that time, there were eleven settlements which spread out from Jamestown. The reason the colony had grown so quickly was due to the new land the colonists needed to plant their tobacco crops.

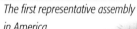

The first representative assembly in America

MASSACHUSETTS BAY FOUNDED		RHODE ISLAND FOUNDED		KING PHILIP'S WAR		GLORIOUS REVOLUTION		GEORGIA FOUNDED	
1629	1634	1636	1649	1675-6	1681	1688	1692	1733	1740-43
	MARYLAND FOUNDED		CHARLES I OF ENGLAND BEHEADED		PENNSYLVANIA FOUNDED		SALEM WITCH TRIALS		GREAT AWAKENING

Establishing a Government

The governor asked each of the eleven settlements to choose two representatives to meet with and advise him from time to time. Accordingly, popular elections were held in the summer of 1619, and on July 30th of that year the first legislative assembly convened. The House of Burgesses was born. Its first meeting was held in the quire (choir loft) of the Jamestown church. The House of Burgesses was the first representative assembly in North America, and it is said to be the ancestor of both the United States Congress and the state legislatures.

Preaching for Tobacco

Virginia ministers were often paid in tobacco. After 1695, the annual salary of a clergyman was fixed by law at 16,000 pounds of tobacco. Because not all tobacco is created equal, a minister who ended up in a parish which raised the lower quality "Oronoko" tobacco received lower pay than a minister who resided in a parish that raised a milder and sweeter variety that brought a higher price.

Here Come the Brides

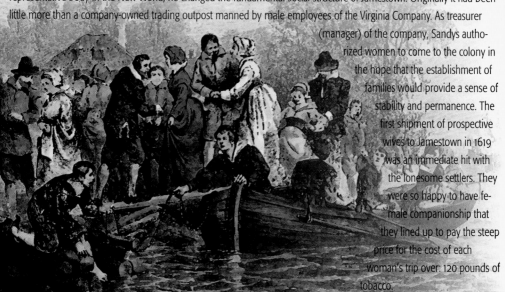

Though Edwin Sandys never set foot in the New World, he left a deep mark there. In addition to establishing the first representative body in the New World, he changed the fundamental social structure of Jamestown. Originally it had been little more than a company-owned trading outpost manned by male employees of the Virginia Company. As treasurer (manager) of the company, Sandys authorized women to come to the colony in the hope that the establishment of families would provide a sense of stability and permanence. The first shipment of prospective wives to Jamestown in 1619 was an immediate hit with the lonesome settlers. They were so happy to have female companionship that they lined up to pay the steep price for the cost of each woman's trip over: 120 pounds of tobacco.

V I R G I N I A   L E A D S   T H E   W A Y

| MARTIN LUTHER'S 95 THESES | | HENRY VIII SPLITS FROM ROME | | REIGN OF QUEEN ELIZABETH I BEGINS | | SPANISH ARMADA DESTROYED | | SIGNING OF MAYFLOWER COMPACT | |
1517   1526   1534   1536   1558   1585   1588   1607   1620   1624
| | TYNDALE'S ENGLISH NEW TESTAMENT | | CALVIN'S *INSTITUTES* PUBLISHED | | FIRST ROANOAK SETTLEMENT | | JAMESTOWN, VIRGINIA FOUNDED | | DUTCH FOUND NEW NETHERLAND |

Seal of the Virginia Company

All Bets Are Off

The Virginia Company hosted a lottery to raise money for ships, crew, and provisions. They kept the lottery running to keep supplies pumping into the struggling settlement. In 1624, King James annulled the Jamestown charter by taking control away from the Virginia Company. The power switch was easy. He simply made the lottery illegal.

King James Takes Over

In spite of the success of tobacco as a cash crop for Jamestown, the Virginia Company was not able to pay any profits to its stockholders. The death rate in the colony was high because of disease and Indian raids. In addition, King James wanted to consolidate power. So, in 1624, the king dissolved the company and took direct control, making Virginia a **royal colony**. Virginia grew and prospered, and in time played a pivotal role in the struggle for American independence.

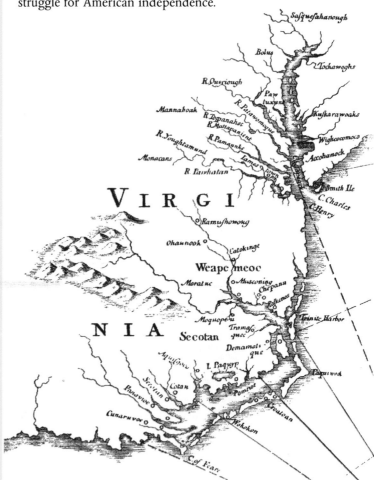

MASSACHUSETTS BAY FOUNDED	RHODE ISLAND FOUNDED	KING PHILIP'S WAR	GLORIOUS REVOLUTION	GEORGIA FOUNDED	
1629	1634	1636	1649	1675-6	1681	1688	1692	1733	1740-43
	MARYLAND FOUNDED	CHARLES I OF ENGLAND BEHEADED	PENNSYLVANIA FOUNDED	SALEM WITCH TRIALS	GREAT AWAKENING

FOR STUDY

CHAPTER 22:
Virginia Leads the Way

Terms

joint stock company

plantation

Lost Colony

Geneva Bible

Virginia Company

London Group

Plymouth Group

Jamestown

Gunpowder Plot

gentry

common storehouse

indentured servant

chattel slavery

House of Burgesses

royal colony

People

John White

Virginia Dare

James I

Guy Fawkes

John Smith

Chief Powhatan

Pocahontas

John Rolfe

Thomas West, Lord De la Warr

Sir Thomas Gates

Sir Edwin Sandys

The first English attempts at colonization were dismal failures due to Indian attacks and laziness on the part of some colonists. Even the first successful attempt at Jamestown was repeatedly beset by near disaster. The English colonists, however, learned from their mistakes and corrected some of them. The discovery of a successful cash crop assured continued growth. The arrival of wives and the establishment of representative government changed the Virginia colony from a frontier company trading post into a permanent home for its members.

Discussion Questions

1. Describe the problems that threatened to end the Jamestown settlement within a year of its founding. How did Capt. John Smith turn this colony around?
2. What two developments caused the settlement to thrive after ten years of struggle?
3. How did the first representative government in the New World come about?

Optional Enrichment Projects

1. Trace the importance tobacco played in the life of the early settlements. What economic role does tobacco have in today's society?
2. Read a historical account of Capt. John Smith and Pocahontas. How does your source deal with Pocahontas's conversion to Christianity?

MARTIN LUTHER'S 95 THESES	HENRY VIII SPLITS FROM ROME	REIGN OF QUEEN ELIZABETH I BEGINS	SPANISH ARMADA DESTROYED	SIGNING OF MAYFLOWER COMPACT
1517	1526	1534	1536	1558	1585	1588	1607	1620	1624
TYNDALE'S ENGLISH NEW TESTAMENT	CALVIN'S *INSTITUTES* PUBLISHED	FIRST ROANOAK SETTLEMENT	JAMESTOWN, VIRGINIA FOUNDED	DUTCH FOUND NEW NETHERLAND

Perspectives

I write the Wonders of the Christian Religion, flying from the depravations of Europe, to the American Strand; and, assisted by the Holy Author of that Religion, I do with all conscience of Truth, required therein by Him, who is the Truth itself, report the wonderful displays of His infinite Power, Wisdom, Goodness, and Faithfulness, wherewith His Divine Providence hath irradiated an Indian Wilderness. I relate the Considerable Matters, that produced and attended the First Settlement of Colonies, which have been renowned for the degree of Reformation, professed and attained by Evangelical Churches, erected in those ends of the earth; and a Field being thus prepared, I proceed unto a relation of the Considerable Matters which have been acted thereupon…. What am I? Nothing.—Sovereign Grace alone Lives in my life, and does what I have done.

Cotton Mather

CHAPTER 23

GOING
Their SEPARATE WAYS

A Reforming of the Reformation

Any discussion of the settlement of New England must begin with a look at two groups of people, **Puritans** and **Separatists.** Both groups were English Reformers who believed that the Reformation had not gone far enough in their country.

Puritans and Separatists wanted the Church of England to give up what remained of Catholic ceremonies and to embrace what they considered to be a more biblical form of worship. Much of Anglicanism, the Puritans maintained, still resembled elements of Catholic "ceremonies": wedding rings as part of the marriage ceremony, clerical vestments, baptizing with the sign of the cross, and kneeling to receive the Lord's Supper (Holy Communion). Since these practices were not found in the Bible, the Puritans asserted, they should not be part of Christian worship. They believed the Bible requires a **regulative principle** for worship— Christians should do only what Scripture explicitly commands and nothing more. The Anglicans, on the other hand, believed that the church was free to order worship in a way that leads to edification of the worshipper as defined by the church.

First coin to bear the legend
"Great Britain"

265

MARTIN LUTHER'S 95 THESES	HENRY VIII SPLITS FROM ROME	REIGN OF QUEEN ELIZABETH I BEGINS	SPANISH ARMADA DESTROYED	SIGNING OF MAYFLOWER COMPACT	
1517	**1526**	**1534**	**1536**	**1558**	**1585**	**1588**	**1607**	**1620**	**1624**
	TYNDALE'S ENGLISH NEW TESTAMENT	CALVIN'S *INSTITUTES* PUBLISHED	FIRST ROANOAK SETTLEMENT	JAMESTOWN, VIRGINIA FOUNDED	DUTCH FOUND NEW NETHERLAND

Archbishop Bancroft

Richard Bancroft was Archbishop of Canterbury from 1604 to 1610. George Abbot followed him in that post until 1633. Together these two leaders of the Church of England vigorously defended the Episcopal form of church government, attacked Presbyterian Puritanism and Roman Catholicism, and sought unsuccessfully to persuade Presbyterian Scotland to adopt England's Episcopal system.

Archbishop Abbot

Church Government

All churches have a form of government, which is technically called an *ecclesiology* (from the Greek word *ekklesia* which means "assembly"). Historically, three forms of church government have prevailed. *Episcopal,* coming from the Greek word for bishop *(episkopos)*, is a form of government where local churches are bound together by means of a "top-down" hierarchy headed by bishops. The Protestant Church in England at the time of the Pilgrim embarkation was Episcopal since bishops made up the hierarchy with the Archbishop of Canterbury being the head bishop. *Presbyterian,* from the Greek word for elder *(presbuteron)*, is a form of church government where members elect elders to rule in the church and represent them at the regional government meetings called presbyteries. Representatives from each church meet annually at a general assembly. This national body of elders handles disputes brought to it by local churches. *Independent* or *congregational* churches follow a type of church government which has no formal ties between churches. Each local church is governmentally independent of every other local church. The Pilgrim churches of New England were congregational.

Leave or Cleave?

Both Puritans and Separatists agreed that further reform was needed. They simply differed on *how* these changes would be accomplished. The Puritans wanted to work within the church to *purify* it. The Separatists believed that the Church of England was beyond reform and that true Christians should *separate* from the corrupt church. Some of these Separatists believed so strongly that the church would not reform itself that they left England altogether and traveled to the New World. A small group of Separatists who settled in Plymouth, Massachusetts, in 1620, would become known as the **Pilgrims.**

In spite of differences over to how to further the Reformation, Puritans and Separatists shared a great number of beliefs. Their worship was similar, as was their theological perspective on nearly every point of doctrine. Both groups rejected the Anglican Church's system of bishops. Both believed in independent congregations. Neither group would use the church's prayer book, and, from the king's point of view, both groups were equally heretical.

C H A P T E R   T W E N T Y   T H R E E

MASSACHUSETTS BAY FOUNDED		RHODE ISLAND FOUNDED		KING PHILIP'S WAR		GLORIOUS REVOLUTION		GEORGIA FOUNDED	
1629	1634	1636	1649	1675-6	1681	1688	1692	1733	1740-43
	MARYLAND FOUNDED		CHARLES I OF ENGLAND BEHEADED		PENNSYLVANIA FOUNDED		SALEM WITCH TRIALS		GREAT AWAKENING

Botched Bibles

Several English Bibles published in the seventeenth century get their nicknames because of typographical errors. The so-called *Murderer's Bible* misprints "murderers" for "murmurers" in Jude 16. Mark 7:27 was made to read: "Let the children first be killed" (instead of "filled"). *The Printer's Bible* laments that "printers" (not "princes") "have persecuted me without cause" (Psalm 119:161). The *Wife-Hater Bible* tells a man to hate his own wife: "If any man come to me, and hate not his father…yea, and his own wife also." "Wife" should read "life." The *Adulterer's* or *Wicked Bible* leaves out an essential "not" and commands, "Thou shalt commit adultery." The king's printers were fined £300 by Archbishop Laud for this notorious typographical error. An Oxford edition of the King James Bible (1717) was known as the *Vinegar Bible* because the chapter heading to Luke 20 had "Vinegar" for "Vineyard" in the title of "The Parable of the Vineyard."

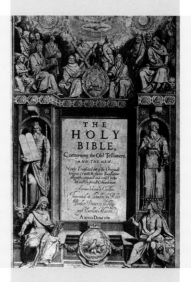

Shakespeare the Psalmist?

Some people believe that the translators of the King James Bible asked William Shakespeare (left) to help them put at least some of the Psalms into English verse. There is not much support for this opinion, but staunch believers in this theory think that Shakespeare left a hidden clue in Psalm 46. Look at a King James Version of the psalm. Count 46 words from the beginning. Then count 46 words from the end (not counting "Selah"). Mere coincidence? We'll never know.

267

G O I N G   T H E I R   S E P A R A T E   W A Y S

MARTIN LUTHER'S 95 THESES		HENRY VIII SPLITS FROM ROME		REIGN OF QUEEN ELIZABETH I BEGINS		SPANISH ARMADA DESTROYED		SIGNING OF MAYFLOWER COMPACT	
1517	1526	1534	1536	1558	1585	1588	1607	1620	1624
	TYNDALE'S ENGLISH NEW TESTAMENT		CALVIN'S *INSTITUTES* PUBLISHED		FIRST ROANOAK SETTLEMENT		JAMESTOWN, VIRGINIA FOUNDED		DUTCH FOUND NEW NETHERLAND

Put No Confidence in Princes

When King James I had assumed the throne at the death of Elizabeth in March of 1603, the Reformers had desperately hoped for royal support of the Reformation. James had been educated in Scotland by followers of John Knox, and the Puritans had hoped that their new king would be open to furthering the Reformation. It soon became painfully clear, however, that James had no interest in Puritan concerns. He claimed the same right to rule the church as had his cousin Elizabeth.

John Knox

Realizing that the Church of England was not going to follow the steps of reform, the Separatists began to form congregations apart from the Anglican parish

King James I

No Idle Threat

What did King James mean when he said that if the Separatists did not conform he would make them leave or do something much worse? Were these vain threats? No indeed. Elder Brewster had published a book critical of the king's plans to reorganize the Church of Scotland. The furious king set out to get Brewster. An author who wrote a similar book was not only fined but was also whipped, pilloried, had his ears cut off, his nose slit, his face branded, and—to emphasize the point—was sentenced to life imprisonment!

Separatists fleeing English officials

C H A P T E R   T W E N T Y   T H R E E

MASSACHUSETTS BAY FOUNDED		RHODE ISLAND FOUNDED		KING PHILIP'S WAR		GLORIOUS REVOLUTION		GEORGIA FOUNDED	
1629	1634	1636	1649	1675-6	1681	1688	1692	1733	1740-43
	MARYLAND FOUNDED		CHARLES I OF ENGLAND BEHEADED		PENNSYLVANIA FOUNDED		SALEM WITCH TRIALS		GREAT AWAKENING

churches. How King James hated these Separatists whom he thought had a "holier than thou" attitude. His intolerance of their religion soon became intense: "I will make them conform, or I will harry them out of the land—or else do worse."

One of these groups was a congregation in the little English village of **Scrooby.** This church had been driven underground to escape persecution. In 1607, the same year that Jamestown was settled, these Scrooby Separatists decided they would leave the country to avoid persecution. However, there was a problem. Under existing law, it was illegal for a family to migrate without a license from the authorities. As a result, initial attempts to leave the country resulted in imprisonment.

Scrooby, England

Protestant martyrs

Ye shalbe led before Princes and rulers for my names sake.
Math. 10.

269

G O I N G   T H E I R   S E P A R A T E   W A Y S

| MARTIN LUTHER'S 95 THESES | HENRY VIII SPLITS FROM ROME | REIGN OF QUEEN ELIZABETH I BEGINS | SPANISH ARMADA DESTROYED | SIGNING OF MAYFLOWER COMPACT |

1517   1526   1534   1536   1558   1585   1588   1607   1620   1624

| TYNDALE'S ENGLISH NEW TESTAMENT | CALVIN'S *INSTITUTES* PUBLISHED | FIRST ROANOAK SETTLEMENT | JAMESTOWN, VIRGINIA FOUNDED | DUTCH FOUND NEW NETHERLAND |

Sailing of the Pilgrims from Plymouth, England

Going Dutch

Finally, this small band of Separatists made their way first to Amsterdam and then on to **Leyden**, Holland, which offered religious freedom to all kinds of Christians. In Leyden, the Separatists enjoyed religious liberty and generally earned the respect of their Dutch neighbors, but they were able to get only the poorest of jobs.

In addition to poor work conditions, these Separatists were concerned that their children were forgetting their English culture, and, even worse, becoming influenced by Dutch worldliness. The English Reformers wanted to live in a culture where God's law was the rule for all of life, and they decided that the Netherlands was not that place. An additional factor prompted them to leave Holland: Their printing press, which was used to print Reformed books to smuggle into England, was destroyed by Dutch soldiers at the request of the king of England. This breach of freedom of the press convinced these Reformers that they must travel even farther to escape the long arm of the English crown. The only other place of refuge which would grant them the freedom they desired was America. Even though they had heard of the terrible death rate in Jamestown during its starving time, these Separatists believed that God was directing them to the New World.

MASSACHUSETTS BAY FOUNDED		RHODE ISLAND FOUNDED		KING PHILIP'S WAR			GLORIOUS REVOLUTION		GEORGIA FOUNDED	
1629	1634	1636	1649	1675-6	1681	1688	1692	1733	1740-43
	MARYLAND FOUNDED		CHARLES I OF ENGLAND BEHEADED		PENNSYLVANIA FOUNDED		SALEM WITCH TRIALS		GREAT AWAKENING

Leyden, Holland

What's His Beef?

Edward Winslow (1595–1655) was a crucial member of the English Separatists in Leyden. He helped fan the flames of religious freedom already burning by printing controversial tracts written by William Brewster. These tracts forced Brewster to go into hiding to avoid the wrath of King James. Winslow also published *Good Newes from New England* (1624), an account showing "the wonderful Providence and goodness of GOD."

In the New World, Winslow became an invaluable ambassador to the Indians and promoted peace with Massasoit. He was instrumental in establishing trade posts in the colonies and is given credit for bringing the first cows to the New World.

271

G O I N G   T H E I R   S E P A R A T E   W A Y S

MARTIN LUTHER'S 95 THESES	HENRY VIII SPLITS FROM ROME	REIGN OF QUEEN ELIZABETH I BEGINS	SPANISH ARMADA DESTROYED	SIGNING OF MAYFLOWER COMPACT
1517 1526	1534 1536	1558 1585	1588 1607	1620 1624
TYNDALE'S ENGLISH NEW TESTAMENT	CALVIN'S *INSTITUTES* PUBLISHED	FIRST ROANOAK SETTLEMENT	JAMESTOWN, VIRGINIA FOUNDED	DUTCH FOUND NEW NETHERLAND

The Saints and the Strangers Look Westward

Before the Leyden Separatists could travel to America, they needed heavy financial support and the permission of a king who despised them. They were able to get financial backing from the Virginia Company, a group of London merchants headed by **Thomas Weston**. It was agreed that the Leyden group would buy shares in the company and would enter into joint partnership with Weston for seven years. Within that time, they would have to share all profits with the London merchants. In 1620, King James finally gave his permission, with the hope that the voyagers would claim more land for England. No doubt he was glad to have these troublemakers an ocean away from him!

The Separatists chose the *Speedwell* to make their voyage, but because of its size, only a small number of the Leyden congregation could make the trip. Their pastor, **John Robinson** (1576–1625), would stay behind. Elder William Brewster would be the spiritual leader of the travelers. Their plan was to

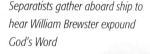

Separatists gather aboard ship to hear William Brewster expound God's Word

272

The Manor House at Scrooby,
William Brewster's residence

William Brewster (1567–1644)
was a spiritual father to most of
the Pilgrims. Brewster traveled on
the Mayflower *to Plymouth where*
he remained a ruling elder for the
rest of his life, preaching "both
powerfully and profitably to the
great contentment of the hearers
and their comfortable edification."

sail to England where they would join other travelers—whom they called "Strangers" because they did not share the Separatists' faith—and a second ship, the *Mayflower*. After their plans were set, the Leyden church paused for a time of fasting and praying. Then those who were staying behind threw a farewell feast for the voyagers. Pastor Robinson gave a final sermon in which he reminded the travelers to put their confidence in God, their Provider.

William Bradford (1590–1657) was one of the Leyden Separatists who made the voyage to the New World. He also recorded an account of their travels and a ten-year (1630–1640) history of the colony in a book, *Of Plymouth Plantation*. Bradford describes the scene as they departed Leyden in the creaky old *Speedwell* on July 22, 1620: "And so they left that good and pleasant city, which had been their resting place near twelve years; but they knew they were *pilgrims,* and lifted up their eyes to the heavens, their dearest country, and quieted their spirits. . . . What sights and sobs and prayers rose from amongst them! What tears gushed from every eye!" Bradford's description of the Separatists as "pilgrims" became a convenient and accurate description of these early Christian colonists.

MARTIN LUTHER'S 95 THESES	HENRY VIII SPLITS FROM ROME	REIGN OF QUEEN ELIZABETH I BEGINS	SPANISH ARMADA DESTROYED	SIGNING OF MAYFLOWER COMPACT
1517	1526	1534	1536	1558	1585	1588	1607	1620	1624
TYNDALE'S ENGLISH NEW TESTAMENT	CALVIN'S *INSTITUTES* PUBLISHED	FIRST ROANOAK SETTLEMENT	JAMESTOWN, VIRGINIA FOUNDED	DUTCH FOUND NEW NETHERLAND

Monkey Business

It is possible that the *Speedwell's* problems were actually faked by the ship's master and some of the crew, so they would not have to make the dangerous journey. This theory gains even more credibility when we consider that the *Speedwell* did not exactly fall apart after the episode. It was employed for many years afterwards as a hardy merchant ship.

A Leaky Launch

The Leyden group traveled from the Dutch harbor of Delft to the English port of Southampton without incident. There they joined the group of Strangers and the second ship, the *Mayflower*. Having been used to transport fine fabrics, cognac, and wine, the *Mayflower* was known as a "sweet ship" because of the pleasant scents below her deck. Some of the new passengers were also traveling to the New World to set up a society faithful to the Bible; others simply sought wealth and adventure. For the most part, these were young people, men and women in their twenties and thirties, ready and eager to meet whatever challenges lay ahead.

The two ships set sail on August 5, 1620, but there was one problem. The *Speedwell* should have been named the "Leakwell." The expedition twice had to sail back to land because winds and choppy waters separated her seams. The *Speedwell* had to be abandoned, and all the passengers and supplies were crammed onto the *Mayflower*. The overloaded ship finally sailed from the port of Plymouth on September 16, 1620. On board were 102 passengers (including 34 children), a number of cats to help keep down the population of mice and rats, and two dogs, a large mastiff and a small spaniel.

The Mayflower *and* Speedwell

274

MASSACHUSETTS BAY FOUNDED		RHODE ISLAND FOUNDED		KING PHILIP'S WAR		GLORIOUS REVOLUTION		GEORGIA FOUNDED	
1629	1634	1636	1649	1675-6	1681	1688	1692	1733	1740-43
	MARYLAND FOUNDED		CHARLES I OF ENGLAND BEHEADED		PENNSYLVANIA FOUNDED		SALEM WITCH TRIALS		GREAT AWAKENING

A cutaway view of the Mayflower

Slowly and Surly

The voyage would prove to be eventful for everyone. The master (captain) of the ship, **Christopher Jones**, decided not to follow the well-known route across the Atlantic which had been pioneered by Columbus. Instead, he chose to sail along the forty-second parallel in order to cut a thousand miles off the journey and avoid the dangers of pirates and Spanish and French warships. Unfortunately, the route he had chosen put the ship squarely in the middle of the **Gulf Stream**, a warm water ocean current which flows out of the Gulf of Mexico in a northeasterly direction across the Atlantic. This route condemned the *Mayflower* to a maximum average speed of only two miles per hour.

The rough seas and the lurching ship soon made many of the travelers seasick. To make matters worse, some members of the crew disliked the Separatists and mocked them in their sickness. One sailor in particular enjoyed telling them that many in their company would probably die before the journey was over and that he looked forward to throwing their bodies overboard. It is ironic that this surly sailor became suddenly ill and died, and *his* became the first body to be buried at sea.

Ocean-Born Baby

Toward the end of the storm, pregnant Elizabeth Hopkins went into labor. The swaying, creaking quarters increased the poor lady's discomfort, even though Katherine Carver and Mary Brewster did all they could to ease her pain. As the wind finally abated, Mrs. Hopkins gave birth to a healthy baby boy. He was named Oceanus by his proud parents.

275

G O I N G   T H E I R   S E P A R A T E   W A Y S

| MARTIN LUTHER'S 95 THESES | HENRY VIII SPLITS FROM ROME | REIGN OF QUEEN ELIZABETH I BEGINS | SPANISH ARMADA DESTROYED | SIGNING OF MAYFLOWER COMPACT |

1517   1526   1534   1536   1558   1585   1588   1607   1620   1624

| TYNDALE'S ENGLISH NEW TESTAMENT | CALVIN'S *INSTITUTES* PUBLISHED | FIRST ROANOAK SETTLEMENT | JAMESTOWN, VIRGINIA FOUNDED | DUTCH FOUND NEW NETHERLAND |

Peril on the High Seas

The greatest problem the *Mayflower* travelers encountered was a massive storm that lashed at the ship with tearing winds and towering waves that were as high as fifty feet. The hatches were bolted down, and the travelers huddled together, cold, wet, and seasick. Then the force of the storm caused one of the main beams that held up the ship's hull to bow and crack under the pressure. All seemed lost. At first, to avoid panic, the master of the ship made no effort to warn the passengers of the potential danger.

Unable to maintain secrecy, the master called together the senior members of his crew and passengers in his quarters to make them aware of the situation. Some of the officers called for the master to return to England. The winds and currents, they claimed, were moving in an easterly direction. In addition, there was hope that they would come upon a friendly ship or a safe haven where they could secure food and shelter until the storm subsided.

No Place to Shop

What would you take on a trip to a new world? Strangely enough, the Pilgrims did not pack one plow or fishing line, but they did leave plenty of room for sundials, candle snuffers, and even a book on the history of Turkey! William Mullins packed 126 pairs of shoes and more than a dozen pairs of boots. Keep in mind that their nearest English neighbors would be more than 500 miles away—at Jamestown in Virginia. Mullins no doubt went overboard to make sure that in the New World wilderness, he would never lack appropriate footwear.

Swords of Plymouth's leaders

After hearing arguments from both sides, Master Jones decided to press on. But the beam would have to be repaired. The ship's carpenter concluded that a metal collar was needed to repair the break. Where would they find such a piece of hardware at sea, more than a thousand miles from civilization? Providentially, the Pilgrims had brought a printing press with its huge iron screw. The mechanism could be used as a giant support clamp to prevent further damage. It was located and attached to the beam, securing the ship. While the high winds continued, Elder Brewster led the travelers in prayer and singing.

After weeks of foul weather, the storms finally abated. The travelers who had been cramped together in the stinking hold eagerly climbed out on the deck. How refreshing it was to see the sky and feel the ocean breezes again! The sick were helped out into the sunshine, so that they too could enjoy the calm weather.

No Shrimp of a Man

Miles Standish (c. 1584–1656) was one of the "Strangers" who accompanied the Pilgrims on the *Mayflower* who turned out to be a valuable asset as captain of the guard. His nickname "Captain Shrimpe" referred to his physical stature, not to his leadership ability. Standish led a mission to survey the land when the *Mayflower* first arrived, and he also served as an envoy to England to negotiate for property rights. At his death, Standish left a small but impressive library.

First seal of Plymouth Colony

From Boat to Barn

The *Mayflower* returned home to England, and, three years after its Plymouth landing, the ship was broken up and sold as lumber. Its salvaged boards were made into a barn about twenty miles from London.

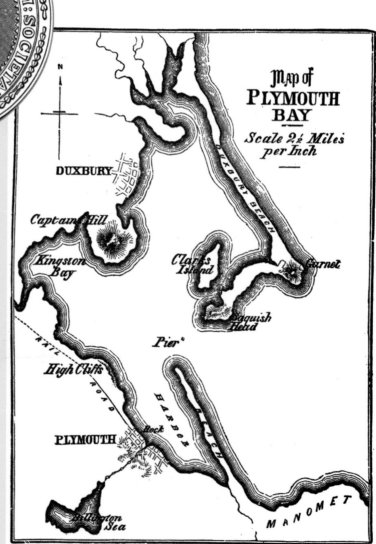

278

MASSACHUSETTS BAY FOUNDED	RHODE ISLAND FOUNDED		KING PHILIP'S WAR		GLORIOUS REVOLUTION		GEORGIA FOUNDED	
1629	1634	1636	1649	1675-6	1681	1688	1692	1733	1740-43
	MARYLAND FOUNDED		CHARLES I OF ENGLAND BEHEADED		PENNSYLVANIA FOUNDED		SALEM WITCH TRIALS		GREAT AWAKENING

New Horizons

It was early on the morning of November 9 when one of the older sailors claimed that he could "smell land." Excitement spread as fast as his words. In the early morning twilight, after more than a nine-week voyage in cramped quarters, the sound of "Land Ho!" echoed through the ship. Elder Brewster led the weary but thankful travelers in singing a musical version of Psalm 100. Describing the event in his history, Bradford wrote:

> *I stand half amazed at this poor people's present condition; and so I think, will the reader, too, when he considers it well. Being thus passed the vast ocean, and a sea of troubles before in their preparations, they had now no friends to welcome them nor inns to entertain and refresh their weather-beaten bodies, nor houses—much less towns—to repair to.... Summer being done, all things had upon them a weather-beaten face, and the whole country, full of woods and thickets, represented a wild and savage view. If they looked behind them, there was the mighty ocean which they had passed, and was now a gulf separating them from all civilized parts of the world.... What, then, could now sustain them but the Spirit of God and His grace?*

Their faith would be tested further. By the time a suitable place for landing had been found, it was late December. The winter was harsh, harsher than anything they had ever experienced.

A Government Built Upon Sandys

While Sir Edwin Sandys (above) was treasurer (manager) of the Virginia Company, he authorized what he believed would be a new settlement within his Virginia colony. William Brewster secured from Sandys a patent to establish a plantation near the mouth of the Hudson River, which at that time was part of Virginia. But delays and bad weather put the Pilgrims off course. Because the Pilgrims had sailed to an area outside the boundaries of Virginia and the government of Sandys, they were forced to create their own government.

279

MARTIN LUTHER'S 95 THESES	HENRY VIII SPLITS FROM ROME	REIGN OF QUEEN ELIZABETH I BEGINS	SPANISH ARMADA DESTROYED		SIGNING OF MAYFLOWER COMPACT	
1517	1526	1534	1536	1558	1585	1588	1607	1620	1624
	TYNDALE'S ENGLISH NEW TESTAMENT	CALVIN'S *INSTITUTES* PUBLISHED		FIRST ROANOAK SETTLEMENT		JAMESTOWN, VIRGINIA FOUNDED	DUTCH FOUND NEW NETHERLAND

FOR STUDY

CHAPTER 23:
Going Their Separate Ways

Terms
Puritans
Separatists
regulative principle
Episcopal
Presbyterian
Independent
Congregational
Pilgrims
Scrooby
Leyden
Speedwell
Mayflower
Of Plymouth Plantation
Gulf Stream

People
Edward Winslow
Thomas Weston
John Robinson
William Bradford
William Brewster
Christopher Jones
Miles Standish

There were many people in England who desired further reformation of the established church. Some, like the members of the Scrooby congregation, decided that the church was beyond reform, and so they separated into their own congregation. Eventually these Separatists left England to seek religious freedom in the Netherlands. When they began to sense that Dutch society was corrupting their children, they jumped at the chance to settle in America where they hoped they and their families would have complete freedom to live out godly lives and develop a Christian commonwealth. Before they would secure this freedom, however, these Pilgrims would endure great hardship.

Discussion Questions
1. What is meant by the "regulative" principle of worship? Why and how did it influence the decisions of the Puritans and Separatists (Pilgrims)?
2. Describe the similarities and differences between the Separatists and Puritans?
3. What caused James I to persecute the Separatists?
4. Why was the New World the best hope for the Separatists?

Optional Enrichment Projects
1. Controversy over how to worship God is still with us. What are the points of contention raised in the twentieth century? How do they compare with the views of the Puritans and Separatists?
2. Read *Of Plymouth Plantation* by William Bradford and describe his account of their first winter and Thanksgiving.

C H A P T E R

24

CARVING A
New World SOCIETY

The Mayflower Compact

Because of bad weather and navigational error, the *Mayflower* had landed in the New World at Cape Cod, which was much further north than the Pilgrims' expected place of landing. As a result, the travelers were outside the jurisdiction of the Virginia Company charter that gave them legal claim to territory specified in the original land grant. Since their charter was now null and void, they were left without the legal power to establish a government. There were some troublemakers on board who gleefully anticipated **anarchy**, hoping to "use their own liberty, for none had power to command them." Rather than let this group of malcontents ruin the enterprise, the Pilgrims drew up a temporary governing document called the **Mayflower Compact**, which would set up a "civil body politic."

281

The Mayflower Compact

The Compact reads in part: "In the name of God, Amen. We whose names are underwritten…having undertaken, for the glory of God, and advancement of the Christian faith, and honor of our king and country, a voyage to plant the first colony in the northern parts of Virginia, do by these present, solemnly and mutually, in the presence of God and one another, covenant and combine ourselves together into a civil body politic, for our better ordering and preservation and furtherance of the ends aforesaid."

The spelling in this portion of the Compact has been modernized. The original document's "ye" was another way of writing "the." It was not pronounced "yee."

MAYFLOWER COMPACT 1620

GOVERNOR BRADFORD'S COPY OF THE MAYFLOWER COMPACT

Preserved in his handwriting in his History of Plymouth Plantation,

OVER 300 YEARS AGO!

*Signing of the
Mayflower Compact*

Number One Governor

John Carver was a wealthy merchant and deacon at the Leyden church. He was instrumental in gaining a grant for the Virginia Company from James I. He served as the first governor of Plymouth Plantation but died during the first sickness.

The Mayflower Compact was a **covenant**, an agreement solemnly made in the presence of God, to establish a government that required the people to submit to the rulers who had authority to enforce it. As the *Mayflower* gently rocked at anchor, the men came up one by one, carefully signed their names to the document, pledged allegiance to the king, and bound themselves to obey all laws enacted. They then selected one of their number, **John Carver** (c. 1576–1621), to be their governor.

C A R V I N G   A   N E W   W O R L D   S O C I E T Y

MARTIN LUTHER'S 95 THESES	HENRY VIII SPLITS FROM ROME	REIGN OF QUEEN ELIZABETH I BEGINS	SPANISH ARMADA DESTROYED	SIGNING OF MAYFLOWER COMPACT
1517 1526 1534 1536 1558 1585 1588 1607 1620 1624
TYNDALE'S ENGLISH NEW TESTAMENT	CALVIN'S *INSTITUTES* PUBLISHED	FIRST ROANOAK SETTLEMENT	JAMESTOWN, VIRGINIA FOUNDED	DUTCH FOUND NEW NETHERLAND

Ready-Made Refuge

When Captain Standish and his men surveyed the land that was chosen for Plymouth Plantation, they found a place perfect for settlement, complete with clearings and grain storage. The reason for these traces of civilization was that, years before, a plague had wiped out the Pawtuxet Indians, who used to inhabit the area. In addition, it seemed that other tribes were afraid of the "cursed" territory and left it alone.

Homecoming

The *Mayflower* travelers sent out men to explore the shores of Cape Cod to look for a suitable place to settle. At first sight, the land was cold and bleak. Their mid-winter arrival would test their faith unlike anything they had ever experienced before. The first Indians they encountered attacked them, but their bows and arrows were no match for English muskets, and the skirmish was quickly over. The Pilgrims would soon learn that not all the natives of this new land were hostile. Some tribes would be their link to survival. As in all things, the Pilgrims looked to God for provision.

It took the Pilgrims several weeks to find a location to settle. They finally decided on a place which had dark, rich soil and plenty of fresh water. They named their new home **Plymouth Plantation.** Soon after their arrival, the Pilgrims began to build the first houses of their colony, living out of the *Mayflower* until they had shelter on land.

The Pilgrims' first settlement

Massachusetts Bay Founded		Rhode Island Founded		King Philip's War		Glorious Revolution		Georgia Founded	
1629	1634	1636	1649	1675-6	1681	1688	1692	1733	1740-43
	Maryland Founded		Charles I of England Beheaded		Pennsylvania Founded		Salem Witch Trials		Great Awakening

Home Sweet Home

The Pilgrims built small frame homes, 14 by 18 feet, out of rough-hewn boards brought with them from England. The houses typically had a fireplace at one end with a ladder up to a loft where children could sleep. Glass was very expensive, so the windows were simply holes with bars of wood to keep out the bats; oiled paper served to let in some light. The roofs were thatched in the English style with layers of marsh grass, and clay was used for caulking their walls.

Death's Grim Harvest

During the very worst part of that severe first winter in America, many of the Pilgrims overworked themselves. The hardships of the ocean crossing, along with a poor diet, weakened them and made them especially susceptible to the flu-like disease which struck the settlers and killed more than half their number. William Bradford describes what it was like:

> But that which was most sad and lamentable was, that in two or three months' time, half of their company died, especially in January and February.... In the time of most distress, there [were] but six or seven sound persons, who, to their great commendation be it spoken, spared no pains night or day, but with abundance of toil and hazard of their own health, fetched them wood, made them fires, dressed them meat, made their beds, washed their loathsome clothes, clothed and unclothed them. In a word, did all the homely and necessary offices for them which dainty and queasy stomachs cannot endure to hear named; and all this willingly and cheerfully, without any grudging in the least, showing herein their true love unto their friends and brethren....I doubt not but their recompense [reward] is with the Lord."

William Bradford, author of the first history of Plymouth Plantation

285

CARVING A NEW WORLD SOCIETY

MARTIN LUTHER'S 95 THESES		HENRY VIII SPLITS FROM ROME		REIGN OF QUEEN ELIZABETH I BEGINS		SPANISH ARMADA DESTROYED		SIGNING OF MAYFLOWER COMPACT	
1517	1526	1534	1536	1558	1585	1588	1607	1620	1624
	TYNDALE'S ENGLISH NEW TESTAMENT		CALVIN'S INSTITUTES PUBLISHED		FIRST ROANOAK SETTLEMENT		JAMESTOWN, VIRGINIA FOUNDED		DUTCH FOUND NEW NETHERLAND

A Pedigreed Pilgrim Portrait

Edward Winslow (below) frequently served as Plymouth's assistant governor and served three terms as governor (1633, 1636, and 1644). Taking seriously Jesus' "Great Commission" to preach the Gospel to all the world, Winslow helped found the "Society for the Propagation of the Gospel among the Indians in New England." His portrait, which was painted in 1651 while he was in England representing his colony, is the only authentic likeness of any of the Pilgrims who came to America on the *Mayflower.*

An Indian Spring

The worst of the sickness was over by the end of February. The coming of spring brought new hope and a great surprise: One day an Indian walked boldly up to a group of Pilgrims who were working in their gardens. He greeted them with the English word "Welcome" and demanded beer. They promptly supplied him with a meal of English food which he ate heartily. His name was **Samoset.** He had learned his English from fishermen.

Later Samoset returned with some other Indians from the **Wampanoag tribe,** as well as the most important Indian the Pilgrims would meet. His name was Tisquantum, the last surviving member of the Pawtuxet tribe. The Pilgrims shortened his name to **Squanto.**

Squanto's tribe had been wiped out by plague, so he adopted the Pilgrims as his own. He taught them how to plant corn, catch fish, trap beaver, and prepare summer fruits for the winter. He also served as interpreter and diplomat in their dealings with other Indian tribes. He was, in the words of Governor Bradford, "A special instrument sent of God for their good beyond their expectation."

286

CHAPTER TWENTY FOUR

Learning the Language

Indian languages are complex, especially Algonquian, the language of Indians of the eastern tribes. It would be twenty years before a primer of the language would be developed in the colonies. Here's a sample of what the Pilgrim settlers were up against:

Nquitpausuckowashâwmen—"There are a hundred of us."

Chénock wonck cuppee-yeâumen?—"When will you return?"

Tasúckqunne cummauchenaûmisz—"How long have you been sick?"

Ntannetéimmin—"I will be going."

No wonder the Pilgrims shortened Tisquantum to Squanto. Providentially for the Pilgrims, Squanto could speak English and a little Spanish.

Squanto leading a group of Pilgrims

Squanto's Mysterious Past

Obviously, the Pilgrims were not the first white men to enter Squanto's life. How did he know so much about the English—their language and culture? Squanto was carried off in 1605 by George Weymouth, an English fisherman, and taken to England where he lived for nine years. Squanto then returned to America as an interpreter for John Smith in 1613. For his services, Smith gave Squanto his freedom. His freedom was short-lived, however. In 1614, he and nineteen others from his tribe were kidnapped by another Englishman and sold into slavery in Malaga, Spain. There he worked as a house servant before managing to escape to England. In 1619, he joined an English expedition headed for the New England coast. When he finally reached home, all Squanto found was an abandoned site. His entire tribe had been destroyed by a plague.

The First Thanksgiving?

There are numerous claims to the first Thanksgiving in America. One of the earliest recorded celebrations occurred a half century before the Pilgrims landed at Plymouth. "A small colony of French Huguenots established a settlement near present-day Jacksonville, Florida. On June 30, 1564, their leader, René de Laudonnière, recorded that 'We sang a psalm of Thanksgiving unto God, beseeching Him that it would please Him to continue His accustomed goodness towards us.'"

In 1610, after a hard winter called "the starving time," the colonists at Jamestown called for a time of thanksgiving. This was after the original company of 490 colonists had been reduced to 60 survivors. The colonists prayed for help that finally arrived by a ship filled with food and supplies from England. They held a prayer service to give thanks.

Massasoit's "Palace"

Harvest Hurrah

The twenty acres of Indian corn which had been planted under the watchful eye of Squanto in the spring of 1621 yielded a bountiful harvest. The Pilgrims were filled with gratitude to God, Who had preserved and blessed them with shelter, food, and the vital help of the Indians. William Bradford—who had been elected governor at the sudden death of John Carver—decided that the Pilgrims needed a day of celebration after their long period of hardship. He called for a time of thanksgiving to God, and he sent out hunters who came back with enough wild turkeys to last a week.

The Pilgrims invited **Massasoit,** chief of the Wampanoag Indians, to their

MASSACHUSETTS BAY FOUNDED		RHODE ISLAND FOUNDED		KING PHILIP'S WAR		GLORIOUS REVOLUTION		GEORGIA FOUNDED	
1629	1634	1636	1649	1675-6	1681	1688	1692	1733	1740-43
	MARYLAND FOUNDED		CHARLES I OF ENGLAND BEHEADED		PENNSYLVANIA FOUNDED		SALEM WITCH TRIALS		GREAT AWAKENING

Giving Thanks at Plymouth

Death took nearly half the company at Plymouth after their landing in December 1620. With the help of Squanto, the English settlers were able to produce an abundant harvest to meet their needs through the winter months. Even after their hardships, Governor Bradford proclaimed a day of thanksgiving and extended an invitation to the local Indians to share in the bounty. They feasted on boiled pumpkins and a variety of corn dishes. The main course consisted of oysters, clams, turkey, venison, and fish. At the end of the meal, Massasoit's brother, Quadequina, came from the woods with a bushel of popcorn in tow.

Massasoit visits the Pilgrims

thanksgiving feast. He came with ninety braves. They brought five deer with them, to the relief of the Pilgrims who were not sure how they were going to feed all their guests. Spread out on the full tables was a feast of venison, duck, goose, eels, lobsters, mussels, and clams, in addition to the parsnips, carrots, turnips, onions, cucumbers, radishes, beets, and cabbage from the Pilgrims' household gardens. Also served were gooseberries, strawberries, plums, and cherries, which had been dried under Squanto's supervision. White and red wine had been prepared from wild grapes growing in the area.

The celebration lasted for three days and featured games such as shooting contests, wrestling matches, and foot races. The following year, Massasoit was again invited to attend the harvest celebration. He must have really enjoyed the first one, because he brought his wife and 120 braves to the second feast.

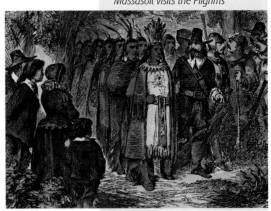

MARTIN LUTHER'S 95 THESES	HENRY VIII SPLITS FROM ROME	REIGN OF QUEEN ELIZABETH I BEGINS	SPANISH ARMADA DESTROYED	SIGNING OF MAYFLOWER COMPACT
1517	1526	1534	1536	1558	1585	1588	1607	1620	1624
TYNDALE'S ENGLISH NEW TESTAMENT	CALVIN'S *INSTITUTES* PUBLISHED	FIRST ROANOAK SETTLEMENT	JAMESTOWN, VIRGINIA FOUNDED	DUTCH FOUND NEW NETHERLAND

The Rest of the Squanto Story

Squanto was indeed a source of help for the Pilgrims, but he was also motivated by selfish advancement. He wanted to gain influence among the colonists and the Indians, so he manipulated groups against each other to create suspicion and conflict while offering himself as a powerful mediator. He once told the Indians that the Pilgrims had control over the plague, that they had buried it under their buildings and could release it whenever they were displeased. The Pilgrims denied this story when they heard it, although they did admit that "the God whom they served had Power to send that or any other Disease upon those that should do any wrong to His people." Later, Squanto tried to spread strife by sending the false message to the Pilgrims that Plymouth was under attack by combined tribes including the Wampanoags.

All for One, and None for All

The Pilgrims' contract with the London Company made it clear that everything they produced in Plymouth belonged to the company and was to be shared by all company members. For the first seven years, the total income of the colony was to be put into a common fund, and out of this the colonists were to draw enough to get their living. At the end of the seven years, the capital and profits, if any, were to be divided between the investors and colonists.

This common storehouse system was a failure from the start. As we have seen from studying the Jamestown colony, this system is a form of communism. The common system never works in any society because it encourages people to become lazy, resentful, and envious. Some depend upon the labor of others and quarrel over who owns what. At the end of three years, conditions were so bad that Governor Bradford abandoned the common storehouse arrangement and assigned each man his own plot of farm

An early meeting in the New World

land. In Bradford's words, it was wrong to believe "that the taking away of property and bringing [the] community into a common wealth would make them happy and flourishing, as if they were wiser than God." Once individual families were made responsible for their own incomes, everyone began to work harder and produce more.

Cain Revisited

One of the "Strangers" who travelled with the Pilgrims on the *Mayflower* was a violent and rude man named John Billington. Billington and his boys were trouble for the Pilgrims from day one. William Bradford called them "one of the most profane families among them" and questioned how they ever managed to slip aboard. Once established in Plymouth, John Billington continued to harangue and anger his neighbors. At last, his temper drove him out of control when he shot a bullet into his neighbor, John Newcomen. Newcomen died of a festering wound and fatal fever, and, after a trial before a jury, Billington was executed, thus having the dubious honor of being the first murderer of Plymouth Colony.

CARVING A NEW WORLD SOCIETY

MARTIN LUTHER'S 95 THESES		HENRY VIII SPLITS FROM ROME		REIGN OF QUEEN ELIZABETH I BEGINS		SPANISH ARMADA DESTROYED		SIGNING OF MAYFLOWER COMPACT	
1517	1526	1534	1536	1558	1585	1588	1607	1620	1624
	TYNDALE'S ENGLISH NEW TESTAMENT		CALVIN'S *INSTITUTES* PUBLISHED		FIRST ROANOAK SETTLEMENT		JAMESTOWN, VIRGINIA FOUNDED		DUTCH FOUND NEW NETHERLAND

William Bradford's house

The Day Plymouth Was Pickled

The original draft of Bradford's *Of Plymouth Plantation* has an unusual history. In 1650, Bradford finished the book, and his manuscript was passed on through many generations. But when the English invaded the colonies during the 1770s in the War for Independence, Bradford's manuscript was taken, along with many other books. It disappeared until 1793, when Bradford's original papers were once again located. If you think they were found in a museum under glass, you are wrong. They were found in a grocery store in Nova Scotia, Canada, where they were being used to wrap fish and pickles!

Sir Edmund Andros and his Great Seal

Plymouth Self-Government

Under Governor Bradford's leadership, the Pilgrims paid off their debt to the English merchants (even though the merchants had failed to send them the supplies they expected) and established a self-supporting community. Because of the Pilgrims' separatist beliefs, few new colonists joined Plymouth Plantation. Nevertheless, the colony did grow slowly and by 1643 contained ten communities. Most Puritans coming from England, however, opted to settle in Plymouth's non-separatist neighbor colony, Massachusetts Bay. In 1686, both Plymouth and Massachusetts Bay were ordered into the **Dominion of New England** by King James II and placed under the authority of **Sir Edmund Andros** (1637–1714).

The Dominion was a union of New England and some Middle Atlantic colonies designed to simplify governing and defense of the region, but the Puritans viewed it as the loss of their independence. Plymouth

292

MASSACHUSETTS BAY FOUNDED		RHODE ISLAND FOUNDED		KING PHILIP'S WAR		GLORIOUS REVOLUTION		GEORGIA FOUNDED	
1629	1634	1636	1649	1675-6	1681	1688	1692	1733	1740-43
	MARYLAND FOUNDED		CHARLES I OF ENGLAND BEHEADED		PENNSYLVANIA FOUNDED		SALEM WITCH TRIALS		GREAT AWAKENING

Plantation hoped to regain its independence when King James II was overthrown in 1688 and Governor Andros was shipped back to England. In 1691, however, Plymouth was joined to the new royal colony of Massachusetts.

The importance of the Plymouth settlement far out weighs its small size and in its example of **covenanted self-government** defined in the Mayflower Compact. The Plymouth Pilgrims were committed to living in terms of God's law as set forth in the Bible. Because of this commitment, they were blessed by God for many years.

A
RELATION OR
Iournall of the beginning and proceedings of the Englifh Plantation fetled at *Plimoth* in NEW ENGLAND, by certaine Englifh Aduenturers both Merchants and others.

With their difficult paffage, their fafe ariuall, their ioyfull building of, and comfortable planting them-felues in the now well defended Towne of NEW PLIMOTH.

AS ALSO A RELATION OF FOVRE feuerall difcoueries fince made by fome of the fame Englifh Planters there refident.

I. In a iourney to PVCKANOKICK the habitation of the Indians grea-teft King Maffafoyt : as alfo their meffage, the anfwer and entertainment they had of him.
II. In a voyage made by ten of them to the Kingdome of Nawfet, to feeke a boy that had loft himfelfe in the woods : with fuch accidents as befell them in that voyage.
III. In their iourney to the Kingdome of Namafchet, in defence of their greateft King Maffafoyt, against the Narrohiggonfets, and to reuenge the fuppofed death of their Interpreter Tifquantum.
IIII. Their voyage to the Maffachufets, and their entertainment there.

With an anfwer to all fuch obiections as are any way made against the lawfulneffe of Englifh plantations in thofe parts.

LONDON,
Printed for *Iohn Bellamie*, and are to be fold at his fhop at the two Greyhounds in Cornhill neere the Royall Exchange. 1622.

Mourt Who?

A great deal of what we know about the Pilgrims comes from **primary historical sources,** eye-witness reports. Their governor, William Bradford, wrote a journal called *Of Plymouth Plantation* which records the colony's struggles in an eloquent history. Another eyewitness account of Plymouth comes from a book called *Mourt's Relation* which is a description of Plymouth by vari-ous people. Mourt apparently had no hand in writing this account. He simply arranged for its publica-tion back in England. Mourt was actually George Morton who at the time was using the name Mourt.

293

MARTIN LUTHER'S 95 THESES	HENRY VIII SPLITS FROM ROME	REIGN OF QUEEN ELIZABETH I BEGINS	SPANISH ARMADA DESTROYED	SIGNING OF MAYFLOWER COMPACT
1517	1526	1534	1536	1558	1585	1588	1607	1620	1624

| TYNDALE'S ENGLISH NEW TESTAMENT | CALVIN'S *INSTITUTES* PUBLISHED | FIRST ROANOAK SETTLEMENT | JAMESTOWN, VIRGINIA FOUNDED | DUTCH FOUND NEW NETHERLAND |

FOR STUDY

CHAPTER 24:
Carving a New World Society

Terms

jurisdiction
anarchy
Mayflower Compact
covenant
Plymouth Plantation
Wampanoag Tribe
communism
Dominion of New England
covenanted self-government
primary historical sources

People

John Carver
Samoset
Squanto
Massasoit
Sir Edmund Andros

Upon their arrival in America, the Separatists faced anarchy. In resolving the problem, they helped lay the foundation for American self-government by drawing up the Mayflower Compact. Their own foolish practice of a form of communism soon brought starvation. God graciously sent aid. In addition, the struggling colonists began to follow economic principles set forth in the Bible. Though the Plymouth colony was never large, the examples it set in the area of government and economics had an enormous impact on the growth of the American nation.

Discussion Questions

1. What unexpected circumstance required the writing and signing of the Mayflower Compact?
2. Why was a written, signed document establishing a government regarded as so important by the people aboard the *Mayflower?* Can the same be said about the United States Constitution? Why?
3. List the providential circumstances and events that the Pilgrims encountered their first few years in Plymouth.
4. Why was the common storehouse system a failure?
5. Define "covenanted self-government" and give examples.

Optional Enrichment Projects

1. Read a complete copy of the Mayflower Compact.
2. Many people believe the U.S. Constitution is an "evolving" document which changes its meaning to meet the needs of each new generation. Others stress the need to understand the document's "original intent." Study the arguments on both sides of the issue and analyze them in light of God's Word. Which view should the Christian have of the Ten Commandments?
3. Research the culture of the tribes encountered by the New England settlers. What did they believe about God, property, justice, the family, and the relationship of the individual to the tribal unit? How did these beliefs help or hinder the way the Indians received the Pilgrims and the Gospel of Jesus Christ?

C H A P T E R

25

NEW ENGLAND's
City Set
Upon a Hill

Charles I

Charles in Charge

In England the Puritans were growing increasingly unhappy about their church and king. At the death of James I in 1625, James's son Charles assumed the throne. **Charles I (1625–1649)** immediately began to use his authority as king in arbitrary and tyrannical ways. After incurring large debts from wasteful wars against France and Spain, Charles called for new taxes. The many Puritans in the House of Commons refused to consider the king's request for new taxes until he considered their requests for reform in the Church of England.

In 1629, Charles decided that the easiest way to get what he wanted was to dismiss Parliament and levy the taxes without its consent.

295

MARTIN LUTHER'S 95 THESES		HENRY VIII SPLITS FROM ROME		REIGN OF QUEEN ELIZABETH I BEGINS		SPANISH ARMADA DESTROYED		SIGNING OF MAYFLOWER COMPACT	
1517	1526	1534	1536	1558	1585	1588	1607	1620	1624

TYNDALE'S ENGLISH NEW TESTAMENT   CALVIN'S *INSTITUTES* PUBLISHED   FIRST ROANOAK SETTLEMENT   JAMESTOWN, VIRGINIA FOUNDED   DUTCH FOUND NEW NETHERLAND

Massachusetts, named for the Massachusetts Indians who inhabited its coast, was the sixth colony to ratify the Constitution on February 6, 1788. State motto: *Ense petit placidam sub libertate quietem,* "By the sword we seek peace, but peace only under liberty."

William Laud, Archbishop of Canterbury

Laud Him or Leave Him

To make matters worse, Charles steadfastly refused to reform the Anglican Church. Not only was he personally opposed to the Reformed faith, he was also greatly influenced by his wife, Henrietta Maria, daughter of Henry IV of France and a fervent Roman Catholic. Throughout the reigns of Elizabeth I and James I, the Puritans had been unable to bring about any substantial reform. When James died and his son Charles became king, the Puritans hoped that perhaps this king would listen to their pleas for true reformation in the Church of England.

Tennis Anyone?

Believing that Sunday should be set aside as a day of rest and worship, the Puritans disapproved of sports on the first day of the week. King Charles I, on the other hand, had nothing but disdain for the Puritans and their view of biblical law. In order to provoke these Reformed-minded Christians, Charles rewrote and published his father's *Book of Sports* which promoted Sunday as a day of recreation. To make matters worse, Archbishop Laud promoted the book and made it required reading in the churches.

C H A P T E R   T W E N T Y   F I V E

MASSACHUSETTS BAY FOUNDED		RHODE ISLAND FOUNDED		KING PHILIP'S WAR		GLORIOUS REVOLUTION		GEORGIA FOUNDED	
1629	1634	1636	1649	1675-6	1681	1688	1692	1733	1740-43
	MARYLAND FOUNDED		CHARLES I OF ENGLAND BEHEADED		PENNSYLVANIA FOUNDED		SALEM WITCH TRIALS		GREAT AWAKENING

It was not long before the Puritans were severely disappointed. King Charles appointed **William Laud** (1573–1645) to be the Archbishop of Canterbury in 1633. Laud was clearly not interested in the changes the Puritans wanted to make. He encouraged Anglican churches to reintroduce Catholic forms of worship such as stained glass windows, crosses, crucifixes, and railed altars. He also called for the Roman Catholic rituals of bowing whenever the name of Jesus was said and making the sign of the cross in baptism. In addition, Laud supported the king's use of the **Court of the Star Chamber** and the **Courts of High Commission** to force people to comply with the new religious practices.

The King's Court Now in Session

The Star Chamber was a room in the palace at Westminster, England, where the king's council met. The room was named for its star-decorated ceiling. From medieval times, the king's council had ruled on specific legal cases that were beyond the jurisdiction of the common courts. By an act of Parliament in 1487, Henry VII strengthened the power of the council so nobles could be put on trial. In 1540, Henry VIII put the committee under his direct control, and it became known as the Court of the Star Chamber. There was no jury, and any punishment could be imposed except the death penalty. In addition, the Star Chamber forced people to testify against themselves. By the time of Charles I, the Star Chamber had gained the reputation of being a "legal" way for the king to get rid of his political enemies. The Courts of High Commission served a similar purpose but were directed at the clergy, especially Puritan ministers. In 1641, Parliament stripped authority from the Court of the Star Chamber and the Courts of High Commission.

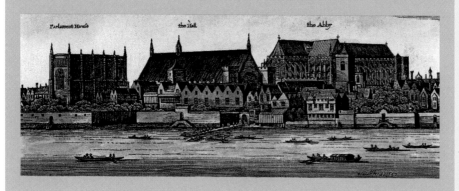

| MARTIN LUTHER'S 95 THESES | HENRY VIII SPLITS FROM ROME | REIGN OF QUEEN ELIZABETH I BEGINS | SPANISH ARMADA DESTROYED | SIGNING OF MAYFLOWER COMPACT |

1517   1526   1534   1536   1558   1585   1588   1607   1620   1624

| TYNDALE'S ENGLISH NEW TESTAMENT | CALVIN'S INSTITUTES PUBLISHED | FIRST ROANOAK SETTLEMENT | JAMESTOWN, VIRGINIA FOUNDED | DUTCH FOUND NEW NETHERLAND |

In a League of Their Own

In an attempt to expand their authoritarian rule, Charles and Laud began to impose their religious views on the Presbyterians in Scotland by forcing them to adopt the Episcopalian form of worship and church government. The Scots refused and in 1638 drafted the **National Covenant**, asserting Scotland's traditional religious rights. In 1643, they drafted the **Solemn League and Covenant** which not only preserved Presbyterianism in Scotland but also proposed to spread the Reformed faith in England and Ireland as well.

The king hoped to force the Scots to comply by sending troops. Instead, the Scots defied the king, defeated his army, abolished episcopacy, and occupied northern England in a military standoff. The Scots even assessed the king daily tribute payments. These Scottish Presbyterians would long remember their battle with English rule.

The Solemn League and Covenant (1643) went further than the National Covenant. The church and government of both England and Scotland agreed "to preserve the Reformed religion in Scotland, while undertaking the reformation of religion in England and Ireland."

Lambeth Palace, the London residence of the Archbishop of Canterbury

Reforming Worship

The *Book of Common Prayer* first appeared in England in 1549. It replaced the complicated Latin Roman Catholic Mass with an English worship service the common people could understand. Scripture readings replaced legends of the saints. The Old Testament was read through each year, the New Testament three times a year, and the Psalms every month. The book attempted to purify worship services from unscriptural practices such as prayer to saints. Even with these reforms, many still opposed it for not going far enough. For example, the term "mass" was still used, and the communion table was still called the "altar," which is the place where sacrifices are performed. This terminology tended to perpetuate the Roman Catholic notion that Christ was being "sacrificed" in a non-bloody ritual. Reformers taught that Christ's one-time death on Calvary was the only sacrifice that was required to meet God's standard of justice.

In 1552, a new *Book of Common Prayer,* which was much more Reformed in its theology and practice, replaced the old one. The two editions of the prayer book illustrate the struggle in the Church of England between the Anglicans who held to the Roman Catholic practices and the Puritans who insisted on the more biblical teachings of the Protestant Reformation.

Book of Common Prayer *title page.*

Charles called Parliament back into session in November of 1640 hoping to gain support against the Scots. Instead, Parliament took advantage of the king's weakened political and military condition by further limiting his powers.

During this period of oppression—from 1630 to 1642—nearly 24,000 Puritans came to New England in what has been described as the **Great Migration.** Many Puritan leaders believed that settlement in America was their last chance to establish a church and civil government pleasing to God and in conformity to His Word.

MARTIN LUTHER'S 95 THESES		HENRY VIII SPLITS FROM ROME		REIGN OF QUEEN ELIZABETH I BEGINS		SPANISH ARMADA DESTROYED		SIGNING OF MAYFLOWER COMPACT	
1517	1526	1534	1536	1558	1585	1588	1607	1620	1624
	TYNDALE'S ENGLISH NEW TESTAMENT		CALVIN'S *INSTITUTES* PUBLISHED		FIRST ROANOAK SETTLEMENT		JAMESTOWN, VIRGINIA FOUNDED		DUTCH FOUND NEW NETHERLAND

Seal of Massachusetts

No Kings Attached

In 1628, a leading group of English Puritans formed the **Massachusetts Bay Company,** a joint stock company with twenty-six stockholders. They received a patent from the Council for New England and secured a charter from King Charles on March 4, 1629, narrowly escaping the coming oppression. This charter or "patent" was the legal foundation of the government of the colony. The patent required that the king be paid one fifth of all gold and silver found in Massachusetts. In addition, the officers of the colony were to be chosen in annual elections by its members, who were called **freemen.**

Unlike other trading company charters of that era, the Massachusetts Bay Company patent did not state that the seat of civil government was to remain in England. This remarkable omission allowed Massachusetts Bay to build a colony without English interference. By transferring the Company's authority to New England, the stockholders could make religious and civil decisions independent of royal control.

FREEMEN
were those persons who possessed a freehold, that is, outright ownership of land. Most of the colonies only allowed freemen the right to vote.

The First Charter of Massachusetts

On March 4, 1629, The Massachusetts Bay Company secured a royal charter. The purpose was so "the people may be so religiously, peaceable, and civilly governed, as their good life and orderly conversation, may win and incite the natives of the country, to the knowledge and obedience of the only true God and Savior of mankind, and the Christian faith, which in our Royal intention is the principal end of this plantation." The Charter repeated the intention of the original patent granted by King James I in 1620: "We...in Hope thereby to advance the enlargement of [the] Christian Religion, to the Glory of God Almighty,...may with Boldness go on to the settling of so hopeful a work, which tends to the reducing and Conversion of such Savages as remain wandering in Desolation and Distress, to Civil Society and Christian Religion...."

C H A P T E R   T W E N T Y   F I V E

MASSACHUSETTS BAY FOUNDED		RHODE ISLAND FOUNDED		KING PHILIP'S WAR		GLORIOUS REVOLUTION		GEORGIA FOUNDED	
1629	1634	1636	1649	1675-6	1681	1688	1692	1733	1740-43
	MARYLAND FOUNDED		CHARLES I OF ENGLAND BEHEADED		PENNSYLVANIA FOUNDED		SALEM WITCH TRIALS		GREAT AWAKENING

On the Road

A small party of Puritans established a foothold in the new colony in 1629, under the leadership of Captain **John Endecott** (*c.* 1599–1665). This group settled in Salem, Massachusetts, and Endecott served as the first governor of Massachusetts Bay.

A year later, **John Winthrop** (1588–1649) paved the way for a mass exodus of English immigrants. Winthrop, who was a **burgess** (owner of a country estate) and a **barrister** (a lawyer), had become a Puritan while studying at Trinity College at Cambridge University. Most of the year, Winthrop was kept busy tending to matters on his estate, but during the winters, when there was less work to be done, he went to London to practice law. There he met others who shared his faith. Winthrop and his companions criticized the spiritual decay of their country and discussed possible solutions.

The question that burdened Winthrop and his Puritan friends was whether it was right for them to leave England and seemingly abandon the country to God's judgment. Being a lawyer, Winthrop decided to argue this case with himself. He wrote up two briefs as though preparing to argue the case both ways in court. When his Puritan friends read his arguments, they were convinced that settling in America was the right thing to do. They asked Winthrop to lead their expedition.

John Winthrop, long-term governor of Massachusetts Bay

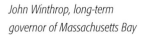

No Maypoles, Please

In 1625, Thomas Morton, an English lawyer, arrived in Massachusetts. Morton saw the land as his own "paradise" and playground. he erected an eighty-foot maypole and invited the neighboring Indians to join him and his friends in dancing, drinking, and riotous celebration. When his Puritan neighbors learned what was going on, John Endecott (above) personally cut down the pagan symbol and hauled Morton into court, where he was sentenced to exile in England.

301

MARTIN LUTHER'S 95 THESES		HENRY VIII SPLITS FROM ROME		REIGN OF QUEEN ELIZABETH I BEGINS		SPANISH ARMADA DESTROYED		SIGNING OF MAYFLOWER COMPACT	
1517	1526	1534	1536	1558	1585	1588	1607	1620	1624
	TYNDALE'S ENGLISH NEW TESTAMENT		CALVIN'S *INSTITUTES* PUBLISHED		FIRST ROANOAK SETTLEMENT		JAMESTOWN, VIRGINIA FOUNDED		DUTCH FOUND NEW NETHERLAND

First Things First

As settlers spread out from Massachusetts Bay, the first thing they did was establish their church. The statement of some thirty of the original settlers at Salem expressed this priority: "We covenant with the Lord and with one another and do bind ourselves in the presence of God to walk together in all His ways according as He is pleased to reveal Himself unto us in His blessed word of truth."

The Light of the World

The Puritan group which sailed from England was enormous compared to the hundred or so Pilgrims who had settled Plymouth Plantation ten years before. Winthrop's fleet of seventeen ships carried almost one thousand men and women with their families, as well as 240 cows and about 60 horses.

On board the flagship *Arbella,* Winthrop gave his fellow travelers an inspiring and challenging message, *A Model of Christian Charity.* Reading this charge helps us to understand the Puritans' hope for their new life: "We must consider that we shall be as a city upon a hill; the eyes of all people are upon us, so that if we shall deal falsely with our God in this work we have undertaken, and so cause Him to withdraw His present help from us, we shall be made a story and a by-word throughout the world."

The phrase "city upon a hill" comes from Jesus' words to His disciples in Matthew 5:14: "You are the light of the world. A city set on a hill cannot be hidden." The message is important: All followers of Jesus Christ will be watched and judged in terms of how faithfully they carry out the demands of the Gospel.

From Eagle to Arbella

The *Arbella* was a ship of 350 tons—about twice the size of the Pilgrims' *Mayflower*—and "manned with 52 seamen and 28 pieces of ordnance [weapons]." She was well stocked with "42 Tonnes of beere" (about 10,000 gallons) and "14 Tonnes of water caske" (about 3,500 gallons) for the ten-week voyage. The ship was originally named *Eagle* and was later rechristened in honor of Lady Arbella Johnson, wife of Isaack Johnson, passengers on the voyage.

A procession of Pilgrims on their way to worship

| MARTIN LUTHER'S 95 THESES | HENRY VIII SPLITS FROM ROME | REIGN OF QUEEN ELIZABETH I BEGINS | SPANISH ARMADA DESTROYED | SIGNING OF MAYFLOWER COMPACT |

| 1517 | 1526 | 1534 | 1536 | 1558 | 1585 | 1588 | 1607 | 1620 | 1624 |

| TYNDALE'S ENGLISH NEW TESTAMENT | CALVIN'S *INSTITUTES* PUBLISHED | FIRST ROANOAK SETTLEMENT | JAMESTOWN, VIRGINIA FOUNDED | DUTCH FOUND NEW NETHERLAND |

MAGISTRATE
A civil officer who administers the law.

A Bible Commonwealth

The Puritans insisted on being "guided by one rule, even the Word of the Most High." They established a church free from the control of the civil magistrates, and they formed a civil government whose magistrates were ordained by God. In each jurisdiction—church and state—the Bible was the standard. The principles of Calvin's Geneva had come to America.

Initially, the government of Massachusetts Bay Colony was solely in the hands of the **General Court,** the legislative assembly composed of shareholders in the Massachusetts Bay Company. The General Court ordered that only church members could hold public office. From this body of eligible voters, a governor, deputy governor, and council of assistants were elected. Since there was no king, Parliament, bishop or judge to overrule them, the members of the General Court could govern in the way they saw fit. With this new political freedom, Winthrop and the Court

MASSACHUSETTS BAY FOUNDED		RHODE ISLAND FOUNDED		KING PHILIP'S WAR		GLORIOUS REVOLUTION		GEORGIA FOUNDED	
1629	1634	1636	1649	1675-6	1681	1688	1692	1733	1740-43
	MARYLAND FOUNDED		CHARLES I OF ENGLAND BEHEADED		PENNSYLVANIA FOUNDED		SALEM WITCH TRIALS		GREAT AWAKENING

opened the way for the whole body of freemen to participate in the government, not just members of the Bay Company. Even with this new freedom, rulers still had the primary duty to enforce the laws of God as they applied to civil government.

The role of church officials in Massachusetts Bay was to instruct the people and offer sound advice based on the Bible. Ministers of the Gospel were not permitted to hold public office, because this was regarded as a breach of the jurisdictional separation between church and state.

Colonization of New England

John Cotton

Communism Comes to New England?

One of the main problems the Puritans had to deal with in their colonies was the economy. People began to complain that they were paying too much for goods and services, so a central court of Massachusetts established price and wage controls. In other words, civil officials determined how much money was a "fair price" to pay for things like food and livestock. Merchants were fined for charging "too much." Just like any other attempt to manage an economy and set prices and wages, these laws did not work. Goods and services remained in short supply, and skilled artisans simply moved to areas where they could make a better wage.

Limiting the Power of Government

John Cotton (1584–1652), a pastor and theologian who emigrated from England to Massachusetts in 1633, had this to say about the limits of governmental authority: "It is…most wholesome for magistrates and officers in church and commonwealth never to affect more liberty and authority than will do them good, and the people good; for whatever transcendent power is given will certainly overrun those that receive it…. It is necessary, therefore, that all power that is on earth be limited, church power or other."

305

MARTIN LUTHER'S 95 THESES		HENRY VIII SPLITS FROM ROME		REIGN OF QUEEN ELIZABETH I BEGINS		SPANISH ARMADA DESTROYED		SIGNING OF MAYFLOWER COMPACT
1517	1526	1534	1536	1558	1585	1588	1607	1620	1624
	TYNDALE'S ENGLISH NEW TESTAMENT		CALVIN'S *INSTITUTES* PUBLISHED		FIRST ROANOAK SETTLEMENT		JAMESTOWN, VIRGINIA FOUNDED		DUTCH FOUND NEW NETHERLAND

Animal Rights Activists?

The Puritans believed in "humane" treatment of animals. In 1641, they wrote in the Massachusetts Body of Liberties this law: "No man shall exercise any tyranny or cruelty towards any brute creature which [is] usually kept for man's use."

Massachusetts Body of Liberties

In order to ensure the liberties of the colonists and the stability of the colony, the leaders of Massachusetts Bay knew they needed a body of written laws. The first comprehensive governing document of the colony was the **Massachusetts Body of Liberties** (1641). It blended laws from England with those of the Bible and combined them with the special circumstances of the colony. This document protected many important liberties that we are familiar with today, such as:

- *Freedom of speech in courts and public assemblies.*
- *The right to trial by jury.*
- *Outlawing of double jeopardy (trying a person twice for the same crime).*

The church was also protected by the Body of Liberties: "Every Church has full liberty to exercise all the ordinances of God, according to the rules of Scripture" (Section 95, part 2). Because the laws were written for all to see, the document had the good effect of limiting the powers of the magistrates and protecting the rights of the citizens.

This Flag Won't Fly

In 1644, John Endecott began to object to the red cross that adorned England's flag. He considered it an emblem of submission to the Roman Catholic Church and a remnant of idolatry. When he saw the flag flying over him in the street of his hometown of Salem, he seized its folds and cut out the cross.

CHAPTER TWENTY FIVE

Harvard's Rules

The "First Rules of Harvard College" in 1643 stated: "Let every Student be plainly instructed, and earnestly pressed to consider well, the main end of his life and studies is, *to know God and Jesus Christ which is eternal life,* John 17.3, and therefore to lay Christ at the bottom, as the only foundation of all sound knowledge and Learning. And seeing the Lord only giveth wisdom, Let every one seriously set himself by prayer in secret to seek it of him, Prov. 2:3."

An early seal of Harvard contained the Latin motto Veritas Christo et Ecclesiae, *which means "Truth for Christ and the Church." The first proposed Harvard seal (1643), which remains in use today, shows a medieval-shaped shield with three open books with clasps. The pages of two books and the front and back covers of one book contain the Latin word* veritas–*truth.*

Reading, Writing, and Reformation

The Puritans believed that in order to bring biblical reformation to a society, it was important to give a godly education to future leaders such as lawyers, magistrates, and pastors. In 1636, only six years after they had settled in Massachusetts Bay, the Puritans established **Harvard College** (above) to provide a proper education for future ministers. They named the college in honor of John Harvard who donated half of his estate and his entire library to the effort. It was possible in those days to enter Harvard at age fourteen—but students had to pass a rigorous entrance examination which was given in Latin!

307

MARTIN LUTHER'S 95 THESES	HENRY VIII SPLITS FROM ROME	REIGN OF QUEEN ELIZABETH I BEGINS	SPANISH ARMADA DESTROYED	SIGNING OF MAYFLOWER COMPACT
1517	1526	1534	1536	1558	1585	1588	1607	1620	1624
TYNDALE'S ENGLISH NEW TESTAMENT	CALVIN'S *INSTITUTES* PUBLISHED	FIRST ROANOAK SETTLEMENT	JAMESTOWN, VIRGINIA FOUNDED	DUTCH FOUND NEW NETHERLAND

The Hornbook

Colonial children normally began their education with a **hornbook.** This was not really a book in the ordinary sense. The Lord's Prayer, the alphabet, numbers, or perhaps vocabulary words broken down by syllables, were printed on a piece of parchment or paper cut to fit the shape of a flat piece of wood that served as the "book." The writing paper was covered with a sheet of animal horn, thin enough to be almost transparent. The covering would protect the paper or parchment underneath. The handle made it easy for students to carry it with them as they studied their lessons.

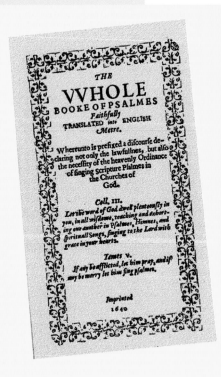

See Jane Read…and Pray

The New England Primer, which made its appearance about 1687, was the first *textbook* to be printed in America. It soon became one of the most influential books ever published in this country. For over a century, it was the most important school book in America. A primer is a first (prime) reader, but this book was far more than that. It first served as a catechism, a book of religious instruction. It taught the alphabet through the use of short poems with Bible references.

In addition to teaching the alphabet, the primer taught the Lord's Prayer, portions of the Westminster Shorter Catechism, and the Apostles' Creed. Students hardly ever owned their own complete copy of the primer; instead, the books were usually taken apart and the individual pages turned into durable hornbooks which could be used to teach hundreds of children. When children had mastered the *New England Primer,* they moved on to the **Bay Psalm Book,** a collection of Psalms written in verse for congregational singing, and the first *book* published in the colonies.

C H A P T E R   T W E N T Y   F I V E

MASSACHUSETTS BAY FOUNDED	RHODE ISLAND FOUNDED	KING PHILIP'S WAR	GLORIOUS REVOLUTION	GEORGIA FOUNDED	
1629	1634	1636	1649	1675-6	1681	1688	1692	1733	1740-43
	MARYLAND FOUNDED		CHARLES I OF ENGLAND BEHEADED		PENNSYLVANIA FOUNDED		SALEM WITCH TRIALS		GREAT AWAKENING

Education Goes Public

A Harvard education was not for everyone. Only those individuals who wanted to take specific leadership roles in society would pursue an advanced education. Even though most colonial children did not go off to college, it was considered very important for everyone to learn the basics of education, especially reading. Reading was essential because of the high value the Puritans placed on studying the Bible.

Most of the early settlers taught their children at home. But in 1647, the Massachusetts General Court passed a law called the **"Old Deluder Satan Act"** which called for the formation of a mandatory common school. The reason given for the establishment of common schools was to make sure children were equipped intellectually and spiritually to fight the devil's deceptive ways. The Act stated that every town of fifty or more families must hire an instructor to teach children how to read and write. Towns with one hundred families or more were required to set up a grammar school "to instruct youth so far as they shall be fitted for the university." This law made it clear that parents, or, in the case of apprenticed children, the masters, had the primary responsibility for paying teachers' salaries.

Because the Massachusetts authorities believed that it was important to pass on sound Christian doctrine to future generations, they made education compulsory and called on everyone in the community to pay for educating the children. The other New England colonies valued education, especially religious education, just as highly. The difference was that most of the other colonies left education completely up to the parents and private groups.

Learning the alphabet and Christian theology in Puritan New England by using the New England Primer

A — In ADAM's Fall We sinned all.

B — Heaven to find, The Bible Mind.

C — Christ crucify'd For sinners dy'd.

D — The Deluge drown'd The Earth around.

E — ELIJAH hid By Ravens fed.

F — The judgment made FELIX afraid.

G — As runs the Glass, Our Life doth pass.

H — My Book and Heart Must never part.

I — JOB feels the Rod, Yet blesses GOD.

K — Proud Korah's troop Was swallowed up

L — LOT fled to *Zoar*, Saw fiery Shower On *Sodom* pour.

M — MOSES was he Who *Israel's* Host Led thro' the Sea.

309

A Puritan Commonwealth

The **Cambridge Platform** of 1648, which was adopted in Puritan New England by 1651, organized a Puritan commonwealth based on the Bible. The following paragraphs from the Platform demonstrate how essential the Bible was to the ordering of society: "It is the duty of the Magistrate to take care of matters of religion and to improve his civil authority for the observing of the duties commanded in the first table [i.e., the first four of the Ten Commandments], as well as for observing of the duties commanded in the second table [i.e., the last six of the Ten Commandments].... Idolatry, Blasphemy, Heresy, venting corrupt and pernicious opinions, that destroy the foundation, open contempt of the word preached, profanation of the Lord's day, disturbing the peaceable administration & exercise of the worship & holy things of God, and the like, are to be restrained, and punished by civil authority."

The Light Dims

By the mid-1600s, the Puritans began to notice a decline of religious zeal. The original Puritan towns had centered on the church. Dwellings were located close to one another so that each church member could encourage his neighbor. In time, some Puritans began to move to the country where land was more plentiful but the church exerted less influence. The original community spirit began to decline.

The second generation was growing up without the same Christian zeal of their parents. In addition, church requirements that members must report a conversion experience made matters worse. Second-generation Puritans were raised in Christian homes. Most of them grew up knowing of God's redeeming grace. Since they could not testify to having a conversion experience, they were not considered full church members. As a result, they could not have their own children baptized. In 1662, the clergy sought to resolve this problem with the **Half-Way Covenant.** Those who wished could become a half-way church member without professing an experience of conversion. They still could not vote or partake of the Lord's Supper, but they could have their children baptized.

Many Puritans complained that the Half-Way Covenant was a compromise of biblical standards. In 1677, **Solomon Stoddard** (1643–1729) of Northhampton took biblical compromise one step further; he offered full communion to anyone who lived an upright life, believing that the Lord's Supper would have a "converting influence." Now it seemed to many Puritans that their mission had been betrayed and that God would punish the colony.

First church building in Salem

In the late 1670s, a great fire destroyed much of Boston. A smallpox epidemic followed. In 1679, the clergy met to discuss the recent events. They drew up a list of sins which they believed had provoked God's wrath: materialism, drunkenness, sleeping during sermons, and especially forgetting their original mission. The Puritans saw the revocation of their charter in 1691 as one more judgment by God. Their "light shining in the wilderness" seemed to grow dim with every passing year.

The Puritans of Massachusetts believed that their sins—compromising God's standards and forgetting their mission—had brought down God's judgment. In addition, some Puritans began to wonder if perhaps the failure of their mission was due to traitors to their faith who lived in their midst.

Not Everyone's Cup of Tea

While it is true that the Puritans restricted voting to male church members who owned property, colonists had more rights than the average Englishman. This is why noted American historian Samuel Eliot Morison could conclude that "Puritanism is an American heritage to be grateful for and not to be sneered at."

How Puritanical Were the Puritans?

The word *puritanical* has come to define anyone who is anti-scientific, rejects education, dresses in dark clothes, and forbids anyone from having fun. While this may be the modern portrayal of the Puritans, it does not describe the real Puritans. What most people think they know of the Puritans comes from Nathaniel Hawthorne's *The Scarlet Letter,* a fictional work written in the nineteenth century which gave a distorted view of Puritans because of Hawthorne's prejudice against them. The Puritans were the most educated people of their day. Harvard College promoted literature, art, and the sciences. Cotton Mather, one of Harvard's most famous graduates, published more than 460 works, could read seven languages, and had a library of nearly 4000 volumes. He supported smallpox inoculations and wrote the first notable work on medicine published in America, *The Angel of Bethesda.* The Puritans were hardly prudes. They drank beer with their meals and rum, a fermented drink made from molasses, at weddings. While recreational sports were forbidden on Sunday, Puritans enjoyed bowling, swimming, archery, skating, and hunting on other days. Their clothing was not drab. Puritans wore colorful clothing. In fact, it was the Quakers who criticized the Puritans for wearing ornate and brightly colored garments.

MARTIN LUTHER'S 95 THESES		HENRY VIII SPLITS FROM ROME		REIGN OF QUEEN ELIZABETH I BEGINS		SPANISH ARMADA DESTROYED		SIGNING OF MAYFLOWER COMPACT	
1517	1526	1534	1536	1558	1585	1588	1607	1620	1624
	TYNDALE'S ENGLISH NEW TESTAMENT		CALVIN'S *INSTITUTES* PUBLISHED		FIRST ROANOAK SETTLEMENT		JAMESTOWN, VIRGINIA FOUNDED		DUTCH FOUND NEW NETHERLAND

FOR STUDY

CHAPTER 25:
New England'
City Set
Upon a Hill

Terms

Court of the Star Chamber
Courts of High Commission
National Covenant
Solemn League and Covenant
Great Migration
Massachusetts Bay Company
freemen
burgess
barrister
A Model of Christian Charity
General Court
Massachusetts Body
of Liberties
Harvard College
hornbook
New England Primer
Bay Psalm Book
"Old Deluder Satan Act"
Cambridge Platform
Half-Way Covenant

People

Charles I
William Laud
Captain John Endecott
John Winthrop
Solomon Stoddard

Charles I of England, along with many leaders of the Anglican Church, severely persecuted Reformed Christians. Therefore, thousands of Puritans fled to the New World to establish a godly community which would serve as a Christian example to the rest of the world. Because the Puritans desired an educated clergy and a church that was able to read God's Word, they established a number of educational institutions. Unfortunately, the children of the Puritans did not all share their parents' zeal for God, and the colony suffered numerous afflictions which appeared to be signs of God's displeasure.

Discussion Questions

1. List the events which forced Charles I to call Parliament back into session after it had been disbanded for over ten years?
2. What unusual omission was made in the patent of the Massachusetts Bay Company? How did this affect the future of the colony?
3. In what sense had Calvin's Geneva come to America with the arrival of the Puritans?
4. Who could vote in the Massachusetts Bay Colony? Why?
5. Why was the ability to read so important to the Puritans in Massachusetts Bay?
6. What events did the Puritans see as evidence of God's displeasure with them?

Optional Enrichment Projects

1. The autocratic attitudes and actions of Charles I and his father James I were due, in part, to a political philosophy much in fashion at the time called the "Divine Right of Kings." Research this theory and critique it from a biblical standpoint.
2. The Massachusetts Puritans saw the judgment of God in their increasing tribulations and loss of self-government. Does this conclusion properly reflect the teachings of the Bible? Is this view of God's judgment still valid today? Why or why not?
3. Research the Solemn League and Covenant. What part did it play in English and Scottish history?

C H A P T E R

26

ROGUE ISLAND:

QUARRELS and QUIRKS

Trouble in Paradise

As we have seen, the Puritans were eager to leave England and the increasing oppression of King Charles I. Those fleeing to America soon learned, however, that they would not be able to escape religious disputes in *New* England either. Even among people who called themselves Puritans there were disagreements and hot-tempered debates.

In 1631, trouble arrived in New England in the person of **Roger Williams** (1603–1683). Williams was a likeable and intelligent man who became good friends with Governor Winthrop. However, while serving as pastor of various Massachusetts churches, Williams began delivering inflammatory messages that the Puritan leadership believed would upset the social and political order of New England.

Rhode Island, founded in 1636, was the last of the original thirteen colonies to ratify the Constitution on May 29, 1790. State motto: "Hope."

313

MARTIN LUTHER'S 95 THESES		HENRY VIII SPLITS FROM ROME		REIGN OF QUEEN ELIZABETH I BEGINS		SPANISH ARMADA DESTROYED		SIGNING OF MAYFLOWER COMPACT	
1517	1526	1534	1536	1558	1585	1588	1607	1620	1624
	TYNDALE'S ENGLISH NEW TESTAMENT		CALVIN'S *INSTITUTES* PUBLISHED		FIRST ROANOAK SETTLEMENT		JAMESTOWN, VIRGINIA FOUNDED		DUTCH FOUND NEW NETHERLAND

Roger Williams

Williams believed that the Church of England had not gone far enough in reforming itself and advocated complete separation from non-Reformed Christians. The Separatists of New England, like Williams, also agreed that the English church was in need of additional reform. In fact, they had been so frustrated with the lack of progress toward full reformation that they had left the church to begin a new work. Even so, they continued in fellowship with Christians who remained members of the English church. They believed that Christians who remained in the Church of England were their brothers and sisters in Christ.

To the colonists of Massachusetts Bay, Williams sounded a lot like the early European Anabaptists—separation and purity no matter what the cost or consequences. As a result, the fragile colony feared that an uprising similar to the one in the German city-state of Münster in 1534 could take place in New England if Williams's views spread among more radical groups.

Good Advice to the Libertines

Puritan preacher John Cotton (right) cautioned those who espouse liberty without restraints: "How far Liberty of Conscience ought to be given to those that truly fear God? And how far restrained to turbulent and pestilent persons, that not only raze the foundation of Godliness, but disturb the Civil Peace where they live?" The concept of unbridled liberties can have a devastating impact on society, because people start believing that their liberty is a license to do whatever they please.

MASSACHUSETTS BAY FOUNDED		RHODE ISLAND FOUNDED		KING PHILIP'S WAR		GLORIOUS REVOLUTION		GEORGIA FOUNDED	
1629	1634	1636	1649	1675-6	1681	1688	1692	1733	1740-43
	MARYLAND FOUNDED		CHARLES I OF ENGLAND BEHEADED		PENNSYLVANIA FOUNDED		SALEM WITCH TRIALS		GREAT AWAKENING

Altogether Revolutionary

"The irresistible fact which confronts the honest and thorough inquirer into the minute history of that time, a fact which cannot be ignored, nor explained away, is that the teaching and influence of Roger Williams—to use the careful language of John Quincy Adams—were 'altogether revolutionary.' Our fathers felt themselves reluctantly compelled to choose between his expulsion, and the immediate risk of social, civil and religious disorganization."—Henry Martyn Dexter, 1876.

John Quincy Adams, the sixth President of the United States

Sir Edward Coke

Cooking up His Own Laws

As a young man, Roger Williams had gained some training in the law by working for one of the leading jurists (lawyers) of England, **Sir Edward Coke** (pronounced "Cook"). Coke opposed arbitrary royal power and championed the common law. He gave Williams a job as a shorthand scribe.

The Wandering Williams

After his arrival in New England, Williams had a hard time settling in a church home. He started his New World wanderings in Boston in February 1631, where he refused the pastorate, because its members were not separatist enough. He then went to Salem in April. By August, he was in Plymouth. The Plymouth church initially welcomed Williams as a fellow separatist until he began teaching that its members were not separated enough from the Church of England. It seems that when the Pilgrims visited England they attended Church of England services. Williams began teaching that Christians who persisted in visiting Anglican churches should be excommunicated. His message was not well received. Williams fled Plymouth in 1633 and returned to Salem that same year.

315

MARTIN LUTHER'S 95 THESES		HENRY VIII SPLITS FROM ROME		REIGN OF QUEEN ELIZABETH I BEGINS		SPANISH ARMADA DESTROYED		SIGNING OF MAYFLOWER COMPACT	
1517	1526	1534	1536	1558	1585	1588	1607	1620	1624
	TYNDALE'S ENGLISH NEW TESTAMENT		CALVIN'S *INSTITUTES* PUBLISHED		FIRST ROANOAK SETTLEMENT		JAMESTOWN, VIRGINIA FOUNDED		DUTCH FOUND NEW NETHERLAND

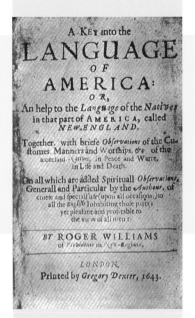

King Charles I at his trial.

The Key to the Charter

In 1643, Williams set sail for England to obtain a charter for the Rhode Island communities. During the long voyage, he wrote *A Key into the Language of America,* a dictionary and study of Native American language in which he described his personal adventures with the Indians. In London, Williams faced the opposition of Massachusetts Bay agents who had come to fight his claim to Rhode Island. Yet in less than ten months Williams had his charter, partly due to the good reputation earned by the speedy publication of his book. In it, Williams told how he had purchased Providence from the Indians, greatly enhancing his claim to the title of that territory.

Separatism Gone Bonkers

Debate again flared up when Williams attacked the Massachusetts Bay Colony for accepting a charter from Charles I. Williams stated that the colony's charter was not legal, arguing that England had not first bought the land from the Indians who lived there. He then questioned whether the colonists had any right to the lands they had settled. He ignored the fact that the settlers did buy the land from the Indians once they came to the New World.

Williams called King Charles I a blasphemer and a "cohort of the Antichrist," claiming that the government of Massachusetts Bay was founded on a "solemn public lie." Many colonists feared that Williams's rantings would get back to England, incur the wrath of the king, and ultimately destroy all they had achieved. Going further, Williams told his congregation that they must separate fully from the other colonial churches which he claimed were "full of antichristian pollution."

He also told his congregation that true Christians should not pray in the presence of unbelievers, and if necessary should stop praying even with their wives and children if they were not believers. Williams became such an extreme separatist that at one point he felt that only he and his wife were pure enough to be part of the church, and he had doubts about his wife.

The magistrates eventually called Williams to appear before the General Court of New England. At that time, Williams retracted most of his statements and issued an apology which was received by the magistrates. Within ten months, however, he began repeating his call for radical separatism, this time expressing it in even stronger terms. Another eight months would pass before he had to appear before the General Court again.

Roger Williams being greeted by Indians

MARTIN LUTHER'S 95 THESES		HENRY VIII SPLITS FROM ROME		REIGN OF QUEEN ELIZABETH I BEGINS		SPANISH ARMADA DESTROYED		SIGNING OF MAYFLOWER COMPACT	
1517	1526	1534	1536	1558	1585	1588	1607	1620	1624
	TYNDALE'S ENGLISH NEW TESTAMENT		CALVIN'S *INSTITUTES* PUBLISHED		FIRST ROANOAK SETTLEMENT		JAMESTOWN, VIRGINIA FOUNDED		DUTCH FOUND NEW NETHERLAND

Rejecting the Reformation

The New England Puritans followed the social and civil polity outlined by John Calvin in Geneva. Calvin taught that church and state were God-ordained institutions that had separate governing jurisdictions. While they were separate *jurisdictionally,* they shared a common *religious* foundation. Church and state were required to rule in terms of the Bible. Williams did not believe that the Bible was the source of law for civil government. His view was totally unacceptable to the Puritans. If the Bible was not the source of law, the Puritans reasoned, then where would ethical norms and standards originate? Williams believed that the source of law was to be found solely "in the people" who used their "reason" in the study of "natural law." Williams wrote in *The Bloody Tenet Yet More Bloody* that "the Sovereign power of the civil authority is founded in the consent of the People…. The…bodies of people…have fundamentally in themselves the root of Power, to set up what Governments and Governors they shall agree upon."

The Puritans asked what would happen if a large number of unbelievers, whose minds were not shaped by the moral laws of the Bible or natural law, seized control of the government through the consent of the people? Williams believed that they could be appealed to by reason alone since **natural law** was available to everyone. The Puritans were not as optimistic as Williams.

Like Williams, the Puritans believed in the consent of the governed. But unlike Williams, the Puritans believed that those who governed were obligated to govern in terms of God's law as found in the Bible. While civil officials represented the people, they first represented God. This meant that sometimes laws were enacted *against* the will of the people.

John Calvin was a harsh critic of the Anabaptists

MASSACHUSETTS BAY FOUNDED	RHODE ISLAND FOUNDED	KING PHILIP'S WAR	GLORIOUS REVOLUTION	GEORGIA FOUNDED	
1629	1634	1636	1649	1675-6	1681	1688	1692	1733	1740-43
MARYLAND FOUNDED	CHARLES I OF ENGLAND BEHEADED	PENNSYLVANIA FOUNDED	SALEM WITCH TRIALS	GREAT AWAKENING

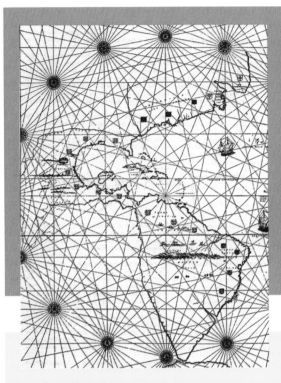

In the Beginning

The first European to view Rhode Island was probably Miguel de Cortereal, a Portuguese navigator who sailed along the coast in 1511. Later, in 1524, the Italian navigator Giovanni da Verrazano explored the region on behalf of France. Some people believe he was responsible for naming it "Rhode Island" because he wrote that it resembled the Mediterranean island of Rhodes. Other people, however, believe that the Dutch navigator Adriaen Block named the region in 1614 when he referred to one of the islands in Narragansett Bay as *Roodt Eylandt* (Red Island) because of the red clay he found there. Either way, Rhode Island remained unsettled by Europeans until after the colonies of Plymouth and Massachusetts were well established.

What is Natural Law?

Natural law is the belief that man has a built-in ability (reason) to understand and live by "self-evident truths" gathered from the natural world. Unfortunately, it is difficult to get people to agree on what laws from nature are "natural" and conform to God's will. This is especially true for atheists since they believe that nature is evolving. What's natural today may not be natural tomorrow; therefore, what people consider to be right today may not be right tomorrow. Because Williams proposed that the civil magistrate should follow natural law and reason, he did not support prayers to open court sessions since unbelievers might be in attendance. In addition, he would not have approved of hanging a copy of the Ten Commandments in court rooms since the civil magistrate is not bound by biblical law.

MARTIN LUTHER'S 95 THESES		HENRY VIII SPLITS FROM ROME		REIGN OF QUEEN ELIZABETH I BEGINS		SPANISH ARMADA DESTROYED		SIGNING OF MAYFLOWER COMPACT	
1517	1526	1534	1536	1558	1585	1588	1607	1620	1624
	TYNDALE'S ENGLISH NEW TESTAMENT		CALVIN'S *INSTITUTES* PUBLISHED		FIRST ROANOAK SETTLEMENT		JAMESTOWN, VIRGINIA FOUNDED		DUTCH FOUND NEW NETHERLAND

Charles II

Christian Motivation for the Founding of Rhode Island

King Charles II renewed Williams's charter for Rhode Island and Providence Plantations in July of 1663. The Charter reads in part: to those "pursuing…their sober, serious and religious intentions, of godly edifying themselves, and one another, in the holy Christian faith and worship as they were persuaded; together with the gaining over and conversion of the poor ignorant Indian natives, in those parts of America, to the sincere profession and obedience of the same faith and worship; whereby, as is hoped, there may, in due time, by the blessing of God upon their endeavors, be laid a sure foundation of happiness to all America."

Rocky Rhode Island

The General Court ordered Williams to leave the colony within six weeks and return to England. His views were considered dangerous to the peace and stability of the colony. **Cotton Mather** (1663–1728), a noted minister and historian of the period, writes the following about Williams in his *Ecclesiastical History of New England* (1702): "Know, then, that about the year 1630 arrived here one Mr. Roger Williams; who being a preacher that had less *light* than *fire* in him, hath by his own sad example, preached unto us the danger of that evil which the apostle mentions in Romans 10:2: 'They have a zeal, but not according to knowledge.'"

Because it was winter, Williams was permitted to remain in the colony until spring. However, before the authorities could send him packing back to England, Williams left the jurisdiction of Massachusetts Bay with twenty supporters. In January 1636, they headed for Narragansett Bay, forty miles south of the Massachusetts colony, and arrived in what is today Rhode Island. There Williams established a settlement, naming it Providence Plantation "in a

Roger Williams fleeing the Massachusetts Bay Colony.

Narragansett Bay

sense of God's merciful providence unto me in my distress." Soon after arriving in the newly-founded Providence, Williams wrote to Governor Winthrop seeking advice on how to run a colony. Without a patent from the king of England, the civil head of the Church of England, Williams and the small band of settlers that followed him were without any legal standing.

In Providence Plantation, Williams was free to make all the wild statements he wanted, but his conviction that the civil government should not legislate in the area of religious beliefs created an environment where religious extremism thrived. Quakers, whose beliefs were even more extreme than those of Williams, flocked to the colony. There they became as much a thorn in Williams's side as Williams had been to the leaders at Massachusetts Bay. Despite this tension, however, he could not do anything to rid his colony of the Quakers, because he had already committed himself to full religious liberty for people of all beliefs. Providence Plantation was now faced with the crisis of **anarchy,** the same fear held by those in the Bay colony.

ANARCHY
From the Greek: *an* "without" + *archos* "ruler." Without government; a state of society in which there is no recognized law or supreme power, or when the laws are not effective and individuals do what they please.

321

Pulling Up the Welcome Mat

Neighboring Connecticut coveted a part of Rhode Island but dreaded the thought of acquiring Rhode Island's cantankerous population along with it. Connecticut Governor John Winthrop, Jr. made it clear that his colony did not want any Rhode Islanders, "for Rhode Island is—pardon necessity's word of truth—a rod to those that love to live in order—a road, refuge, asylum to evil [doers]."

> **ANTINOMIANISM**
> From the Greek: *anti* (against) + *nomos* (law). An antinomian maintains that under the Gospel era, the law is of no use or obligation for the Christian.

Doctrines of Gangrene

When Anne Hutchinson went through her trial, the magistrates questioned her closely on many of her teachings and found her unable to support her views biblically. John Cotton condemned her by saying, "Your opinions frett like a Gangrene, and spread like a Leprosie…and will eate out the very Bowells of Religion."

Hearing Voices

Anne Hutchinson (1591–1643) proved to be a different kind of threat to Massachusetts Bay soon after Roger Williams was banished in 1636. She began well enough with neighborhood groups to discuss the previous Sunday's sermon, a practice she brought with her from England while under John Cotton's ministry. However, when she began preaching her own messages that often contradicted the day's sermon, she got into trouble. She argued that since believers possess the Holy Spirit, they do not have to follow the requirements of the law. Since salvation is by grace alone, Mrs. Hutchinson insisted, the law has no place in the believer's life. While she was not calling on Christians to be lawless, the Puritan ministers believed that her views would lead to **antinomianism.**

Trial of Mrs. Hutchinson

Mrs. Hutchinson taught that it was not possible to tell if someone was a Christian through his obedience to God's law. How could it be determined then? Only through divine revelation—and, more specifically, divine revelation that came through *her*. She began elevating herself to the status of prophetess, saying that she was able to discern who was saved and who was not. When she claimed that most of the clergymen in the colony were unregenerate, her troubles mounted.

A Prophetess Without Honor

Mrs. Hutchinson concluded that all the ministers were guilty of teaching false doctrine, except John Cotton, Sir Harry Vane (the governor of the colony), and her brother-in-law, John Wheelwright. Called before the General Court in 1638, Mrs. Hutchinson defended her position by again claiming a direct revelation from God. The colonial authorities were not impressed. They questioned whether she could discern if this "inner revelation" was really from God or her own imagination. Some wondered if Satan might be the source of these inner promptings. Once again *sola Scriptura* was at the heart of the matter.

The possibility of a rebellion was always a concern of the colonists. What if a self-appointed prophet claimed that God had given special instructions to gather a group of followers and take up arms against the government? The awful specter of Münster was always in view.

After Mrs. Hutchinson's brief trial, the court banished her from the colony. Since it was winter, and she was pregnant, she did not have to depart until spring. When spring arrived, she and some of her followers made their way to Rhode Island. After quarreling with Roger Williams in 1642, she moved to Long Island in New Netherland and then to what is now Pelham Bay, New York, where she and her family, except for one child, were massacred by Indians.

Sir Harry Vane, governor of Massachusetts

Rumors of Divine Wrath

Some people believed that God took vengeance on Anne Hutchinson for her errors in a number of peculiar ways. Especially horrible were the reports of "monstrous births." Mary Dyer, a follower of Anne, was said to have given birth to a grotesque creature complete with horns, claws and scales. In addition, Cotton Mather wrote that eyewitnesses claimed that Anne "was delivered of some *thirty* monstrous births at once," a highly unlikely story.

The massacre of Anne Hutchinson

323

MARTIN LUTHER'S 95 THESES		HENRY VIII SPLITS FROM ROME		REIGN OF QUEEN ELIZABETH I BEGINS		SPANISH ARMADA DESTROYED		SIGNING OF MAYFLOWER COMPACT	
1517	1526	1534	1536	1558	1585	1588	1607	1620	1624
	TYNDALE'S ENGLISH NEW TESTAMENT		CALVIN'S *INSTITUTES* PUBLISHED		FIRST ROANOAK SETTLEMENT		JAMESTOWN, VIRGINIA FOUNDED		DUTCH FOUND NEW NETHERLAND

"Professor of the Mysteries of Christ"

Providence attracted a number of free thinkers who took advantage of the colony's open society. **Samuel Gorton** (c. 1592–1677) left England in pursuit of his own brand of religious freedom. Upon his arrival in New England in 1637, he was banished from Boston and Plymouth for preaching odd and disturbing doctrines. He denied the Trinity and taught that heaven and hell did not exist. His attacks on the legitimacy of the colonial government in Massachusetts bordered on anarchy. Gorton considered his views to be far superior to the orthodox Puritans, so much so that he called himself "professor of the mysteries of Christ." Even Roger Williams considered Gorton's views to be extreme.

The Colony Matures

As we have seen, the early years of Providence were filled with turmoil and controversy. Settlers argued over politics and religion. Some left to form new settlements when they could not get along in Providence. One group of people felt that their liberty was being threatened because Williams was not following the established English law. In 1643, they left to found the settlement of Warwick. Eventually three independent settlements, in addition to Providence, were established in Rhode Island: Warwick, Portsmouth, and Newport.

By 1647, Williams had succeeded in uniting the four settlements in a loose confederacy. In that year, the first assembly of the Colony of Rhode Island and Providence Plantation met at Portsmouth. In 1654, Roger Williams became president of the settlements. Nine years later, King Charles II granted Rhode Island a second charter which made the colony a royal colony.

A plainly dressed Quaker

Yankee Slaveholders

Most people think of slavery as a practice belonging only to the southern states, but in the New England colony of Rhode Island, slaves were a very important part of the economy. In the bustling seaport of Newport, they comprised a tenth of the population around 1700 and outnumbered indentured servants eleven to one. On nearby Jamestown Island, slaves made up fully a seventh of the population. The earliest slaves were Africans imported from the island of Barbados in the Caribbean and Indians, many of whom had been captured and enslaved during King Philip's War. While Rhode Island plantation owners reaped profits from slave labor, the greatest profits from slavery went to Rhode Island mariners who transported slaves from Africa to other colonies in the holds of their ships. However, as the growing slave trade led to increased prosperity in Newport, Quakers began to question the morality of the practice. Soon they began to oppose the slave trade and excommunicate fellow Quakers who refused to free their slaves.

From Rhode Island College to Brown College

Because the colony of Rhode Island had been founded by Roger Williams, who said his main goal was providing a place where Christians could exercise their freedom of conscience, Rhode Island College was careful to make no theological demands upon any of its students, so long as they were Protestants. Its Charter in 1764 stated: "That into this liberal and catholic institution shall never be admitted any religious tests: But on the contrary all the members hereof shall forever enjoy full, free, absolute and uninterrupted liberty of conscience: And that the places of Professors, Tutors, and all other officers... shall be free and open for all denominations of Protestants." In 1804, the name was changed to Brown College in memory of Nicholas Brown, who had endowed the school with a large sum of money.

ROGUE ISLAND: QUARRELS AND QUIRKS

| MARTIN LUTHER'S 95 THESES | HENRY VIII SPLITS FROM ROME | REIGN OF QUEEN ELIZABETH I BEGINS | SPANISH ARMADA DESTROYED | SIGNING OF MAYFLOWER COMPACT |

1517 1526 1534 1536 1558 1585 1588 1607 1620 1624

TYNDALE'S ENGLISH NEW TESTAMENT   CALVIN'S *INSTITUTES* PUBLISHED   FIRST ROANOAK SETTLEMENT   JAMESTOWN, VIRGINIA FOUNDED   DUTCH FOUND NEW NETHERLAND

Yo-Ho-Ho
and a Bottle of Rum

Rum is an alcoholic drink distilled from fermented sugarcane or molasses. The drink was first known as "kill-devil."

Rhode Island prospered greatly as a royal colony. Because the coastal areas proved excellent for farming, great plantations sprang up there and on the islands in Narragansett Bay. Slaves tilled the soil, raised cattle, sheep, and horses, and produced large amounts of cheese. Merchants in the port city of Newport built large fleets of sailing ships which carried the products of the plantations in the other English colonies in North America and the West Indies.

Merchants also participated in the highly profitable **triangular trade.** This three-way trade shipped New England rum to Africa where it was exchanged for African slaves. The slaves were sent to the islands of the West Indies where they produced sugar. The sugar in turn was sent on to New England where it was turned into vast quantities of rum to quench the thirst of the sailors and to purchase more slaves. Despite the great profits that Rhode Islanders were making in the slave trade, that colony became the first to prohibit the importation of slaves in 1774, on the eve of the War for Independence.

Rhode Island State House

FOR STUDY

CHAPTER 26:
Rogue Island: Quarrels and Quirks

Terms

natural law

Rhode Island

Providence Plantation

anarchy

antinomianism

triangular trade

People

Roger Williams

Sir Edward Coke

Cotton Mather

Anne Hutchinson

Samuel Gorton

The Puritans believed in an orderly society where Scripture alone is the final authority in matters of belief and conduct. However, a few in their midst challenged that order, placed private revelations above Scripture, and threatened the stability of society with their disruptive teachings. When Roger Williams could not get along with Massachusetts authorities, he left and founded Rhode Island, but soon faced problems similar to the ones he had created in Massachusetts. Similarly, Anne Hutchinson rejected God's Law and could not get along with either the Puritans or Williams.

Discussion Questions

1. Explain Roger Williams's brand of separatism. What were his basic arguments? What were their major flaws?
2. Contrast Williams's view of the relationship between church and state with that of the Puritans and Pilgrims.
3. Why was Anne Hutchinson put on trial and later ordered to leave Massachusetts Bay?
4. What was the "triangular trade"?
5. Is there a difference between the separation of *church* and state and the separation between *religion* and state? Explain

Optional Enrichment Projects

1. Those who disagreed with the Massachusetts Puritans, no matter what their theological quarrel, all had in common a problem with the idea of "law," where it came from, who it applied to, and how it was administered. Research and discuss the concepts of natural law, revelational (biblical) law, and antinomianism, especially as they relate to the various people who lived in New England.
2. Roger Williams and Anne Hutchinson are regarded as colonial heroes in most modern textbooks and reference books. Now that you know some of "the rest of the story," why do you think they are put in such a positive light? From the point of view of biblical Christianity, do they deserve all the honors they are usually accorded? Why or why not?

Perspectives

Roger Williams believed that the sources of the state should be sought in the secular rather than in the spiritual order. The right of magistrates is natural, human, civil, not religious. The officer of the state gains nothing and loses nothing by being a Christian, or by not being. Likewise, the Christian merchant, physician, lawyer, pilot, father, master are not better equipped for fulfilling their social function than are the members of any other religion. There can be no such thing as a Christian business, or a Christian profession of law or medicine. These vocations stand in their own right. No state may claim superiority over any other state by virtue of being, or professing to be, Christian. The state is not irreligious; it is simply non-religious. As for the church, Williams said it was like a college of physicians, a company of East India merchants, or any other society in London, which may convene themselves and dissolve themselves at pleasure. Roger Williams's ideas in these matters were and are overstatements and oversimplifications of the problem. Indeed, he followed the logic of his own thinking so far that he outgrew the visible organized church, even of his own independent kind, and finally parted with all institutional religion.

William L. Sperry

CHAPTER 27

SATAN Comes to Paradise

"The giving up of [believing in] witchcraft is in effect the giving up of the Bible."—John Wesley (1703–1791)

Traitors in their Midst

The problems Massachusetts had with Roger Williams and Anne Hutchinson were nothing compared to the events that took place in 1692. In that year, some Puritans in the village of Salem, Massachusetts, discovered what they believed to be the worst of traitors in their midst.

Many people today remember the Puritans for only one thing: the **Salem Witchcraft Trials.** They wrongly judge the Puritans solely on the basis of the witch trials, often believing the myth that hundreds of people were burned at the stake under harsh and superstitious Puritan authorities. In fact, witchcraft trials were not peculiar to Salem or the Puritans but were common throughout England and the rest of Europe. However, we cannot ignore the serious nature of the Salem trials where people were sentenced to death.

329

MARTIN LUTHER'S 95 THESES		HENRY VIII SPLITS FROM ROME		REIGN OF QUEEN ELIZABETH I BEGINS		SPANISH ARMADA DESTROYED		SIGNING OF MAYFLOWER COMPACT	
1517	1526	1534	1536	1558	1585	1588	1607	1620	1624
	TYNDALE'S ENGLISH NEW TESTAMENT		CALVIN'S *INSTITUTES* PUBLISHED		FIRST ROANOAK SETTLEMENT		JAMESTOWN, VIRGINIA FOUNDED		DUTCH FOUND NEW NETHERLAND

Samuel Parris

The Law of Massachusetts Colony

"If any man or woman be a witch (that is, hath or consulteth with a familiar spirit) they shall be put to death."

Witchcraft and Weirdness

During the winter of 1691–1692, several young girls in Salem Village began to gather in secret to discuss their future. Soon they began to experiment with magic, hoping to discover a means of fortunetelling. They then started to act oddly, having seizures and making bizarre speeches.

The father of one of the girls was a minister, **Samuel Parris.** He was concerned about his daughter's bizarre behavior and became convinced that a witch was attempting to attack his ministry. A rumor of demon possession spread quickly. Other parents came forward and admitted that their daughters were also acting strangely. The community immediately demanded that the girls involved be questioned. After several hours of examination, the girls named three local women as witches: Sarah Good, Sarah Osborne, and a half-Indian, half-African slave from the West Indies named **Tituba.** Sarah Good and Sarah Osborne both denied the charges. Tituba confessed that she had been a witch.

Salem: A Village Divided

Some historians theorize that witchcraft accusations were partially due to economic tensions that existed between Salem Town and Salem Village. The town was one of the busiest and wealthiest ports in Massachusetts. The village, on the other hand, did not prosper unless it invested in the commerce of Salem Town. Eventually, Salem Village divided into two factions: pro-town and anti-town. The anti-town faction favored political independence from Salem Village while the pro-town forces thwarted any move toward independence. During the witchcraft trials, the anti-town forces controlled the interrogations. Although this is a simplistic view of the Salem affair, it is interesting that most of those accused of witchcraft were *supporters* of Salem Town.

Map of Salem Village, 1692

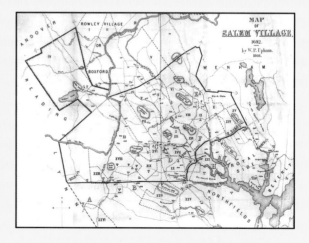

MASSACHUSETTS BAY FOUNDED		RHODE ISLAND FOUNDED		KING PHILIP'S WAR		GLORIOUS REVOLUTION		GEORGIA FOUNDED	
1629	1634	1636	1649	1675-6	1681	1688	1692	1733	1740-43
	MARYLAND FOUNDED		CHARLES I OF ENGLAND BEHEADED		PENNSYLVANIA FOUNDED		SALEM WITCH TRIALS		GREAT AWAKENING

On a Mushroom Trip?

The girls who were involved in the initial accusations claimed that they were bewitched by eating "witch cakes" which made them see weird visions and go into convulsions. Many people discount their story as mischievous, childish pranks. Others, however, take the "witch cake" story seriously. The theory goes that the cake which the girls claimed they had eaten may have been made with grain contaminated with a fungus called *ergot*. If so, the girls could have been gradually ingesting a powerful hallucinogenic drug similar to lysergic acid diethylamide, "LSD."

Tituba and the girls

She claimed that she was tormented by Satan, describing him as "a thing all over hairy, all the face hairy, and a long nose." The magistrates believed her story because her body was marked in such a way that gave the impression that she had been tormented. Of course, there was no proof that the *devil* had marked her body. She was released while Sarah Osborne and Sarah Good remained in jail to await trial. Eventually, Sarah Good was convicted and hanged on July 19, 1692 with four other accused witches. Sarah Osborne died in prison in May of 1692.

The imprisonment of the accused witches did not cure the girls of their odd behavior. Instead, they claimed to have had strange visions. One of them said she was taunted by little birds, and others insisted that they were visited by ghosts. The hysteria grew, and many more people were arrested and accused of practicing witchcraft.

Death warrant of Bridget Bishop, a condemned witch

331

| MARTIN LUTHER'S 95 THESES | HENRY VIII SPLITS FROM ROME | REIGN OF QUEEN ELIZABETH I BEGINS | SPANISH ARMADA DESTROYED | SIGNING OF MAYFLOWER COMPACT |

1517   1526   1534   1536   1558   1585   1588   1607   1620   1624

| TYNDALE'S ENGLISH NEW TESTAMENT | CALVIN'S *INSTITUTES* PUBLISHED | FIRST ROANOAK SETTLEMENT | JAMESTOWN, VIRGINIA FOUNDED | DUTCH FOUND NEW NETHERLAND |

George Jacobs, on trial because of false accusations, was one of the nineteen people condemned and hanged in Salem in 1692

Off to See the Wizard

One of the accused witches was a former pastor of the Salem Village church, George Burroughs. Although Burroughs was a minister, his brief stay in town had won him more enemies than friends. When he was charged with being a wizard, few locals would vouch for his character. The strange fact of the case was that Burroughs could not defend himself. In fact, he even pretended to possess supernatural powers. Eventually he was convicted, not of witchcraft, but of perjury. He paid for his crime with his life.

Trial by Error

One important condition helped prepare the way for the hysteria which was to follow. Many people had noted the decline in piety among the children and grandchildren of the original Puritan settlers. Ministers warned that the people could expect to see signs of God's displeasure and wrath. Indeed, New England had already experienced many such signs. Some began to feel that they had already been punished for their decline in piety and wondered if there might be yet other causes of God's anger.

When the residents of Salem discovered what they believed to be evidence of witchcraft in their midst, they concluded that they had found the real cause of God's displeasure. Many feared that if the leadership did not take drastic measures soon, this witchcraft might provoke further punishment from God.

Combined with this heightened sense of God's displeasure, another of the key problems in the initial stages of this witchcraft frenzy was the fact that Massachusetts was temporarily without a court system. The original Massachusetts charter had recently

been revoked, and the colony was waiting for England to send both a new governor and a new constitution for the colony. When the new governor, **William Phips,** finally arrived, he visited Salem to look into the witchcraft problem. Convinced that the witches might be real, Phips established a court to try the accused.

The Bible requires that any evidence given against a person must be confirmed by the testimony of **two witnesses** (DEUTERONOMY 19:15). Because the court ignored this principle, even the strangest evidence was allowed to stand with no confirmation. Some witnesses gave testimony based on what they claimed were visits by bizarre apparitions. Others claimed to have suffered from mysterious afflictions, including sudden pains. In some cases, the witnesses were supposedly rendered mute by witchcraft, so their grunts and convulsions were entertained as evidence. Much "evidence" was simply confirmed by the girls' convulsions in the presence of the accused. While the court questioned the validity of some testimony, many of the accused were still found guilty of witchcraft in spite of a lack of validated evidence.

Keeping the Rumors Afloat

One of the strangest testimonies against an accused witch was the story that a woman was so possessed of Satan that she floated to the ceiling of a room, and no one could pull her down.

A fanciful interpretation of a witchcraft trial

| MARTIN LUTHER'S 95 THESES | HENRY VIII SPLITS FROM ROME | REIGN OF QUEEN ELIZABETH I BEGINS | SPANISH ARMADA DESTROYED | SIGNING OF MAYFLOWER COMPACT |

1517   1526   1534   1536   1558   1585   1588   1607   1620   1624

TYNDALE'S ENGLISH NEW TESTAMENT   CALVIN'S *INSTITUTES* PUBLISHED   FIRST ROANOAK SETTLEMENT   JAMESTOWN, VIRGINIA FOUNDED   DUTCH FOUND NEW NETHERLAND

Increase Mather's approach to the witch trials was designed to bring the series of events under control

The Clergy to the Rescue

At the onset of the witchcraft hysteria, many of the colony's clergy believed that trials by the civil court would solve the crisis. As the trials continued and bizarre testimony came to light, however, many pastors changed their minds. **Increase Mather** (1639–1723), prominent Boston minister and president of Harvard College, led a protest against the trials. "It is better that ten suspected witches should escape than one innocent person should be condemned," he declared. Mather was careful to point out that while he did not doubt the possibility of witchcraft, he did object to the loose rules for admitting evidence. Mather pointed out the Bible's requirement that an accusation must be confirmed by two witnesses. He asserted that without the proper regulation of evidence, there was no safeguard to prevent Satan from deceiving the court into convicting the innocent. In fact, most of the ministers of Massachusetts Bay opposed the way the trials were conducted. Mather's way of dealing with those accused of witchcraft involved prayer, fasting, counsel, and evangelism; all the cases he dealt with in this fashion came to a peaceful conclusion.

Mather's argument, plus the fact that the governor's wife had herself been accused of being a witch, convinced Governor Phips to change the court's rules of evidence and to free from jail those who were accused of witchcraft. *After this change, no one ever again was convicted of witchcraft.*

Harvard College

C H A P T E R T W E N T Y S E V E N

MASSACHUSETTS BAY FOUNDED		RHODE ISLAND FOUNDED		KING PHILIP'S WAR		GLORIOUS REVOLUTION		GEORGIA FOUNDED	
1629	1634	1636	1649	1675-6	1681	1688	1692	1733	1740-43
	MARYLAND FOUNDED		CHARLES I OF ENGLAND BEHEADED		PENNSYLVANIA FOUNDED		SALEM WITCH TRIALS		GREAT AWAKENING

Like a Roaring Lion

Many Puritan theologians of the day believed that they were living at the end of history. Earthquakes, plagues, wars, and the appearance of comets were considered to be prophetic signs. Their interpretations of various Bible prophecies indicated to them that Satan had to be loosed in the last days. It was easy for them to believe in stories of demonic possession. After all, they believed that Satan was prowling around "like a roaring lion, seeking whom he will devour" (1 Peter 5:8).

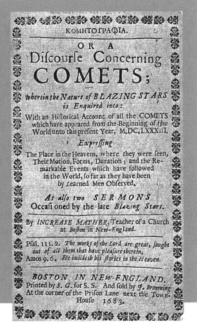

Name Your Poison

The Bible states, "Thou shalt not suffer [permit] a witch to live" (Exodus 22:18). The Hebrew word translated **"witch"** in the King James Version of the Bible is best rendered "sorceress." The Septuagint, a second-century B.C. Greek translation of the Old Testament, used the Greek word *pharmakeia* for the Hebrew word translated **"sorceress."** (The English word "pharmacy" is derived from the Greek word *pharmakeia*.) Witches in seventeenth-century Europe and America were considered to be experts in potions and strange concoctions designed to poison their victims.

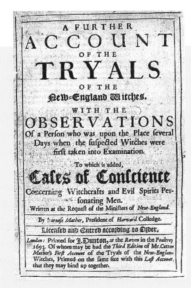

It Takes Two

"On the evidence of two witnesses or three witnesses, he who is to die shall be put to death; he shall not be put to death on the evidence of one witness" (Deuteronomy 17:6). Likewise, the Law of Massachusetts Bay Colony stated, "No man shall be put to death without the testimony of *two or three witnesses* or that which is equivalent thereunto."

335

MARTIN LUTHER'S 95 THESES	HENRY VIII SPLITS FROM ROME	REIGN OF QUEEN ELIZABETH I BEGINS	SPANISH ARMADA DESTROYED	SIGNING OF MAYFLOWER COMPACT
1517	1526	1534	1536	1558	1585	1588	1607	1620	1624
TYNDALE'S ENGLISH NEW TESTAMENT	CALVIN'S *INSTITUTES* PUBLISHED	FIRST ROANOAK SETTLEMENT	JAMESTOWN, VIRGINIA FOUNDED	DUTCH FOUND NEW NETHERLAND

Cotton Mather

Bewitched or Befuddled?

What about all the evidence of occult practices given during the trials? Was it pure invention, or was some of it true? Much of the testimony given against the accused witches was never truly confirmed, but some was reliable—in particular, **self-incriminating evidence.** Several of the accused freely admitted to practicing magic. The slave girl Tituba not only described the devil but also showed the court her voodoo dolls. Others pretended to possess supernatural powers and were convicted in part by their own testimony.

The fits and seizures of the "bewitched" girls seemed quite real to themselves as well as to others. Even respectable men like Cotton Mather substantiated the girls' strange behavior as being demonic. The *cause* of their convulsions, whether satanic or psychological, is another issue altogether. Nevertheless, several of the young girls who had begun the craze admitted they had lied.

Of the 160 people who were accused of "covenanting with evil spirits," nineteen were hanged, four died in prison, and one was crushed to death with heavy weights. No one, contrary to popular depictions, was "burned at the stake." Although the number of actual deaths is small when compared with European statistics, the witch-craft episode had a devastating effect on the colony. Many people who had been involved in bringing accusations later publicly repented of their role in the matter. The General Court of Massachusetts eventually voted a cash award to all the surviving victims.

Salem's bout of witch trials was a time of great social and

I Beg Your Pardon

Samuel Sewall (1652–1730), one of nine judges who presided over the Salem trials, wrote a confession of error in 1697 and had it read publicly, the only judge to do so. It reads that he "Desires to take the Blame and Shame of it, Asking pardon of Men, And especially desiring prayers that God, who has an Unlimited Authority, would pardon that Sin. . . ." Sewall also published *The Selling of Joseph* (1700), the first American work condemning slavery.

MASSACHUSETTS BAY FOUNDED		RHODE ISLAND FOUNDED		KING PHILIP'S WAR			GLORIOUS REVOLUTION		GEORGIA FOUNDED	
1629	1634	1636	1649	1675-6	1681	1688	1692	1733	1740-43
	MARYLAND FOUNDED		CHARLES I OF ENGLAND BEHEADED		PENNSYLVANIA FOUNDED		SALEM WITCH TRIALS		GREAT AWAKENING

spiritual upheaval. Despite the relatively small number of people who were actually convicted and executed for witchcraft, many others were caught up in the frenzy. Dabbling with the devil is no light matter. The Puritans were right to wonder whether God was judging their colony for neglecting His law.

Title page from The Wonders of the Invisible World *(1693) written by Cotton Mather to defend the reality of supernatural manifestations of evil*

Pressed to Death

The few who were executed during the witchcraft trials were hanged. All, that is, except for **Giles Corey**; he was crushed to death. Under the practice of the time, a person who confessed to a serious crime lost all his property. However, if the accused "stood mute," then he was to the ancient, painful, and *unbiblical* punishment of being slowly pressed to death. If he endured the ordeal without confessing, then his heirs could inherit his estate.

Corey had earlier accused his wife of being a witch. However, when he was himself accused, he changed his mind about his wife. He then willed all his property to the two sons-in-law who had stood by his wife. In order to save his estate, Corey stood mute in court. When he was found guilty, instead of suffering a relatively merciful hanging, Corey was forced to lie down with a large, flat rock placed on his chest. The executioner slowly added more and more rocks until Corey either confessed his guilt or died. If he cried out a plea, he would be spared a slow, painful death, but his family would receive none of his estate. Corey thought only of his family's well-being and endured the crushing weight without confessing. His last words were, "More weight, more weight."

| MARTIN LUTHER'S 95 THESES | HENRY VIII SPLITS FROM ROME | REIGN OF QUEEN ELIZABETH I BEGINS | SPANISH ARMADA DESTROYED | SIGNING OF MAYFLOWER COMPACT |

1517　1526　1534　1536　1558　1585　1588　1607　1620　1624

| TYNDALE'S ENGLISH NEW TESTAMENT | CALVIN'S *INSTITUTES* PUBLISHED | FIRST ROANOAK SETTLEMENT | JAMESTOWN, VIRGINIA FOUNDED | DUTCH FOUND NEW NETHERLAND |

Setting the Record Straight

Secular historians like to exaggerate the events of the Salem witchcraft trials in order to lay the mistakes of history solely at the feet of "religious zealots" like the Puritans. Underlying this negative judgment of the Salem affair is the general denial of the supernatural. How can there be witches and witchcraft when there is no such thing as a spiritual world? The humanistic mind that rejects God also rejects the existence of Satan and demons.

No doubt many mistakes were made in Salem in an unrelenting attempt to drive the devil out of Massachusetts and bring order to a society struggling with growing pains. But it is important to realize that these mistakes were not brought about by Puritanism; in fact, they were the result of *abandoning* Bible-based, Puritan principles. In addition, we must not use the single event of the Salem witchcraft trials to dismiss all the achievements of America's early pioneers.

Trial of Giles Corey

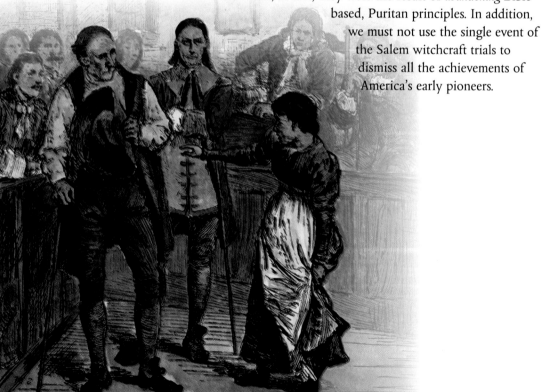

MASSACHUSETTS BAY FOUNDED		RHODE ISLAND FOUNDED		KING PHILIP'S WAR		GLORIOUS REVOLUTION		GEORGIA FOUNDED	
1629	1634	1636	1649	1675-6	1681	1688	1692	1733	1740-43
	MARYLAND FOUNDED		CHARLES I OF ENGLAND BEHEADED		PENNSYLVANIA FOUNDED		SALEM WITCH TRIALS		GREAT AWAKENING

FOR STUDY

CHAPTER 27:

Satan Comes to Paradise

Terms

Salem Witchcraft Trials

two witnesses

witch

sorceress

self-incriminating evidence

People

Samuel Parris

Tituba

William Phips

Increase Mather

Cotton Mather

Samuel Sewall

Giles Corey

In the late 1600s, the Puritans began to see many signs of God's displeasure. In 1692, they saw the greatest sign of all: witchcraft in their midst. For a people who placed such emphasis upon following God's laws set forth in the Bible, their response was surprisingly unbiblical. Allowing unsubstantiated evidence and ignoring the biblical requirement for two or more witnesses simply encouraged the witchcraft hysteria. And, although there were no more than twenty people who died during the trials, the Puritans' image has suffered for their departure from biblical law. Nevertheless, it was members of the clergy, following God's laws, who eventually set things right.

Discussion Questions

1. How do the events of the Salem Witchcraft Trials support the requirement that all of life, legal procedures included, must be based on the Bible?

2. What problems in Salem's court system gave rise to the witchcraft trials?

3. Who spearheaded the protest against Salem's witchcraft trials? How did he approach the situation?

Optional Enrichment Projects

1. Most modern people base their view of the Salem trials on a play rather than on the historical record. Read or attend a performance of *The Crucible* by Arthur Miller. How accurate is Miller's history, his portrayal of the main characters, and his understanding of Puritan theology? What conclusions does Miller wish his audience to reach as a result of his play?

2. The Puritans are often condemned because of the witchcraft trials. Study recent accounts of using the testimony of children without any related evidence in convicting adults of crimes. Compare these modern-day "witch-hunting" episodes with what happened in Salem in 1692.

| MARTIN LUTHER'S 95 THESES | HENRY VIII SPLITS FROM ROME | REIGN OF QUEEN ELIZABETH I BEGINS | SPANISH ARMADA DESTROYED | SIGNING OF MAYFLOWER COMPACT |

1517   1526   1534   1536   1558   1585   1588   1607   1620   1624

| TYNDALE'S ENGLISH NEW TESTAMENT | CALVIN'S *INSTITUTES* PUBLISHED | FIRST ROANOAK SETTLEMENT | JAMESTOWN, VIRGINIA FOUNDED | DUTCH FOUND NEW NETHERLAND |

Perspectives

The fundamental error here seems to have been an insufficient appreciation of Christ and His word. Those who do not love Him fully will grasp at other means, including occult ones, to order their lives. The body of Christ must lead people on into the fullness of Christ. The negative approach, including warnings against occult activity, is also necessary. However, it is by itself ineffective and moreover at times self-defeating....

Finally, the error was deepest when it was decided to treat the problem with civil means, rather than evangelical means. When Cotton Mather had his way, he treated the afflicted with fasting, prayer, counseling, and evangelism, and he saw every case cured. It would not do to divide the world into mutually exclusive "secular" and "religious" realms. Neither would it do to place our hopes and our faith in a physical/political problem solver—even if it is a Christian-dominated theocracy.

Kirk House

C H A P T E R   T W E N T Y   E I G H T

MASSACHUSETTS BAY FOUNDED	RHODE ISLAND FOUNDED		KING PHILIP'S WAR		GLORIOUS REVOLUTION		GEORGIA FOUNDED	
1629	1634	1636	1649	1675-6	1681	1688	1692	1733 1740-43
	MARYLAND FOUNDED	CHARLES I OF ENGLAND BEHEADED		PENNSYLVANIA FOUNDED		SALEM WITCH TRIALS		GREAT AWAKENING

C H A P T E R

28

New England
BURSTING AT THE SEAMS

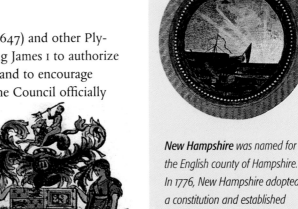

Council for New England

In 1620, **Sir Ferdinando Gorges** (1566–1647) and other Plymouth Company investors persuaded King James I to authorize the creation of the Council for New England to encourage English settlement in America. In 1622, the Council officially turned over a large tract of land—known today as New Hampshire and Maine—to Gorges and the governor of the English colony in Newfoundland, **John Mason** (1586–1635).

*Seal of the Council
of New England*

New Hampshire was named for the English county of Hampshire. In 1776, New Hampshire adopted a constitution and established itself as the first independent American state. It was the ninth colony to ratify the Constitution on June 21, 1788. State motto: "Live Free or Die."

341

| MARTIN LUTHER'S 95 THESES | HENRY VIII SPLITS FROM ROME | REIGN OF QUEEN ELIZABETH I BEGINS | SPANISH ARMADA DESTROYED | SIGNING OF MAYFLOWER COMPACT |

1517 1526 1534 1536 1558 1585 1588 1607 1620 1624

| TYNDALE'S ENGLISH NEW TESTAMENT | CALVIN'S *INSTITUTES* PUBLISHED | FIRST ROANOAK SETTLEMENT | JAMESTOWN, VIRGINIA FOUNDED | DUTCH FOUND NEW NETHERLAND |

The Pains of Persecution

Persecution under Charles I was widespread. One man by the name of Dr. Leighton published a paper against Charles's court, so he was fined £10,000 and publicly whipped and pilloried. He then had both ears sawn off, his nostrils slit, and his cheeks branded with the letters S.S., which stood for "Sower of Sedition." Another man, William Prynne, was also charged with treason, and his ears were cut off. A few years later, he published a book against the corruptions of the Church of England; since he did not have any more ears to cut off, he was punished by having the stumps of his ears sawn off.

Unfriendly Neighbors

In 1629, because of a series of disputes, Mason and Gorges agreed to divide the territory. Gorges received a section of land which became Maine. Mason acquired what is today New Hampshire, naming the territory after his native county of Hampshire, England. Gorges wanted to create great estates in America with a nobility patterned after that in England. His scheme had no place for Puritans whom he considered a threat to the established order. Therefore, Gorges and his associates were furious to discover Puritans in Massachusetts living in a land Gorges believed belonged to him.

In the 1630s, Gorges began legal proceedings against Massachusetts Bay, claiming that the colony had received its original land grant from the Council for New England through deception. Tensions ran so high that the General Court of Massachusetts expected Gorges to invade their colony. King Charles I not only sided with Gorges but also revoked the charter by which the Bay Colony governed itself. He claimed Massachusetts for the crown and appointed Gorges as its royal governor. Fortunately for Massachusetts, Charles was too busy fighting Parliament to enforce his actions in America. Gorges, at age seventy, was too old to

New Hampshire State House

Portsmouth, New Hampshire

342

Massachusetts Bay Founded	Rhode Island Founded	King Philip's War	Glorious Revolution	Georgia Founded

1629   1634   1636   1649   1675-6   1681   1688   1692   1733   1740-43

| Maryland Founded | Charles I of England Beheaded | Pennsylvania Founded | Salem Witch Trials | Great Awakening |

Cromwell, the Lord Protector

In England, a major conflict arose between King Charles I and Parliament. At this time, Parliament was controlled by Puritans, and they disliked Charles's disdain for reform. In addition, Charles alienated himself from Parliament by refusing to acknowledge its authority and attempting to rule England as a dictator. This conflict eventually erupted into the **English Civil War** in 1642. During the war, Puritans rallied around one of their leaders, **Oliver Cromwell** (1599–1658), a former member of Parliament. Cromwell had risen quickly to the rank of general, organizing the **New Model Army** to oppose the king. His valiant soldiers, who sang the Psalms as they marched into battle, came to be nicknamed "Ironsides" because of their fighting ability.

When the king refused to accept a constitutional monarchy or any loss of power, Cromwell had him put on trial. Charles was found guilty of treason and on January 30, 1649, was beheaded. Four years later, Cromwell ruled the country as the **Lord Protector**, a title granted to him because he *protected* the interests of the realm. He fought for a constitution that would provide for rule by Parliament, rather than rule solely by a king. Each new Parliament was marked by disputes and divisions. In the mid-1650s, Cromwell's health began to fail, and on September 3, 1658, he died. His son Richard (1626–1712) succeeded him as Lord Protector, but he did not have the strong character of his father and resigned within a year of taking office. In 1660, Charles II was restored to the throne, thus ending the Puritan Revolution.

The nursery rhyme "Humpty Dumpty" was written with King Charles I in mind. He was the ruler who sat on the wall of his autonomous authority, high above his subjects. As is true with all brands of pride, Charles's conceit had a great fall. After the king was tried and executed, no one could put his shattered government together again.

343

N E W   E N G L A N D   B U R S T I N G   A T   T H E   S E A M S

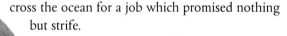

MARTIN LUTHER'S 95 THESES	HENRY VIII SPLITS FROM ROME	REIGN OF QUEEN ELIZABETH I BEGINS	SPANISH ARMADA DESTROYED	SIGNING OF MAYFLOWER COMPACT
1517	1526	1534	1536	1558	1585	1588	1607	1620	1624
TYNDALE'S ENGLISH NEW TESTAMENT	CALVIN'S INSTITUTES PUBLISHED	FIRST ROANOAK SETTLEMENT	JAMESTOWN, VIRGINIA FOUNDED	DUTCH FOUND NEW NETHERLAND

John Winthrop, Jr.,
governor of
Connecticut

Connecticut was named after the
Algonquian word Quinnehtukqut,
meaning "beside the long tidal
river," referring to the Connecticut
River. Connecticut was the fifth
colony to ratify the Constitution
on January 9, 1788. State motto:
Qui transtulit sustinet, "He who
transplanted still sustains."

cross the ocean for a job which promised nothing
but strife.

Governor Winthrop of Massachusetts believed
strongly that the Puritan colonies of New
England should be unified, so in the early
1640s, Massachusetts began to take over the
settlements in Maine and New Hampshire. By
the next decade, the two future states were part
of the Bay Colony. However, in 1660, following
the restoration of Charles II to the throne of
England, the heirs of Gorges began to assert the
claim that Maine rightfully belonged to them. In 1664,
an English board of commissioners agreed and ordered Maine
restored to the Gorges family. In 1677, Massachusetts regained
Maine by buying the area from the Gorges family. The territories
remained unified until 1820. New Hampshire was declared a
separate colony in 1679.

Thomas Hooker leads
colonists to Connecticut

MASSACHUSETTS BAY FOUNDED		RHODE ISLAND FOUNDED		KING PHILIP'S WAR		GLORIOUS REVOLUTION		GEORGIA FOUNDED	
1629	1634	1636	1649	1675-6	1681	1688	1692	1733	1740-43
	MARYLAND FOUNDED		CHARLES I OF ENGLAND BEHEADED		PENNSYLVANIA FOUNDED		SALEM WITCH TRIALS		GREAT AWAKENING

Cutting Loose

Thomas Hooker (1586–1647) was a Puritan preacher in England who was forced to leave when Archbishop Laud came to power and made him one of his arch-enemies. Hooker fled to Holland and then to New England where he became the minister of a church at Cambridge, Massachusetts. He became friends with John Winthrop. Although Hooker agreed with Winthrop on most issues, he disagreed with him over the Bay Colony's political affairs, believing that Winthrop's rule was too authoritarian. In 1636, Hooker led a group of a hundred people on a 120-mile trek overland to settle the fertile land of the Connecticut River Valley. They called their new colony Connecticut.

Thomas Hooker

Hooker's group **John Winthrop, Jr.** (1606–1676) as their governor. In 1639, they adopted a set of laws called the **Fundamental Orders of Connecticut.**

One Colony Under God

The Fundamental Orders of Connecticut, which many people consider the first written constitution in America, began by pointing out that "where a people are gathered together the word of God requires that to maintain the peace and union of such a people there should be an orderly and decent Government established according to God. . . ." With this in mind, the inhabitants of Connecticut joined together "to maintain and preserve the liberty and purity of the gospel of our Lord Jesus which we now profess, as also the discipline of the Churches, which according to the truth of the said gospel is now practiced among us. . . ." The Fundamental Orders required that the governor take an oath in which he promised to "further the execution of justice according to the rule of God's word. So help me God, in the name of the Lord Jesus Christ."

345

NEW ENGLAND BURSTING AT THE SEAMS

MARTIN LUTHER'S 95 THESES	HENRY VIII SPLITS FROM ROME	REIGN OF QUEEN ELIZABETH I BEGINS	SPANISH ARMADA DESTROYED	SIGNING OF MAYFLOWER COMPACT
1517 1526	1534 1536	1558 1585	1588 1607	1620 1624
TYNDALE'S ENGLISH NEW TESTAMENT	CALVIN'S *INSTITUTES* PUBLISHED	FIRST ROANOAK SETTLEMENT	JAMESTOWN, VIRGINIA FOUNDED	DUTCH FOUND NEW NETHERLAND

Goody, Goody Twoshoes

The colonists believed that good literature had two purposes: to delight and to instruct. One of the favorite fictional books published in the colonies was *The History of Little Goody Twoshoes*. Although the term "goody twoshoes" has a negative meaning today, back then it was a compliment. Goody (or Mrs.) Twoshoes was an industrious and godly woman who went through many trials but was eventually rewarded for her virtues.

Haven on Earth

In 1637, a group of London Puritans led by John Davenport (1597–1670) traveled from England to New England. Forced to flee the persecutions of Archbishop Laud, Davenport had earlier spent time in Holland. Like the Pilgrims before him, Davenport had found Holland too liberal for his Puritan beliefs. After a brief return to London, he decided to sail to Puritan New England. He spent a short time in Massachusetts Bay Colony and concluded that

John Davenport

the colony was too lax, so he decided to establish a Puritan colony more pure than the one he had just left. He and his followers bought some land from the Indians and settled a colony which they named **New Haven.**

Goody Twoshoes.

First Sunday in New Haven

346

New Haven was dedicated to upholding biblical principles in all areas—family, church, and state. **New Haven's Fundamental Articles** of 1639 stated that "the word of God shall be the only rule to be attended unto in ordering the affairs of government in this plantation." Twelve godly men were elected as head of the colony. As New Haven grew and prospered, it gave birth to many other communities. In 1643, they joined together as the Colony of New Haven. New Haven was very much like Massachusetts Bay, but somewhat more strict in its observance of God's laws. In 1662, King Charles II gave Governor John Winthrop, Jr. of Connecticut a new charter which included New Haven. Citizens of New Haven were not happy at first that their colony had been absorbed by its neighbor, but within a few years they agreed to a peaceable union of the colonies.

Yalies to Live by Rules of God's Word

Yale College was founded in 1701 because many people in New England felt that Harvard was drifting away from the Calvinistic theology on which it had been founded. Among the rules for Yale students in 1745, one stated: "All Scholars Shall Live Religious, Godly and Blameless Lives according to the Rules of God's Word, diligently Reading the holy Scriptures the Fountain of Light and Truth; and constantly attend upon all the Duties of Religion both in Publick and Secret."

MARTIN LUTHER'S 95 THESES		HENRY VIII SPLITS FROM ROME		REIGN OF QUEEN ELIZABETH I BEGINS		SPANISH ARMADA DESTROYED		SIGNING OF MAYFLOWER COMPACT	
1517	1526	1534	1536	1558	1585	1588	1607	1620	1624
	TYNDALE'S ENGLISH NEW TESTAMENT		CALVIN'S *INSTITUTES* PUBLISHED		FIRST ROANOAK SETTLEMENT		JAMESTOWN, VIRGINIA FOUNDED		DUTCH FOUND NEW NETHERLAND

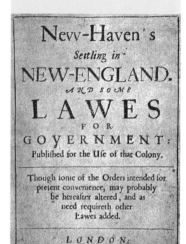

Where's Vermont?

Vermont was not one of the original thirteen colonies. The territory that makes up present-day Vermont was claimed by New Hampshire and New York. New Connecticut, the original name of Vermont, declared itself an independent republic on January 15, 1777. In July 1777, Vermont adopted its first constitution and its present name. Vermont joined the union on March 4, 1791, as the fourteenth state.

United States of New England

In 1643, the New England colonies—Massachusetts Bay, Plymouth, Connecticut, and New Haven—banded together to form a defense against the Dutch, French, and hostile Indians. This coalition was called the **New England Confederation.** These colonies shared more than their desire for security against hostile forces. They all believed in a limited civil government whose purpose was to advance the cause of the Christian faith. The Confederation maintained its solidarity long enough to see the colonies through a conflict with the Indians, **King Philip's War.**

War-Path Indians

The Puritans had enjoyed a long period of peace and friendship with the Wampanoag Indians under their ruler Massasoit. But in 1675 when Massasoit died, peace died with him. His son **Metacomet,** who was known as **"King Philip,"** became the Wampanoag chief. Philip had become increasingly dissatisfied with his tribe's relations with the growing English population.

When the English colonists started hearing reports from friendly Indians that Philip had been talking with their Dutch and French rivals, they became suspicious. In January of 1675, a Christian Indian by the name of John Sassamon, who had once

English colonists fighting Indians during King Philip's War

348

been a friend of Philip, was murdered because he had told the leaders at Plymouth that Philip was organizing a general uprising against the English settlers. An eyewitness to the murder gave information which led to the arrest of three Wampanoags. They were tried by a jury of English settlers and Indians, convicted of murder, and then hanged. Tensions mounted. On June 24, the Wampanoags attacked the Massachusetts town of Swansea and killed eleven colonists. King Philip's War had begun.

The war quickly spread, with the Mohegans, Pequots, and Niantic tribes allied with the English against the Wampanoags, Nipmucks, and Narragansetts. Christian Indians James Quannapohit and Job Kattenanit brought the news that about 400 Indians were planning a raid on the town of Lancaster. The attack occurred on February 9, 1676.

When one considers the number of deaths in relation to the total population, King Philip's War was the bloodiest conflict in American history. Whole sections of New England were depopulated as people fled the onslaught or were massacred before they could get away. Twenty years or more passed before some settlers could return to their farms and towns.

King Philip

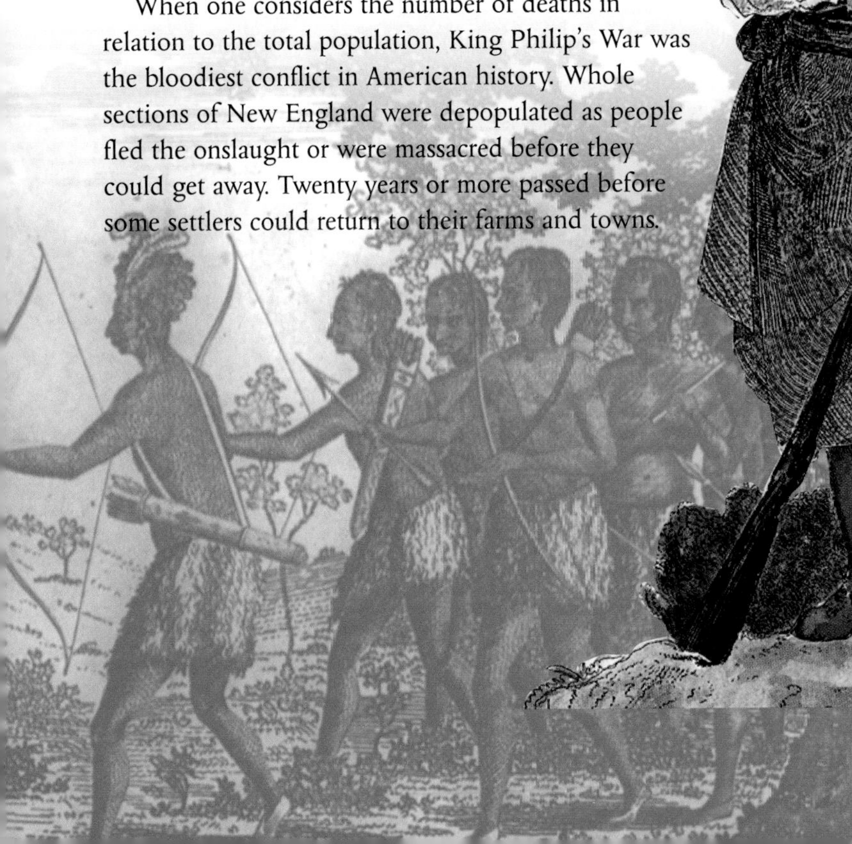

349

NEW ENGLAND BURSTING AT THE SEAMS

MARTIN LUTHER'S 95 THESES	HENRY VIII SPLITS FROM ROME	REIGN OF QUEEN ELIZABETH I BEGINS	SPANISH ARMADA DESTROYED	SIGNING OF MAYFLOWER COMPACT
1517	1526	1534	1536	1558	1585	1588	1607	1620	1624
	TYNDALE'S ENGLISH NEW TESTAMENT	CALVIN'S *INSTITUTES* PUBLISHED	FIRST ROANOAK SETTLEMENT	JAMESTOWN, VIRGINIA FOUNDED	DUTCH FOUND NEW NETHERLAND

A Ransomed Captive

During King Philip's War, **Mary Rowlandson** (c. 1635–1678) and her three children were captured, separated, and forced into slavery by hostile Indians. After three months, her husband ransomed Mary and their children, although their youngest child died in captivity. Mary told her story in her book, *The Captivity and Restoration of Mrs. Mary Rowlandson* (left).

"There were twelve killed, some shot, some stabbed with their spears, some knocked down with their hatchets. . . . There was one who was chopped into the head with a hatchet, and stripped naked, and yet was crawling up and down. It is a solemn sight to see so many Christians lying in their blood, some here, and some there, like a company of sheep torn by wolves, all of them stripped naked by a company of hell-hounds roaring, singing, ranting, insulting, as if they would have torn our very hearts out. Yet the Lord by His almighty power preserved a number of us from death, for there were twenty-four of us taken alive and carried captive."

First published in 1682, Mary Rowlandson's narrative was the first book published in America to be written by a woman. Her bloody ordeal did not cause Mrs. Rowlandson to despair. Instead, she praised God for her affliction, saying that trials cause people to depend more fully on God: "We must rely on God Himself, and our whole dependence must be on Him. . . . I have learned to look beyond present and smaller troubles, and to be quiet under them, as Moses said, Exodus 14:13, 'Stand still and see the salvation of the LORD.'"

The Dominion of New England

Under James II, England attempted to control the colonies of New England by appointing as governor **Sir Edmund Andros** (pronounced "Andrews"). Andros was, above all, loyal to the throne of England. This new union of colonies was named the **Dominion of New England.** When Andros stepped off the British ship *Kingfisher* in 1686 to implement the king's decree, he was probably the most unpopular man in Massachusetts. First, he was a member of the Church of England attempting to rule a Puritan colony. Second, he had been the governor of New York during King Philip's War and had refused to aid New England.

A mere three hours after his arrival, Andros insulted the Puritans by demanding a building in which to hold an Anglican service.

MASSACHUSETTS BAY FOUNDED		RHODE ISLAND FOUNDED		KING PHILIP'S WAR		GLORIOUS REVOLUTION		GEORGIA FOUNDED	

1629   1634   1636   1649   1675-6   1681   1688   1692   1733   1740-43

| MARYLAND FOUNDED | CHARLES I OF ENGLAND BEHEADED | PENNSYLVANIA FOUNDED | SALEM WITCH TRIALS | GREAT AWAKENING |

Charter Oak

When the New England colonies were forced to join the newly-formed Dominion of New England, they actually violated their colonial charters. Thus when Sir Edmund Andros arrived in America in 1686, one of his first tasks was to collect those charters which were still in the hands of the colonists and alter them to lend legality to the Dominion. The citizens of Connecticut, however, refused to cooperate and hid their charter in an oak tree near Hartford (inset left). After the Dominion was overthrown, they recovered the charter and resumed their government. The famous oak tree fell in 1856.

Five days later, he added insult to injury by celebrating Christmas, a Roman Catholic holiday. Andros's decision to tax land owners further infuriated many of the colonists who believed that the Bible does not authorize such a tax. Andros also tried to reform the judicial system and make it conform more to English practices. He ordered all writs to be issued in the king's name and required that when taking an oath a witness must kiss the Bible rather than simply place one hand on it while raising the other. Many believed that this requirement was another attempt to introduce Roman Catholicism into the colony.

By far the greatest objection the Puritans had to Andros was his attempt to require residents of Massachusetts to obtain new titles to their lands from the king's men in the king's name. Besides being a costly nuisance, Puritans saw this as nothing less than idolatry. In their minds, this requirement was a violation of the First Commandment because the colonists would be required to recognize the crown, and not God, as the ultimate authority.

N E W   E N G L A N D   B U R S T I N G   A T   T H E   S E A M S

MARTIN LUTHER'S 95 THESES		HENRY VIII SPLITS FROM ROME		REIGN OF QUEEN ELIZABETH I BEGINS		SPANISH ARMADA DESTROYED		SIGNING OF MAYFLOWER COMPACT	
1517	1526	1534	1536	1558	1585	1588	1607	1620	1624
	TYNDALE'S ENGLISH NEW TESTAMENT		CALVIN'S *INSTITUTES* PUBLISHED		FIRST ROANOAK SETTLEMENT		JAMESTOWN, VIRGINIA FOUNDED		DUTCH FOUND NEW NETHERLAND

Andros had been under orders to make swift changes in New England society. To do so, he ruled with an iron fist. Andros, however, was the mere servant of the Roman Catholic king of England, James II. Protestants rejoiced when King James was driven from the throne and forced to flee England during the **Glorious Revolution**. When word of the revolution reached the colonies, New Englanders saw their opportunity to rid themselves of a hated tyrant. They deposed and arrested Andros in a colonial "glorious revolution." Andros escaped but was later recaptured attempting to flee disguised as a woman. Angry Puritans shipped him back to England as a prisoner.

James II

Governor Andros attempting to flee the colony disguised as a woman

WILLIAM & MARY.

Glorious Revolution

King James II (1685–1688) was a practicing Roman Catholic, the first Catholic English king in over a century. Anglicans feared that he might destroy the Church of England but tolerated him because they thought that he would soon be succeeded by his daughter, Mary. Mary was a Protestant and was married to a Protestant, William of Orange, the *stadholder*, or governor, of the Netherlands.

However, in 1688, the unexpected happened: James and his wife produced a male heir. Protestants of England knew that James would raise his son as a Roman Catholic and that a whole new generation of Roman Catholics would rule England if he took the throne. This was too much. Prominent members of the government decided to get rid of King James by inviting **William and Mary** to come from the Netherlands to take the English throne. The Protestant rulers agreed, and when they arrived in November 1688, James's supporters deserted him, and he was forced to flee the country. Happily, the revolution was completed without the loss of life, which is why the Glorious Revolution is sometimes called the "bloodless revolution."

Andros's rule during the Dominion of New England was a turning point in relations between England and her American colonies. The failure of England to exercise dominion over the colonies was a warning to the crown that each colony could and would manage its own affairs. For more than seventy years after Andros's departure, the colonies experienced virtual independence from the mother country which allowed the colonists to continue developing the institutions of self-government.

N E W   E N G L A N D   B U R S T I N G   A T   T H E   S E A M S

MARTIN LUTHER'S 95 THESES		HENRY VIII SPLITS FROM ROME		REIGN OF QUEEN ELIZABETH I BEGINS		SPANISH ARMADA DESTROYED		SIGNING OF MAYFLOWER COMPACT	

1517   1526   1534   1536   1558   1585   1588   1607   1620   1624

TYNDALE'S ENGLISH NEW TESTAMENT   CALVIN'S *INSTITUTES* PUBLISHED   FIRST ROANOAK SETTLEMENT   JAMESTOWN, VIRGINIA FOUNDED   DUTCH FOUND NEW NETHERLAND

WUSKU WUTTESTAMENTUM

Matthew 5:1-3 in Eliot's New Testament reads: "Nauont moochequshaoh, ogquodchuau wadchuut, kah na matapit, ukkodnetuh taéneumoh peyauónuk. Kah woshwunum wuttoon, ukkuhkootomauuh noowau. Wunnánumôog kodtummungeteahoncheg, a newutche wuttaihécu kesukque ketassootamóonk." Members of some Algonquian-speaking tribes like the Ojibways are able to understand the passage, especially when it is read aloud.

Was Joshua a Mugwump?

The Massachusetts Indian tribe for whom John Eliot translated the Bible died out long ago, and there are now only a few Indians or scholars alive who can read the book. One word in Eliot's Bible, however, has become a part of the American language. The word the Algonquians used for a "great chief" is "mukxuomp" or "mugwump." This is the word that Eliot used in his translation to describe the Bible's great leaders, like Joshua or Gideon. However, in 1884, the word was applied to independent Republicans who refused to support their party's candidate. That is why today the word "mugwump" is used to describe a political maverick, someone who refuses to conform to his group.

"Apostle to the Indians"

The English colonists believed that one of the main purposes for settling in the New World was to bring Christianity to the Indians. Perhaps the best known of the New England missionaries was **John Eliot** (1604–1690). Eliot was born and raised in England. After graduating from Cambridge University in 1622, he was ordained a minister in the Church of England. Eliot began his career as a teacher at a school in England run by Thomas Hooker, the man who founded Connecticut. Because of Eliot's Puritan beliefs, he was persecuted by Archbishop Laud and forced to flee England. He came to Massachusetts Bay in 1631, shortly after the colony was established, and became a teacher at the Church of Christ in Roxbury. He held this position for nearly sixty years until his death.

Shortly after arriving in America, Eliot began to study the difficult language of the local Indians. By 1646, he had learned enough to enable him to begin to preach the Gospel to them in their own language.

MASSACHUSETTS BAY FOUNDED		RHODE ISLAND FOUNDED		KING PHILIP'S WAR		GLORIOUS REVOLUTION		GEORGIA FOUNDED	
1629	1634	1636	1649	1675-6	1681	1688	1692	1733	1740-43
	MARYLAND FOUNDED		CHARLES I OF ENGLAND BEHEADED		PENNSYLVANIA FOUNDED		SALEM WITCH TRIALS		GREAT AWAKENING

Society for the Propagation of the Gospel

Eliot's pioneering work in evangelism among the Indians led to the establishment in 1649 of the **Society for the Propagation of the Gospel** in New England. Indians who converted to Christianity became known as "praying Indians." By 1660, Eliot's work had led to the founding of the first Indian church at Natick, Massachusetts. In time, Eliot trained a number of Indians as Christian workers, twenty-four of whom became preachers. The outbreak of King Philip's War in 1675 dealt a severe blow to the church, though it continued on until the death of its last native pastor in 1716.

Most "praying Indians" preferred to live with other Indians rather than move into the English settlements. By 1674, Eliot had some 3600 Indian converts whom he gathered into fourteen self-governing communities. Here Eliot arranged for them to have land, housing, clothing, and jobs. His great work among the Indians earned Eliot the title "Apostle to the Indians."

The King Versus the King of Kings

John Eliot wrote a little book called the *Christian Commonwealth* which stirred up a major controversy with royalists back in England. The book describes an ideal Christian commonwealth guided in all matters by God's law. According to Eliot, all earthly authorities must bow before Christ as the King of kings and acknowledge that the Bible alone reveals the law of God. "Much is spoken of the rightful Heir of the Crown of England," he stated, "and of the injustice of casting out the right Heir; but Christ is the only right Heir of the Crown of England (Ps. 2:8) and of all other Nations also (Rev. 11:15)." Eliot wrote the book in the midst of the Puritan rule of Oliver Cromwell in England, just after King Charles I had been beheaded. In 1660, however, the Stuarts were restored to the throne when King Charles II came to power. The leaders of Massachusetts Bay Colony feared that the king—who saw himself, not Christ, as the supreme ruler of England—would view *The Christian Commonwealth* as a seditious attack on his throne, so they ordered the book to be suppressed.

NEW ENGLAND BURSTING AT THE SEAMS

| MARTIN LUTHER'S 95 THESES | HENRY VIII SPLITS FROM ROME | REIGN OF QUEEN ELIZABETH I BEGINS | SPANISH ARMADA DESTROYED | SIGNING OF MAYFLOWER COMPACT |

1517   1526   1534   1536   1558   1585   1588   1607   1620   1624

TYNDALE'S ENGLISH NEW TESTAMENT   CALVIN'S *INSTITUTES* PUBLISHED   FIRST ROANOAK SETTLEMENT   JAMESTOWN, VIRGINIA FOUNDED   DUTCH FOUND NEW NETHERLAND

Dartmouth College in the eighteenth century

Native Collegians

The colonists of New England were very much involved in Indian mission work. Around 1754, Reverend Eleazar Wheelock of Connecticut, at his own expense and on his own estate, established a school where he "clothed, maintained and educated a number of the children of the Indian natives, with a view to their carrying the gospel in their own language, and spreading the knowledge of the great Redeemer among their savage tribes. . . ." The school grew beyond the ability of private donors to meet its expenses. The colony of New Hampshire then stepped in to take over what it considered a worthy work, and from these efforts, Dartmouth College was born. The 1769 charter of the college stated: "Know ye therefore that we, considering the premises and being willing to encourage the laudable design of spreading Christian knowledge among the savages of our American wilderness . . . [grant that a college be established in New Hampshire] by the name of Dartmouth College, for the education and instruction of youths of the Indian tribes in this land in reading, writing, and all parts of learning, which shall appear necessary and expedient, for civilizing and christianizing the children of pagans. . . ."

Eliot did not limit his missionary work to the Indians. He persuaded a number of colonists to send their African servants to him for biblical instruction. Near the end of his life, Eliot gave seventy-five acres of land for the teaching of Indians and Africans.

John Eliot had other interests as well. In 1640, he helped prepare a metrical version of the Psalms called the *Bay Psalm Book,* which was the first book printed in New England. He translated many Christian works into the language of the local Indians, the most important of which was the Bible. Eliot's translation of the New Testament, first printed in 1661, and the Old Testament, first printed in 1663, together constituted the first edition of the Bible printed in North America. With the help of his sons, Eliot also produced an Indian grammar.

Eliot was known far and wide for his great learning, pious lifestyle, practical wisdom, and zeal to proclaim the Gospel to the lost. The great Puritan minister Cotton Mather summed up Eliot's life with these words: "He that writes of Eliot, must write of charity, or say nothing."

The Big Six

Present-day **New England** includes Maine, New Hampshire, Vermont, Massachusetts, Rhode Island, and Connecticut.

John Eliot preaching to the Indians

MARTIN LUTHER'S 95 THESES		HENRY VIII SPLITS FROM ROME		REIGN OF QUEEN ELIZABETH I BEGINS		SPANISH ARMADA DESTROYED		SIGNING OF MAYFLOWER COMPACT		
1517	1526	1534	1536	1558	1585	1588	1607	1620	1624
	TYNDALE'S ENGLISH NEW TESTAMENT		CALVIN'S *INSTITUTES* PUBLISHED		FIRST ROANOAK SETTLEMENT		JAMESTOWN, VIRGINIA FOUNDED		DUTCH FOUND NEW NETHERLAND	

FOR STUDY

CHAPTER 28:
New England Bursting at the Seams

Terms

English Civil War
New Model Army
Lord Protector
Fundamental Orders
of Connecticut
New Haven
New Haven's
Fundamental Articles
Yale College
New England Confederation
King Philip's War
Dominion of New England
Glorious Revolution
Society for the Propagation
of the Gospel

People

Sir Fernando Gorges
John Mason
Oliver Cromwell
Thomas Hooker
John Winthrop, Jr.
Metacomet, "King Philip"
Sir Edmund Andros
Mary Rowlandson
King James II
William and Mary
John Eliot

Both Puritans and non-Puritans established new colonies in New England: Maine, New Hampshire, Connecticut, and New Haven. Continued growth led to bloody conflict between the colonists and the Indians. Meanwhile, momentous events back in England, a civil war and a revolution, left their marks on the colonies. In a foreshadowing of the events leading up to the American Revolution, England briefly tightened the clamps on colonial liberties and self-government through the short-lived Dominion of New England. However, not all of New England's growth brought turmoil. Thousands of Indians came to know the saving grace of Christ through the efforts of the Puritans.

Discussion Questions

1. How was Gorges and his colony of Maine a threat to the Puritan colony of Massachusetts Bay?
2. What was the purpose of the founding of the various New England colonies according to the Fundamental Orders of Connecticut, New Haven's Fundamental Orders, and the charter of the New England Confederation?
3. Explain why the Puritans opposed Governor Edmund Andros.
4. What effect did these events in England have on the colonies of New England: the English Civil War; the Restoration of Charles II and James II; and the Glorious Revolution?

Optional Enrichment Project

1. Read the account of Mary Rowlandson's experience in *The Captive*. Make note of aspects of her narrative that surprise or inspire you. What passages in the Bible comforted and strengthened her? What advice does she give to the reader?

MASSACHUSETTS BAY FOUNDED	RHODE ISLAND FOUNDED		KING PHILIP'S WAR		GLORIOUS REVOLUTION		GEORGIA FOUNDED	
1629	1634	1636	1649	1675-6	1681	1688	1692	1733 1740-43
	MARYLAND FOUNDED		CHARLES I OF ENGLAND BEHEADED		PENNSYLVANIA FOUNDED		SALEM WITCH TRIALS	GREAT AWAKENING

CHAPTER 29

New Netherland

Becomes NEW YORK

The Low Lands Reach New Heights

In 1607, the English navigator **Henry Hudson** was hired by a company of London merchants to find a more direct passage to Asia. He coasted the shores of Greenland and came within eight degrees of the North Pole before ice forced him to give up his quest. Hudson made a second voyage but again failed to find the Northwest Passage, the elusive water route to Asia.

In 1609, Hudson was hired by the Dutch East India Company to search for the Northwest Passage. He made his way to the coastal waters of Virginia in his ship, the *Half Moon,* and then followed the coastline north until he reached the mouth of a river which he named after himself. Along the Hudson River, the explorer established trading posts as far north as **Fort Orange,** the site of New York's present-day capital, Albany. Even though he did not find a northwest water route to the East, Hudson did establish the basis for Dutch claims to one of the richest regions of fur-bearing animals south of Canada. In addition, he brought back glowing reports of rich forests and abundant fishing waters.

New York, named in honor of the Duke of York and Albany who later became King James II, was the eleventh colony to ratify the Constitution on July 26, 1788. State motto: Excelsior, "Ever Upward."

359

MARTIN LUTHER'S 95 THESES	HENRY VIII SPLITS FROM ROME	REIGN OF QUEEN ELIZABETH I BEGINS	SPANISH ARMADA DESTROYED	SIGNING OF MAYFLOWER COMPACT
1517 1526	1534 1536	1558 1585	1588 1607	1620 1624
TYNDALE'S ENGLISH NEW TESTAMENT	CALVIN'S *INSTITUTES* PUBLISHED	FIRST ROANOAK SETTLEMENT	JAMESTOWN, VIRGINIA FOUNDED	DUTCH FOUND NEW NETHERLAND

Henry Hudson sailing up the Hudson River

Mutiny on the Hudson

Henry Hudson's fourth voyage to the New World (which was funded not by the Dutch but by the English) allowed him to discover even more territory as he sailed into Hudson Bay. However, the voyage also brought him disaster. His crew mutinied and set him adrift. Hudson was never heard from again.

Henry Hudson's last voyage

Hudson's discoveries opened the area to future business ventures. In 1621, a group of merchants called the **Dutch West India Company** received a commercial land grant. This grant, consisting of indefinite property boundaries, was named **New Netherland.** The first settlers arrived in 1623 to set up trading posts. In 1626, **Peter Minuit** (1580–1638), the first director-general of New Netherland, purchased Manhattan Island from the Indians. The new village and capital was named **New Amsterdam** (the site of present-day New York City).

The main interest of the Dutch West India Company was the development of the fur trade. Therefore, the founders gave little attention to making the settlement attractive to colonists. Unlike English colonies that were forming at that time, New Netherland's charter did not even mention religion. With the exception of a few persecuted religious groups—Protestant refugees from Catholic Belgium, Huguenots from France, and the Walloons, French-speaking Hollanders—the majority of those who came to New Netherland were not pursuing religious freedom.

MASSACHUSETTS BAY FOUNDED	RHODE ISLAND FOUNDED		KING PHILIP'S WAR		GLORIOUS REVOLUTION		GEORGIA FOUNDED	
1629	1634	1636	1649	1675-6	1681	1688	1692	1733	1740-43
	MARYLAND FOUNDED		CHARLES I OF ENGLAND BEHEADED		PENNSYLVANIA FOUNDED		SALEM WITCH TRIALS		GREAT AWAKENING

Manhattan is sold

Let's Make a Deal!

In 1626, the governor of the Dutch colony, Peter Minuit, decided that Manhattan—or "Hill Island" as the Algonquians called it—was well worth having. He made an offer of sale to the Canarsee Indians, who occupied the land along with the Weckquaesgeeks, even though neither tribe owned the tract of land or even recognized ownership in the European sense. Even so, Minuit's instructions from Holland were clear: "In case the said Island is inhabited by some Indians…these should not be driven away by force or threats, but should be persuaded by kind words or otherwise by giving them something, to let us live amongst them." The price they settled upon was "the value of sixty guilders" (about $24) worth of beads, knives, axes, clothes, and rum.

The Dutch arrive at New Netherland

361

NEW NETHERLAND BECOMES NEW YORK

MARTIN LUTHER'S 95 THESES		HENRY VIII SPLITS FROM ROME		REIGN OF QUEEN ELIZABETH I BEGINS		SPANISH ARMADA DESTROYED		SIGNING OF MAYFLOWER COMPACT	
1517	1526	1534	1536	1558	1585	1588	1607	1620	1624
	TYNDALE'S ENGLISH NEW TESTAMENT		CALVIN'S *INSTITUTES* PUBLISHED		FIRST ROANOAK SETTLEMENT		JAMESTOWN, VIRGINIA FOUNDED		DUTCH FOUND NEW NETHERLAND

Early view of Manhattan

Seal of New Amsterdam

MONOPOLY

In economic terms, a **monopoly** (from two Greek words: *mono* = one + *polein* = to sell) exists when a government forbids people to sell certain goods by granting one organization the exclusive right of doing business. Monopolies stifle competition, cause inefficiency, inhibit innovation, and keep prices artificially high.

Maintaining a Monopoly

For many years before New Netherland was established, the fur trade was already a thriving industry in that area. The highly prized pelts that came from America were much less expensive than those from Russia and Scandinavia. This enterprise appealed to Amsterdam merchants who outfitted small ships to engage in a very profitable fur trade with the Indians.

After the Dutch West India Company began operations in 1623, the economic condition of the area began to change. The Company was granted a trade **monopoly**, so freedom and economic enterprise were restrained. Settlers who had ventured inland were ordered to return to the area around New Amsterdam, so trade could be controlled and the monopoly maintained. Allowing individuals access to the interior, the Company reasoned, would encourage competition and lower its profits.

America Returns to the Middle Ages

In 1629, the Dutch West India Company began to expand its efforts beyond trading by encouraging further colonization. Any stockholder in the Company could obtain a large estate—a **patroonship**—if he could settle it with fifty people within four years. The patroonship revived a feudalistic lifestyle that ran counter to the new American spirit of self-reliance and independence. The patroon supplied cattle, the necessary tools for farming, and buildings, whereas the tenants paid rent and gave the patroon first option to purchase surplus crops. Tenants could not hunt or fish without the patroon's permission, nor could they grind their grain except at his mill.

While the tenants were exempted from colonial taxation for ten years, they were compelled to stay on the original estate for the entire period. To leave was forbidden by law, a condition similar to medieval serfdom. The Dutch maintained this feudal

Crooks, Beware!

The first day of court in New Amsterdam was opened with prayer that God would bless the justice system of that colony "to the general good of the community, and to the maintenance of the church, that we may be praised by them that do well, and a terror to evil-doers [ROMANS 13:4]."

New Amsterdam's harbor brought increasing prosperity to the area

363

N E W   N E T H E R L A N D   B E C O M E S   N E W   Y O R K

| MARTIN LUTHER'S 95 THESES | HENRY VIII SPLITS FROM ROME | REIGN OF QUEEN ELIZABETH I BEGINS | SPANISH ARMADA DESTROYED | SIGNING OF MAYFLOWER COMPACT |

1517   1526   1534   1536   1558   1585   1588   1607   1620   1624

| TYNDALE'S ENGLISH NEW TESTAMENT | CALVIN'S *INSTITUTES* PUBLISHED | FIRST ROANOAK SETTLEMENT | JAMESTOWN, VIRGINIA FOUNDED | DUTCH FOUND NEW NETHERLAND |

Lord and Father

The word **patroon** is derived from the Latin words *pater,* "father," and *patronus,* "protector." From early Roman times, landowners—patrons—supplied financial support and legal aid to dependents called "clients." In turn, the clients cultivated the patrons' lands, fought for them in time of war, and supported them or their relatives in elections. In a similar way, the patroons of New Netherland received perpetual land tenure and the right to establish courts and appoint officials. Traces of the patroon system remained until New York abolished perpetual leases in 1846.

system by mandating that settlers lease land rather than allowing them to purchase the land outright. This arrangement meant that the Dutch government could maintain almost complete control over New Netherland. Under this medieval arrangement, the settlers had no stake in the future of the colony since inheritance was impossible.

Because settlers were denied the freedom to own land, to choose where to live, and to compete economically in the lucrative fur trade, it is no wonder that the rate of settlement in the colony was slow. Why would anyone risk the hazards of sea travel to become a feudal vassal in New Netherland when fertile land was so easily obtainable elsewhere in America? Many gifted and industrious settlers simply by-passed New Netherland and moved on to New England or Pennsylvania. By 1629, only three hundred people lived in the capital of New Amsterdam. When the English took possession of the province in 1664, the total population of New Netherland was fewer than eight thousand.

Plan of the City of New York

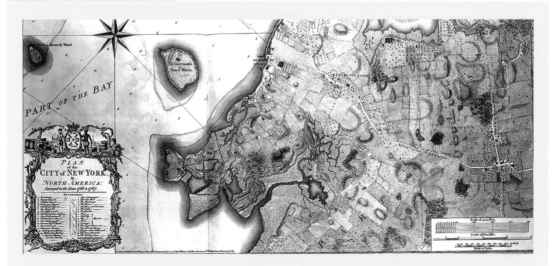

From Monopoly to Freedom

Political policy in New Netherland was a mirror image of its restrictive economic policies. Governmental control was concentrated in the director general and the Council of Five appointed by the Amsterdam Chamber. They ran the entire government by controlling its legislative, executive, and judicial functions. Colonists had no voting privileges.

Over time, however, some powerful patroons began to resist the government's trade monopoly. In response to this act of defiance, the Dutch West India Company began to apply its restrictive regulations with greater force. Conditions worsened in 1638 with the arrival of a new director general, Amsterdam merchant **Willem Kieft** (1599–1647). Kieft reduced the governing council from five members to one and made it a high crime to appeal his decisions to the Netherlands. Kieft damaged the economy further by outlawing all trade of any commodity unless he granted a special license.

Eventually, however, freedom won out. The Company decided to end its monopolistic practices and allow land ownership. The effect of increased economic freedom was astounding. Settlers flocked to the colony, and in one year the number of farms on Manhattan Island quadrupled.

Growth of New York under English rule

365

MARTIN LUTHER'S 95 THESES		HENRY VIII SPLITS FROM ROME		REIGN OF QUEEN ELIZABETH I BEGINS		SPANISH ARMADA DESTROYED		SIGNING OF MAYFLOWER COMPACT	
1517	1526	1534	1536	1558	1585	1588	1607	1620	1624
	TYNDALE'S ENGLISH NEW TESTAMENT		CALVIN'S *INSTITUTES* PUBLISHED		FIRST ROANOAK SETTLEMENT		JAMESTOWN, VIRGINIA FOUNDED		DUTCH FOUND NEW NETHERLAND

Israel Finds a Home in America

In 1654, the French privateer *St. Catherine* brought twenty-three Jewish refugees from Brazil to New Netherland. Governor Stuyvesant protested to the Dutch West India Company against this settlement. The Company instructed the governor to permit them to live and trade in the colony. Later, under English control, Governor Nicolls stressed the right to freedom of worship.

A Public Relations Nightmare

In addition to almost wrecking New Netherland's economy, Director Kieft bungled what once had been good relations with the Algonquins. Because of a series of inept policies implemented by Kieft, the Algonquins called for an all-out war on the Dutch. Entire Dutch communities were wiped out by the raids. (It was during this war that Anne Hutchinson and members of her family were massacred by Indian raiders.) By 1644, almost all the Dutch settlers were forced to abandon their homes and fields and to retreat behind the wall of Fort Amsterdam (now Wall Street). The colonists were so desperate to rid themselves of their incompetent director that an assassination attempt was made. It failed, and the man who fired the shot was instantly killed and his head publicly displayed as a warning to other anarchists.

Kieft's solution to a faltering economy and social disaster was to raise taxes on those who had lost everything in the wars with the Indians. Kieft was finally removed from office in 1645 and was replaced in 1647 by **Peter Stuyvesant** (1592–1672).

Peter Stuyvesant

New York Harbor

So What Else Is New?

Some settlers of New Netherland sent a written complaint to the Dutch West India Company in 1650: "Great distrust has also been created among the inhabitants on account of Heer Stuyvesant being so ready to confiscate. There scarcely comes a ship in or near here which, if it does not belong to his friends, is not re-garded as a prize by him.…Confiscating has reached such a pitch in New Netherland that nobody who has any visible prop-erty considers it to be at all safe. Besides this, the country…is so taxed, and is burdened and kept down in such a manner that the inhabitants are not able…to undertake any enterprise."

A Duke Gets His Own State

Stuyvesant was nearly as bad a governor as Kieft. He suppressed all political dissent and jailed his critics. He also established unreasonable restrictions against hospitality shown to Quakers. Anyone who took in a Quaker for the night, the governor decreed, would be fined. For these and other actions, the colo-nists turned against Stuyvesant and looked for relief from his oppressive style of governing.

Relief came one summer's day in 1664 when Governor Stuyvesant was confronted by an English naval force of one thousand men. The reason for the English attack was that Dutch ownership of the strategic waterways of New Amsterdam made New Netherland an economic and military threat to the English colonies. Dutch warships could strike English ships bound to and from New England and the southern colonies. The English also believed that they had legal title to the land. James, the Duke of York (who would later become King James II), had received a patent to settle the area from his brother King Charles II, who claimed the land for England based on the explorations of John Cabot more than 150 years earlier.

Peg-Leg Peter

Peter Stuyvesant became gover-nor of New Netherland in 1647. His most distinctive feature was his wooden leg which was bound together with bands of silver which is why it was sometimes re-ferred to as his "silver leg."

A Dutch man-of-war

| MARTIN LUTHER'S 95 THESES | HENRY VIII SPLITS FROM ROME | REIGN OF QUEEN ELIZABETH I BEGINS | SPANISH ARMADA DESTROYED | SIGNING OF MAYFLOWER COMPACT |

1517   1526   1534   1536   1558   1585   1588   1607   1620   1624

| TYNDALE'S ENGLISH NEW TESTAMENT | CALVIN'S *INSTITUTES* PUBLISHED | FIRST ROANOAK SETTLEMENT | JAMESTOWN, VIRGINIA FOUNDED | DUTCH FOUND NEW NETHERLAND |

James, Duke of York
(later James II)

The English force was small, but there was so much political dissent in New Netherland that the governor could muster only 450 men capable of bearing arms. Even Stuyvesant's own son rejected his father's call to fight. Before even one shot was fired, Stuyvesant surrendered.

Following the capture of New Netherland, King Charles made his brother, the Duke of York, absolute proprietor of the colony. The duke's power was so complete that for nearly two decades he governed without any representative assembly. New Netherland was renamed **New York Province**, New Amsterdam was renamed the City of New York, and Fort Orange was renamed **Albany**, after one of the Duke of York's titles.

The Fading Light of King's College

King's College was the first college established in New York. An advertisement appeared in the *New York Mercury* on June 3, 1754, announcing the opening of the college: "The chief thing that is aimed at in this college is to teach and engage the children to know God in Jesus Christ and to love and serve Him in all sobriety, godliness, and righteousness of life. . . ." The original shield of King's College (now Columbia University), adopted in 1755, shows a seated woman with the Hebrew name for *Jehovah* (YHWH) above her head. The Latin motto around her head reads "In Thy light we see light" (PSALM 36:9). The Hebrew phrase on the ribbon is *Uri El* ("God is my light"), an allusion to Psalm 27:1. At the feet of the woman is the New Testament passage commanding Christians to desire the pure milk of God's Word (1 PETER 2:1-2). Columbia's present seal has only one line remaining from the original, the Latin phrase "In Thy light we see light."

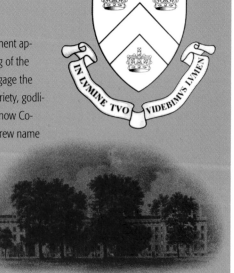

MASSACHUSETTS BAY FOUNDED		RHODE ISLAND FOUNDED		KING PHILIP'S WAR		GLORIOUS REVOLUTION		GEORGIA FOUNDED	
1629	1634	1636	1649	1675-6	1681	1688	1692	1733	1740-43
	MARYLAND FOUNDED		CHARLES I OF ENGLAND BEHEADED		PENNSYLVANIA FOUNDED		SALEM WITCH TRIALS		GREAT AWAKENING

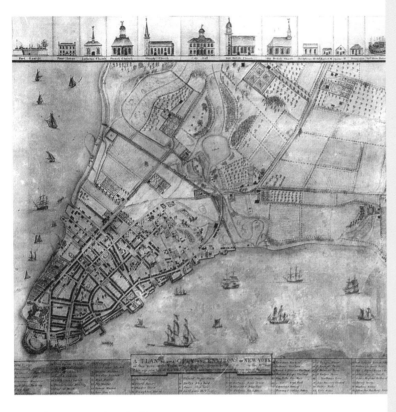

Lower Manhattan

These Church Doors Are Open

The West India Company made the Dutch Reformed Church the established church of New Netherland. It pledged to maintain the national religion "as it is at present preached and practiced by public authority in the United Netherlands," and to send over and support "good and suitable preachers, school-masters and comforters of the sick." Taxes were levied for the construction of church buildings and the support of the clergy.

Although the Reformed Church was the established church of New Netherland, religious dissenters were welcomed and were promised "liberty of conscience according to the custom and manner of Holland." Toleration remained a characteristic of the colony for most of its existence.

Regulations and Rebellion

The colony, stretching from Maine to Maryland, proved too large an area to govern, so the duke immediately began to give away portions to his friends. He also appointed as governor of the colony **Richard Nicolls** (1624–1672), who had led the force which captured New Amsterdam. Within four months, Governor Nicolls published a code known as the **Duke's Laws,** which preserved the duke's absolute authority in New York, yet gave the people local control over their affairs. These laws enforced religious toleration, guaranteed freedom of conscience, and required every town to build and maintain a church. They protected property rights and freedom of trade and immigration. New Yorkers enjoyed far more liberty under English rule than they had under the Dutch Company government.

New Jersey's Religious Heritage

The earliest settlers in New Jersey were Puritans who came from the eastern end of Long Island, New York. They settled at Elizabethtown where the first colonial legislative assembly convened to transfer the chief features of New England laws to the statute book of New Jersey. The New Jersey constitution of 1776 stipulated that "no person shall ever…be deprived of the inestimable privilege of worshipping Almighty God in a manner agreeable to the dictates of his own conscience." A citizen of New Jersey would not be compelled by state law "to attend any place of worship, contrary to his own faith and judgment." Neither would he be "obliged to pay tithes, taxes, or any other rates, for the purpose of building or repairing any church or churches, places of worship, or for the maintenance of any minister or ministry."

These religious liberty provisions did not disestablish Protestant Christianity. They merely stated that the civil government could not establish "any one religious sect…in preference to another." The constitution did give Protestants special constitutional privileges in that "no Protestant inhabitant of this Colony shall be denied the enjoyment of any civil right, merely on account of his religious principles; but that all persons, professing a belief in the faith of any Protestant sect…shall be capable of being elected into any office or profit or trust, or being a member of either branch of the Legislature." The following instructions from the legislature of New Jersey to its delegates in Congress in 1777 exemplifies the Christian sentiments of the men who directed the civil and military concerns of the Revolution: "We hope you will habitually bear in mind that the success of the great cause in which the United States are engaged depends upon the favor and blessing of Almighty God; and therefore you will neglect nothing which is competent to the Assembly of the States for promoting *piety* and *good morals* among the people at large."

New Jersey's history of Christian foundations goes back as far as 1683 with the drafting of the "Fundamental Constitution for the Province of East New Jersey." Religious liberty was upheld, and every civil magistrate was required to affirm and swear a binding oath to Jesus Christ. Following this requirement, we read: "Nor by this article is it intended that any under the notion of liberty shall allow themselves to avow atheism, irreligiousness, or to practice cursing, swearing, drunkenness, profaneness, adultery, murdering, or any kind of violence." Marriage was defined by "the law of God."

What Do Wall Street and Santa Claus Have In Common?

The Dutch introduced ice skating and sleighing to American culture. They enriched the English language with such words as "spook" (ghost), "brief" (letter), "boss," "scow" (boat), "yacht," and "dope" (as in, "give me the inside dope"). New York's Broadway was originally the Dutch *Breede Wegh*. Wall Street, the hub of New York's financial district and the New York Stock Exchange, is so named because it stands on the site of a wall that had been built across Manhattan Island in 1653 to protect settlers from Indian attacks. Famous New Yorkers have Dutch ancestry, such as Presidents Martin Van Buren (left) and Theodore Roosevelt. The Dutch were the first to establish parochial schools, which they formed to keep alive Dutch language, traditions, culture, and religion, which they feared English rule might destroy. Probably the best-known Dutch contributions to American culture are the Easter egg and Santa Claus. In fact, St. Nicholas, who was the basis of the Santa Claus character, was the patron saint of New Amsterdam.

Wall Street

In the 1670s, the new governor of New York, Major Edmund Andros, was confronted by unhappy residents of Long Island who demanded a representative assembly. They threatened to withhold taxes if they did not receive adequate representation. Andros supported their demand, although the Duke of York argued that such bodies would "prove destructive to, or very oft disturb, the peace of the government wherein they are allowed." Andros insisted, and the Duke relented.

The first representative assembly passed a **Charter of Liberties and Privileges,** which guaranteed property rights and protected the liberties of Englishmen. The duke approved the charter, but later, after he became King James II, rescinded it when he ordered New York into the newly formed Dominion of New England in 1686.

The Dominion of New England was no more popular in New York than it was in New England, so when rumors of the Glori-

| MARTIN LUTHER'S 95 THESES | HENRY VIII SPLITS FROM ROME | REIGN OF QUEEN ELIZABETH I BEGINS | SPANISH ARMADA DESTROYED | SIGNING OF MAYFLOWER COMPACT |

| 1517 | 1526 | 1534 | 1536 | 1558 | 1585 | 1588 | 1607 | 1620 | 1624 |

| TYNDALE'S ENGLISH NEW TESTAMENT | CALVIN'S *INSTITUTES* PUBLISHED | FIRST ROANOAK SETTLEMENT | JAMESTOWN, VIRGINIA FOUNDED | DUTCH FOUND NEW NETHERLAND |

Seal of the Carterets

ous Revolution in England reached the colony, a German immigrant named **Jacob Leisler** seized power and governed New York for more than a year. Leisler took over a colony beset with bitter political divisions, and he himself made many enemies. When the new monarchs of England, William and Mary, sent a new royal governor to New York, Leisler hesitated in turning over his power. For this, his enemies branded him a traitor and had him tried for treason and executed. The new royal governor finally granted New York its representative assembly in 1691. In 1695, Parliament belatedly reversed Leisler's conviction, but New Yorkers were by this time bitterly divided into factions which would last well into the era of the War for Independence from England.

Carteret Landing in New Jersey

The Two Jerseys Become One

Three months after the Duke of York had received the charter for New York, he transferred the part between the Hudson and Delaware Rivers, known as the **Province of Nova Caesaria**, to two friends, **Lord John Berkeley** and **Sir George Carteret**. The duke gave these men the land as repayment for the losses they had suffered in the English Civil War. This area was renamed **New Jersey** in honor of Carteret's birthplace, the Isle of Jersey in the English Channel,

This grant was the beginning of years of confusion and conflict. Before the governor of New York, Richard Nicolls, learned of the duke's grant, Nicolls had already given permission for a group of New Englanders to settle in eastern New Jersey. Nicolls promised the settlers an elective assembly and liberty of conscience in exchange for a small rent. The problem was that Berkeley and Carteret began offering a different group of colonists the same deal. The result was chaos. One group of colonists claimed that Nicolls had authorized their assembly, while others claimed that Berkeley or Carteret had authorized theirs. In fact, all of them were wrong. Neither Nicolls, Berkeley, nor Carteret had any authority to set up a colonial government. Only the Duke of York could do that. The Duke could give away parts of his land to his friends, but the government was still his alone. The duke unfortunately showed little interest in the peace and welfare of the New Jersey colonists.

By 1674, Berkeley had experienced enough of the strife in New Jersey, so he sold his western half of the colony to a group of English Quakers. This led to an official division of the region into East and West Jersey. Eventually, the West Jersey proprietors went bankrupt, and those of East Jersey did not fare much better. In 1702, both groups surrendered their charters to the king who reunited New Jersey as a royal colony.

Seal of East Jersey

New Jersey *was named for the Isle of Jersey, which Sir George Carteret, one of the original proprietors of the colony, had defended against the Puritans in the English Civil War. New Jersey was the third colony to ratify the Constitution on December 18, 1787. State motto, Libertas et Prosperitas, "Liberty and Prosperity."*

MARTIN LUTHER'S 95 THESES		HENRY VIII SPLITS FROM ROME		REIGN OF QUEEN ELIZABETH I BEGINS		SPANISH ARMADA DESTROYED		SIGNING OF MAYFLOWER COMPACT	
1517	1526	1534	1536	1558	1585	1588	1607	1620	1624
	TYNDALE'S ENGLISH NEW TESTAMENT		CALVIN'S *INSTITUTES* PUBLISHED		FIRST ROANOAK SETTLEMENT		JAMESTOWN, VIRGINIA FOUNDED		DUTCH FOUND NEW NETHERLAND

FOR STUDY

CHAPTER 29:
New Netherland Becomes New York

While the English were colonizing the coast of North America, the Dutch carved out their own strategically located colony of New Netherland, from which they hoped to reap rich profits. They brought their unique culture and customs, including an order of society left over from Middle Age feudalism. The English could not tolerate Dutch competition for long and soon incorporated New Netherland into their own growing empire, renaming it New York.

Terms

Fort Orange
Dutch West India Company
New Netherland
New Amsterdam
monopoly
patroonship
patroon
New York Province
Albany
Duke's Laws
Charter of Liberties
and Privileges
Province of Nova Caesaria
New Jersey

People

Henry Hudson
Peter Minuit
Willem Kieft
Peter Stuyvesant
Richard Nicolls
Jacob Leisler
Lord John Berkeley
Sir George Carteret

Discussion Questions

1. The Dutch West India Company was virtually a government unto itself with extensive powers over its colonies. What aspects of its economic and political policies proved unworkable in New Netherland?

2. Compare and contrast the founding and administration of Massachusetts Bay colony with that of New Netherland. Consider religious, economic, and political policies.

3. Both the Dutch West India Company in New Netherland and Sir Fernando Gorges in Maine tried to establish a medieval system in the New World. Why did both efforts fail?

4. Discuss the interior turmoil and foreign problems that resulted in New Netherland becoming New York. How did the English deal with religious differences once they took control?

Optional Enrichment Projects

1. Research the history of the Dutch West and East India Companies. How important were these companies and how wide was their influence? What present-day conditions or complications may be traced back to these commercial empires?

2. What conclusions might be drawn from the lack of success of the Dutch in the New World?

C H A P T E R

30

Quaking
in PENN's WOODS

Could We Just Get a Little Peace?

William Penn (1644–1718) was an Englishman who was converted to Quaker beliefs while he was a student at Oxford University. Upon his arrival at the university, Penn had first been influenced by Puritan doctrines. The essence of Quaker doctrine is the belief that there is a spark of the divine in every person. Penn's new religious convictions, and those of his fellow Quakers, would soon compel him to look for a sanctuary where they hoped to be free from persecution.

In 1681, young William appealed to King Charles II for a grant of land in America in repayment of a £16,000 debt the king owed to his father for loans and back salary. Ignoring his advisors who opposed the idea, the king granted Penn the land lying north of Maryland and west of the Delaware River. Penn named the land **Pennsylvania** ("Penn's Woods") in honor of his father, **Admiral Sir William Penn** (1621–1670). Penn described his colony as "a Holy Experiment . . . that an example may be set up to the nations."

William Penn

375

QUAKING IN PENN'S WOODS

| MARTIN LUTHER'S 95 THESES | HENRY VIII SPLITS FROM ROME | REIGN OF QUEEN ELIZABETH I BEGINS | SPANISH ARMADA DESTROYED | SIGNING OF MAYFLOWER COMPACT |

1517   1526   1534   1536   1558   1585   1588   1607   1620   1624

TYNDALE'S ENGLISH NEW TESTAMENT   CALVIN'S *INSTITUTES* PUBLISHED   FIRST ROANOAK SETTLEMENT   JAMESTOWN, VIRGINIA FOUNDED   DUTCH FOUND NEW NETHERLAND

Quaking in Their Boots

George Fox (1624–1691) was the founder of the **Religious Society of Friends** (1647), which is more commonly known as the **Quakers**. The story of how the Religious Society of Friends came to be known as Quakers is in dispute. One version claims that the Friends were dubbed "Quakers" by an English judge in 1650, when Fox and some of his disciples reputedly "quaked" when sentenced to prison for blasphemy. Fox gives a different account in his journal. He writes that the name was first given to the Friends by Justice Bennet "because I bid them, Tremble at the Word of the Lord."

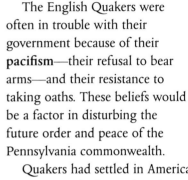

George Fox

Pennsylvania was named in honor of William Penn's father. The Latin word sylvania *means "woodland." Pennsylvania was the second colony to ratify the Constitution on December 12, 1787. State motto: "Virtue, Liberty, and Independence."*

The English Quakers were often in trouble with their government because of their **pacifism**—their refusal to bear arms—and their resistance to taking oaths. These beliefs would be a factor in disturbing the future order and peace of the Pennsylvania commonwealth.

Quakers had settled in America prior to Penn's charter, but they had never found a place where they felt secure. Their thinly dispersed numbers and radical religious and political ideas had never allowed them much in the way of political influence. Puritan Massachusetts was not open to them, and even the radically open-minded Roger Williams of Rhode Island had found it difficult dealing with their eccentricities. Penn hoped that his group could remain true to Quaker beliefs by making a fresh start in the newly chartered Pennsylvania. What began as a "holy experiment," however, ended in a loss of political power. As we shall see, the utopian hopes of Quaker idealism were soon dashed on the rock of man's sinful nature.

A Quaker on trial

376

Differences make a Difference

The Quaker style of government differed from that of the Puritans in neighboring New England in almost every way. Even their church services provide a study in contrasts. A Puritan church service included singing, Bible reading, and prayer; the most important part of the service was the preaching of God's Word. This emphasis was clearly seen in the raised pulpit at the front of the Puritan meeting house. By contrast, the Quakers had no sermons. They believed that each man, woman, and child had an **Inner Light,** the Spirit of Christ within them. During worship, anyone who had something to share could speak. Sometimes, however, the worshipers might sit for an hour with no one uttering a word.

The informal attitude that Quakers had toward church organization also affected the way they viewed civil government. Puritans believed that the Bible is the only infallible standard for ethical living and for governing the individual, family, church, and civil government. If a Christian's conscience conflicted with the Bible, Puritans chose the Bible over the dictates of one's

No Respect!

The Quakers were so determined that everyone be treated alike—an unbiblical and impractical view of equality—that they would not address anyone with titles of honor, like sir, madam, lady, or lord. Instead, they called each other "thee" and "thou" (which were terms of familiarity, not formality, as is sometimes thought).

A Quaker meeting

Martin Luther's 95 Theses		Henry VIII Splits from Rome		Reign of Queen Elizabeth I Begins		Spanish Armada Destroyed		Signing of Mayflower Compact	
1517	1526	1534	1536	1558	1585	1588	1607	1620	1624
	Tyndale's English New Testament		Calvin's *Institutes* Published		First Roanoak Settlement		Jamestown, Virginia Founded		Dutch Found New Netherland

Proprietary Colonies

Charter colonies created by royal land grants were called **proprietary colonies**. Pennsylvania, Maine, New York, New Jersey, Maryland, the Carolinas, and Georgia all began as proprietary colonies. In a proprietary transaction, territorial and political powers were bestowed upon a single person or a small group. In the case of Pennsylvania, Penn's charter included a provision that he could rule only with the consent of an assembly of freemen. Furthermore, the Privy Council—a body of advisors selected by the king—could veto Pennsylvania's actions. By 1776, only Maryland and Pennsylvania remained proprietary colonies.

conscience. Quakers, on the other hand, believed that only Jesus, and not the Bible, is the Word of God. For the Quakers, therefore, the Bible is only "a *secondary* rule, subordinate to the Spirit."

This difference might seem like a needless quibble over words and fine points of theology, but the Puritans considered the Quakers' views "plainly destructive of Civil Society." How could a colony survive when one person's Inner Light might differ from the Inner Light of others? Without the Bible as the infallible Word of God, what could serve as the ultimate standard? How could a commonwealth function in an orderly fashion if a person's Inner Light might direct him or her to act contrary to established law? Anarchy would be the result. What about non-Quakers? How would they be governed in a society where they dismissed the Quaker notion of the Inner Light? As theologian John Cotton wrote in 1636, "If the people be governors, who shall be governed?"

Penn's first visit to his colony

378

Penn's Great Treaty

In 1683, shortly after his arrival in his new colony, William Penn made his "Great Treaty" with the Delaware Indians, which has been described as "the only treaty not sworn to and never broken." Penn's fairness in dealing with the Indians and his care to pay them well for their land resulted in good relations between Europeans and Indians during Penn's lifetime.

William Penn makes "Great Treaty" with Delaware Indians

QUAKING IN PENN'S WOODS

| MARTIN LUTHER'S 95 THESES | HENRY VIII SPLITS FROM ROME | REIGN OF QUEEN ELIZABETH I BEGINS | SPANISH ARMADA DESTROYED | SIGNING OF MAYFLOWER COMPACT |

1517   1526   1534   1536   1558   1585   1588   1607   1620   1624

| TYNDALE'S ENGLISH NEW TESTAMENT | CALVIN'S INSTITUTES PUBLISHED | FIRST ROANOAK SETTLEMENT | JAMESTOWN, VIRGINIA FOUNDED | DUTCH FOUND NEW NETHERLAND |

Compromise Comes Calling

From their earliest days in England, Quakers had refused to take oaths. Eventually English law had compromised by allowing Quakers to make a simple affirmation "in the presence of Almighty God." All others were still required to "swear." Even so, the law had prohibited Quakers from holding any public office, giving evidence in criminal cases, or serving as jurors. In Pennsylvania, however, the colonial authorities liberalized English law in order to allow Quakers to hold public office. Quakers ran the government for many years without requiring oaths, although they received much criticism from Anglicans and others who felt that "simple affirmations" were not binding. The controversy over oath-taking remained a divisive issue in Pennsylvania politics throughout the colonial era.

When non-Quaker English immigrants began settling the colony in greater numbers, they raised objections about Quaker peculiarities related to government. Could rulers be trusted who did not swear allegiance to the king? Could one believe a witness who would not take a simple oath to tell the truth? Could confidence be placed in a juror to carry out his duties to weigh evidence impartially if he would not take an oath to do so?

Perhaps the most controversial issue, however, was the Quakers' refusal to bear arms to defend the colony. In the dangerous environment of colonial New England, pacifism could result in the death of Quakers and non-Quakers alike. Because of its location, Pennsylvania was vulnerable to both hostile

William Penn holding the "Great Treaty"

MASSACHUSETTS BAY FOUNDED		RHODE ISLAND FOUNDED		KING PHILIP'S WAR		GLORIOUS REVOLUTION		GEORGIA FOUNDED	
1629	1634	1636	1649	1675-6	1681	1688	1692	1733	1740-43
	MARYLAND FOUNDED		CHARLES I OF ENGLAND BEHEADED		PENNSYLVANIA FOUNDED		SALEM WITCH TRIALS		GREAT AWAKENING

French military forces and ruthless Indians. The colony needed a militia, but Quakers refused to serve. Therefore, non-Quaker officials were appointed to command the militia. Even the deputy-governor of Pennsylvania (the person holding the executive powers in the colony on behalf of the proprietors) was a non-Quaker. Related to this issue was the question of taxes. Should Quakers be made to pay taxes to fund a militia they did not support? Gradually the Quakers began to realize that their high ideals were no match for the day-to-day affairs of running a growing colony.

To Swear or Not to Swear

The Quakers had difficulty with English law because it required people who testified in court or sat on juries to "swear an oath" to tell the truth. George Fox believed that Jesus taught that all oath-taking was sinful. He appealed to Jesus' words in Matthew 5:34 to support his view: "But I say to you, make no oath at all. . . ." A closer reading suggests that Jesus is condemning frivolous oath-taking. The Old Testament does not condemn swearing to tell the truth in a court of law; in fact, it requires it. The law said, "you shall . . . swear by His name" (DEUTERONOMY 6:13; 10:20). Even God is said to have "guaranteed with an oath" as a way of confirming His word to those who lacked faith (HEBREWS 6:17). Jesus responded when the high priest put him under oath (MATTHEW 26:63–64). The apostle Paul took oaths (ROMANS 1:9; 2 CORINTHIANS 1:23; 1 THESSALONIANS 2:5, 10). While the Quakers were well-intentioned, they seem to have missed the true meaning of Jesus' words: Those who follow Him must speak the truth, not just when an oath is taken.

| MARTIN LUTHER'S 95 THESES | HENRY VIII SPLITS FROM ROME | REIGN OF QUEEN ELIZABETH I BEGINS | SPANISH ARMADA DESTROYED | SIGNING OF MAYFLOWER COMPACT |

1517   1526   1534   1536   1558   1585   1588   1607   1620   1624

| TYNDALE'S ENGLISH NEW TESTAMENT | CALVIN'S INSTITUTES PUBLISHED | FIRST ROANOAK SETTLEMENT | JAMESTOWN, VIRGINIA FOUNDED | DUTCH FOUND NEW NETHERLAND |

Paradise Lost

By the mid-eighteenth century, events forced the Quakers to choose one of two options: compromise their principles or withdraw from governmental affairs. Pacifism had become an increasingly dangerous position as the colonies were required to fend off enemies. Tensions mounted over the role that Quaker Pennsylvania would play in defense of the colonies. Spain had gone to war against England in the **War of Jenkins' Ear** (1739–1743), and France had also waged war with England. Since Pennsylvania was a colony of England, France and Spain were technically also at war with Pennsylvania. As Spanish privateers made their way to the Delaware River, many people wondered how the Quakers in the Assembly would respond. Conflict

Philadelphia in 1682

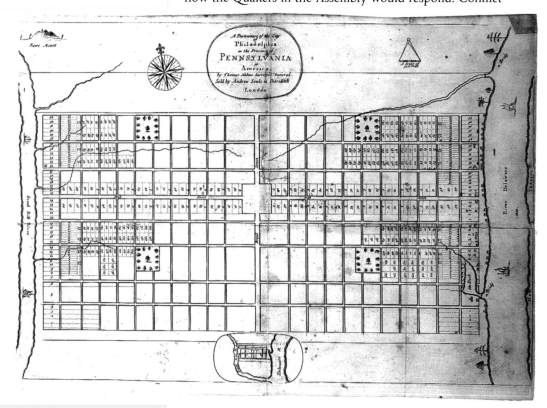

Lend Me Your Ear

In 1739, a naval war erupted between England and Spain when the Spanish intercepted the British merchant ship *Rebecca,* which they claimed was trading with their colonies in violation of Spanish laws. After ransacking the cargo hold of the *Rebecca,* the Spanish sent a message to other British "smugglers" by cutting off one of the ears of the ship's captain, **Robert Jenkins.** Jenkins carried his lopped-off ear in a little box wrapped in a handkerchief and often showed it to remind his fellow Englishmen of Spanish cruelty. The incident outraged British public opinion and led to a declaration of war, which became known as the "War of Jenkins' Ear" (1739–1743). In 1743, the war became a part of a larger struggle known in Europe as the **War of the Austrian Succession** (1740–1748), and in the American colonies as **King George's War** (1744–1748), named for England's King George II. Britain—along with Austria, Holland, and many lesser powers—fought not only Spain, but also France, Prussia, and many other lesser powers. In 1748, the **Peace Treaty of Aix-la-Chapelle** ended the war and returned nearly all of the many conquests of the war.

immediately arose between the non-Quaker governor and the pacifist Quakers how the situation should be handled.

In 1745, the Assembly finally granted £3,000 to help the war effort. The money was to be spent on "bread, flour, wheat, *or other grains."* The "other grains" was understood by all to mean gunpowder. Many Quakers still refused to back down from their pacifist stance. A compromise party—steering a course between the proprietors and the Quakers—was conceived in 1747 under the leadership of **Benjamin Franklin** (1706–1790), who would become a member of the Pennsylvania Assembly in 1751. Pennsylvania could no longer stay out of the war, Franklin argued in his political pamphlet *Plain Truth* (1747), since it is the duty of governments to protect the people. If the Quakers wanted to maintain their religious views and avoid compromising their principles, they should step down and allow others to govern. Franklin then developed a plan that would raise money for a voluntary militia. His pamphlet must have done the job, because a ten-thousand-man militia was soon recruited.

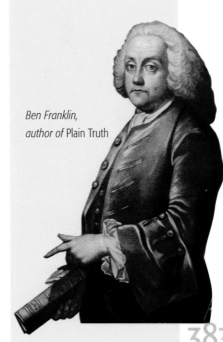

Ben Franklin, author of Plain Truth

Martin Luther's 95 Theses	Henry viii Splits from Rome	Reign of Queen Elizabeth i Begins	Spanish Armada Destroyed	Signing of Mayflower Compact
1517	1526	1534	1536	1558	1585	1588	1607	1620	1624
	Tyndale's English New Testament	Calvin's *Institutes* Published	First Roanoak Settlement	Jamestown, Virginia Founded	Dutch Found New Netherland

The Pennsylvania Deutsche

The so-called Pennsylvania Dutch who arrived as early as 1683 were not from Holland. They actually came from Germany. The reason for the confusion of terms is that the German name for Germany is *Deutschland*. During the colonial era, people from Holland were known as Netherlanders.

Philadelphia on the Delaware River

On the War Path

In addition to Spanish and French hostilities, Pennsylvania was also troubled by Indian hostilities in the latter part of 1755. Indian uprisings had led to massacres along the western border of the colony. The Quakers believed that **diplomacy** alone was the best way to handle the situation. On the other hand, while Franklin and his followers believed that diplomacy was needed, they also called for military defense.

Part of the reason for the Quakers' idealism came from the fact that the Assembly was in Philadelphia, hundreds of miles from the western frontier of the colony. Many of them had never witnessed an Indian attack. However, the western settlers and their representatives knew first-hand how brutal some of the Indian tribes could be.

CHAPTER THIRTY

MASSACHUSETTS BAY FOUNDED	RHODE ISLAND FOUNDED	KING PHILIP'S WAR	GLORIOUS REVOLUTION	GEORGIA FOUNDED	
1629	1634	1636	1649	1675-6	1681	1688	1692	1733	1740-43
MARYLAND FOUNDED	CHARLES I OF ENGLAND BEHEADED	PENNSYLVANIA FOUNDED	SALEM WITCH TRIALS	GREAT AWAKENING

In 1756, the die-hard Quakers who insisted on no military intervention began to relent. First of all, the non-Quaker population of Pennsylvania began to put pressure on them to give up their political authority. It was one thing for Quakers to die for their own beliefs, non-Quakers reasoned; it was another thing to ask others to die for them. Second, many Quakers compromised their pacifist position and set themselves against their fellow Quakers. Third, when English authorities heard of the Indian massacres, they threatened to disqualify Quakers from holding office. Finally, when the non-Quaker governor and council declared war against the Indians, six prominent Quaker assemblymen resigned. Quaker political dominance had ended even though some Quakers continued to hold seats in the Assembly.

Some Quakers believed that once hostilities subsided, they could re-enter politics. It was not to be. The coming revolution with England made it impossible for Quakers to participate in the Assembly and still hold to their pacifist ideals. Revolution was simply a synonym for war.

Pennsylvania in 1706

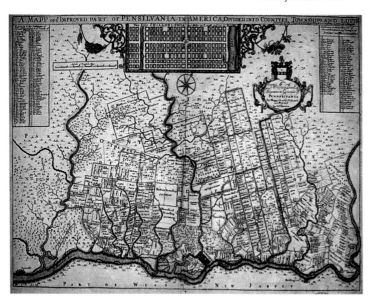

A Trinitarian Oath

A 1705 act of the Pennsylvania legislature, designed to regulate the number of assembly members, required that to serve as a civil magistrate a person had to "profess to believe in Jesus Christ, the saviour of the world" and profess "faith in God the Father and in Jesus Christ his eternal Son, the true God, and in the Holy Spirit, one God blessed for evermore."

385

QUAKING IN PENN'S WOODS

| MARTIN LUTHER'S 95 THESES | HENRY VIII SPLITS FROM ROME | REIGN OF QUEEN ELIZABETH I BEGINS | SPANISH ARMADA DESTROYED | SIGNING OF MAYFLOWER COMPACT |

1517   1526   1534   1536   1558   1585   1588   1607   1620   1624

| TYNDALE'S ENGLISH NEW TESTAMENT | CALVIN'S *INSTITUTES* PUBLISHED | FIRST ROANOAK SETTLEMENT | JAMESTOWN, VIRGINIA FOUNDED | DUTCH FOUND NEW NETHERLAND |

Quakers in the White House

Herbert Hoover, the 31st President of the United States, and Richard M. Nixon, the 37th President, were raised as Quakers.

Pennsylvania's Constitution

The Pennsylvania Constitution of 1776 required that those who serve in the legislature "believe in one God, the Creator and Governor of the universe, the Rewarder of the good and the Punisher of the wicked" and "acknowledge the Scriptures of the Old and New Testaments to be given by Divine inspiration."

Finding Their Niche

As the Quakers lost political influence due to their extreme and impractical political views, they focused their energies on social concerns such as prison reform and humane care for the insane. They were also some of the first people to speak out against the slave trade, and they refused to buy goods made with slave labor. The Quaker **John Woolman** (1720–1772) was a vociferous critic of slavery. Woolman, a tailor by trade, toured the colonies after 1746 to argue against slaveholding, especially among his Quaker brethren. In Rhode Island, Quaker shipowners had long taken part in the slave trade, but Woolman (right) persuaded them to abandon the practice. Within two generations, Philadelphia, the "city of brotherly love," then the state's capital, had become a thriving metropolis with excellent schools and the best hospitals and charitable institutions in the colonies. The Quakers had finally found their place in society.

Colonial Philadelphia

Delaware Up For Grabs

Many European nations claimed the area that is now Delaware. The Spanish claimed it, along with the rest of America, based on the voyages of Columbus. The English claimed Delaware because of Cabot's voyages in the area, including the territory in the Virginia grant and later in the grant to Lord Baltimore. It was **Captain Samuel Argall,** an Englishman from Virginia, who gave Delaware its name in honor of Lord De la Warr, the governor of Virginia. The Dutch also claimed Delaware on the basis of Henry Hudson's 1609 expedition along its coast which resulted in the discovery of Delaware Bay and River. In 1631, twenty-eight Dutchmen tried to establish claim to Delaware by building a colony they called Zwaanendael ("Valley of Swans"), but their colony was wiped out by Indians the following year.

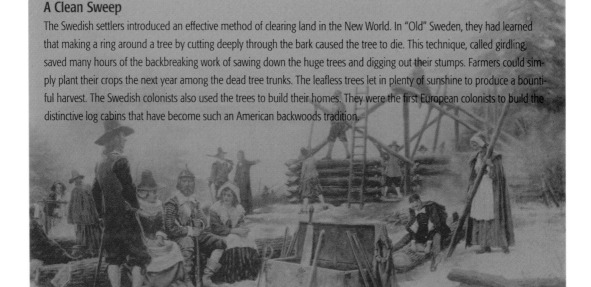

A Clean Sweep

The Swedish settlers introduced an effective method of clearing land in the New World. In "Old" Sweden, they had learned that making a ring around a tree by cutting deeply through the bark caused the tree to die. This technique, called girdling, saved many hours of the backbreaking work of sawing down the huge trees and digging out their stumps. Farmers could simply plant their crops the next year among the dead tree trunks. The leafless trees let in plenty of sunshine to produce a bountiful harvest. The Swedish colonists also used the trees to build their homes. They were the first European colonists to build the distinctive log cabins that have become such an American backwoods tradition.

Delaware was named for Lord De la Warr (Sir Thomas West), governor of colonial Virginia. It was the first colony to ratify the Constitution on December 7, 1787. State motto: "Liberty and Independence."

The Swedes made the strongest claim to Delaware because they were first to establish a permanent colony there. Led by **Peter Minuit,** who had been the first Dutch director-general (governor) of New Netherland, Swedish settlers founded the colony of **New Sweden** in 1638 and built Fort Christina, named for the queen of Sweden, on the site of modern-day Wilmington. They then purchased land from the Indians as far upriver as Trenton, New Jersey, and built a village on the future site of Philadelphia. The hard-working Swedes outlawed slavery in New Sweden and, although they themselves were Lutherans, welcomed all Christians.

The Dutch in New Netherland tolerated the Swedes because the two groups had been allies in a recent European war, had cooperated in their American trading ventures, and were united in a common dislike of the English. However, Swedish fur-traders cut deeply into Dutch profits, so in 1655 the Dutch governor of New Amsterdam, Peter Stuyvesant, led seven vessels and several hundred men into Delaware Bay and demanded the surrender of New Sweden. The Dutch acquired New Sweden without blood-

The Delaware River was an important reason for Philadelphia's rapid growth

388

C H A P T E R   T H I R T Y

Massachusetts Bay Founded		Rhode Island Founded		King Philip's War		Glorious Revolution		Georgia Founded	
1629	1634	1636	1649	1675-6	1681	1688	1692	1733	1740-43
Maryland Founded		Charles I of England Beheaded		Pennsylvania Founded		Salem Witch Trials		Great Awakening	

shed. Nine years later, the Dutch turned the area over to the English when the Duke of York's fleet captured New Amsterdam. The Duke of York in turn sold Delaware in 1682 to William Penn, who had just established Pennsylvania and wanted direct access to the Atlantic Ocean. Penn called his new acquisition the Three Lower Counties on the Delaware—a rather long name that was soon shortened to simply Delaware.

The residents of Delaware were never happy with Quaker rule and demanded independence. In 1704, William Penn granted Delaware a separate assembly, although it was still subject to the authority of the governor of Pennsylvania. Over the years, Delaware developed considerable self-government, provided leaders in the movement for independence from England, and became the first state to ratify the United States Constitution.

Wlliam Penn

Ho-Hum

At the beginning, New Sweden had no resident pastor and had to be satisfied with an elderly man sitting and reading sermons during the church services. One settler describes how this lack of clergy "inspired" the young people of the colony: "The youth who came were fonder of riding races than of attending Divine service. There was no order, no reverence among the people. It was time for God to help them, for all human help had failed."

MARTIN LUTHER'S 95 THESES	HENRY VIII SPLITS FROM ROME	REIGN OF QUEEN ELIZABETH I BEGINS	SPANISH ARMADA DESTROYED	SIGNING OF MAYFLOWER COMPACT
1517	1526	1534	1536	1558	1585	1588	1607	1620	1624
	TYNDALE'S ENGLISH NEW TESTAMENT	CALVIN'S *INSTITUTES* PUBLISHED	FIRST ROANOAK SETTLEMENT	JAMESTOWN, VIRGINIA FOUNDED	DUTCH FOUND NEW NETHERLAND

FOR STUDY

CHAPTER 30:
Quaking in Penn's Woods

William Penn began his colony as yet another "Holy Experiment." His Quaker beliefs, however, sometimes differed from those of the Bible. This caused not only religious conflict but problems of government, particularly when that government was forced to deal with the problem of protecting its people from others who did not share the Quakers' pacifistic views. Meanwhile, Delaware passed through Swedish and Dutch hands before coming under the control of the Duke of York, who later sold it to Penn.

Terms

Pennsylvania
pacifism
Religious Society of Friends
Quakers
Inner Light
War of Jenkins' Ear
War of
the Austrian Succession
King George's War
Peace Treaty of Aix-la-Chapelle
diplomacy
New Sweden
Delaware

People

William Penn
Admiral Sir William Penn
George Fox
Robert Jenkins
Benjamin Franklin
John Woolman
Capt. Samuel Argall
Peter Minuit

Discussion Questions

1. The question of the nature and purpose of oaths and vows is very important. What part did they play in the early history of Pennsylvania? Using a concordance, find out what the Bible commands regarding oaths and vows.
2. Explain John Cotton's statement, "If the people be governors, who shall be governed?"
3. What realities of colonial life challenged Quaker governance of Pennsylvania? What role did Benjamin Franklin play in the conflict?

Optional Enrichment Projects

1. Research the origins and beliefs of the early "Quakers" or Religious Society of Friends. How do these beliefs compare with Scripture? Where does the Society stand on the issues of today?
2. One result of the Quakers' reform efforts was the "penitentiary." Under their influence attempts were made to rehabilitate prisoners through hard work and meditation—to make them penitent. Is this biblical? What is the biblical model for dealing with lawbreakers?

C H A P T E R

31

A Place of Refuge:

Building MARYLAND

Claiborne and Calvert

In 1631, **William Claiborne** (*c.* 1587–1677), who had been a prominent official in the government of Virginia, led a hundred settlers into **Chesapeake Bay** where he established a trading post on Kent Island. This was the first colonial settlement in the region which became Maryland. Because he founded it before anyone had been officially granted title to the area, Claiborne and his trading post would be the center of controversy for many years.

During this period, King Charles I attempted to secure loyal supporters in his confrontation with Parliament by offering English gentlemen large land grants to colonize New England. One of these gentlemen was **George Calvert** (*c.* 1580–1632). Calvert had held several government

"Henrietta Land"

King Charles I, who gave Lord Baltimore the grant of Maryland, named it after his Roman Catholic wife Queen Henrietta Marie (above). The colony's original name, "Terra Mariae," means "Land of Marie," *terra* being the Latin word for "land" or "earth." Eventually, the colony became "Mary Land," which later became the more familiar "Maryland." Maryland was the seventh colony to ratify the Constitution on April 28, 1788. State motto: *Fatti maschii, parole femine*, "Manly deeds, womanly words."

| MARTIN LUTHER'S 95 THESES | HENRY VIII SPLITS FROM ROME | REIGN OF QUEEN ELIZABETH I BEGINS | SPANISH ARMADA DESTROYED | SIGNING OF MAYFLOWER COMPACT |

1517   1526   1534   1536   1558   1585   1588   1607   1620   1624

TYNDALE'S ENGLISH NEW TESTAMENT   CALVIN'S *INSTITUTES* PUBLISHED   FIRST ROANOAK SETTLEMENT   JAMESTOWN, VIRGINIA FOUNDED   DUTCH FOUND NEW NETHERLAND

posts, had served on the Council for New England, and had received a large grant of land in Newfoundland. Then he converted to Roman Catholicism. Since his conversion made him less desirable in the English government, he resigned, but he was still given the title **Lord Baltimore.**

Entrance to Chesapeake Bay

Lord Baltimore at first hoped to found a colony on Newfoundland. That project failed, so he headed south to Jamestown. Baltimore liked this area so much that he sailed to England to ask the king for a grant of land south of Virginia. He failed to get what he asked for. Instead he was given a grant farther up Chesapeake Bay to the north of Virginia. The English were just beginning to realize that their future rivals in America might be the Dutch, and they believed that locating Baltimore's settlement to the north might help check the spread of the Dutch who were beginning to appear along the Delaware and Hudson Rivers.

The Charter of 1632 granted Maryland to Lord Baltimore. The land grant proved both a disappointment and a blessing to him. He was disappointed to receive only about ten million acres of land, far less than he had expected. In addition, Maryland's boundaries were so vague that they caused troubles that were not entirely resolved until the Constitution of 1787 was adopted.

On the other hand, the Charter of 1632 made Lord Baltimore absolute monarch of Maryland with enormous power within his colony. Baltimore never exercised those absolute powers, however, because the colonists, who were accustomed to English liberties and who saw those liberties being practiced in neighboring Virginia, would never have tolerated a proprietor who behaved like a king. Furthermore, Baltimore himself was a gentleman who believed that authority carried with it the responsibility for the welfare of those under his authority, so he was careful not to abuse his power.

Sadly, Lord Baltimore died before the Maryland charter received the king's seal. Maryland passed on to Calvert's oldest

*George Calvert,
First Lord Baltimore*

Monarch of Maryland

If the Charter of 1632 disappointed Lord Baltimore with the size of the tract it granted, it more than made up for this lack in the powers it granted. The Charter made Lord Baltimore absolute lord and proprietor of Maryland. He was "Lieutenant-General, Admiral, Chief, Captain, and Commander, as well by sea as land." He owned all of the land in his own name. He could pass all of his power and holdings on to his heirs. He controlled all branches of the colony's government and could appoint all colonial officers. He was absolute master over the courts and the judges and could try any and all civil and criminal cases as he saw fit. He could establish and lay out all towns and cities. He could bestow titles to whomever he pleased. He alone could initiate legislation, although the colonists were entitled to give their advice and consent to laws which he proposed. He even had the right to pardon criminals, to disallow laws, and to levy taxes. In theory, Lord Baltimore actually held more power in Maryland than the king wielded in England.

Charter of 1632

393

| MARTIN LUTHER'S 95 THESES | HENRY VIII SPLITS FROM ROME | REIGN OF QUEEN ELIZABETH I BEGINS | SPANISH ARMADA DESTROYED | SIGNING OF MAYFLOWER COMPACT |

1517 1526 1534 1536 1558 1585 1588 1607 1620 1624

| TYNDALE'S ENGLISH NEW TESTAMENT | CALVIN'S *INSTITUTES* PUBLISHED | FIRST ROANOAK SETTLEMENT | JAMESTOWN, VIRGINIA FOUNDED | DUTCH FOUND NEW NETHERLAND |

son **Cecilius, the Second Lord Baltimore** (*c.* 1605–1675). Fortunately, the elder Baltimore passed on not only his title and lands but also the fine qualities of his character.

Founding of Maryland

Cecilius Calvert with his grandson

Planting the Plantation

The younger Lord Baltimore quickly set out to colonize Maryland. As a Roman Catholic, he earnestly desired to establish a refuge for oppressed English Catholics. He also knew that he could not build a successful colony with Catholics alone, so he appealed to all Englishmen to come to Maryland, regardless of religion.

In 1633, the first colonists set sail for Maryland aboard two ships, the *Ark* and the *Dove,* under the leadership of **Leonard Calvert** (1606–1647), young Lord Baltimore's brother. The party included two Jesuit priests, seventeen gentlemen and their families, and about two hundred craftsmen, servants, and farm laborers. Although their leaders were Roman Catholic, the majority of the colonists were Protestant. In fact, at no time in Maryland's history were Catholics in the majority.

The Calverts had learned from Virginia's mistakes and brought along only people who would establish farms and trading posts or practice useful trades. To attract settlers, the proprietor offered a hundred acres for each man, his wife, and every servant, and fifty acres for each child under sixteen. Anyone who brought five other settlers with him was rewarded with two thousand acres plus the right to erect an English-style **manor** with all its privileges, including the exacting of **royalties** from tenants.

After a four-month voyage, the first Marylanders reached Virginia in March, 1634, where Governor Harvey gave them a warm welcome and an offer of help. The governor's council, however, was not so warm, insisting that "they would rather knock their cattle on the heads than sell them to Maryland." The *Ark* and *Dove* soon departed and sailed on to Maryland where the colonists landed on March 25. Some men were chosen to search out the land for a site for their first settlement. They made peace

Medal of Cecilius Calvert, Second Lord Baltimore, and his wife.

Keeping Peace on the Dove

Although a Roman Catholic, Lord Baltimore was adamant that Maryland be open to *all* Christians. In fact, both Protestants and Catholics sailed to the colony in the first two ships, the *Ark* and the *Dove*. To keep the peace on the voyage, Baltimore instructed the passengers to keep quiet about religion. Peaceful relations with the Indians was also a primary goal in the colony. When Maryland colonists first arrived, Governor Leonard Calvert made a special effort to meet with Indian tribes on the Maryland side of Chesapeake Bay. He established particularly friendly relations with the Yaocomico Indians, who sold huts and fields to the Marylanders.

395

MARTIN LUTHER'S 95 THESES	HENRY VIII SPLITS FROM ROME	REIGN OF QUEEN ELIZABETH I BEGINS	SPANISH ARMADA DESTROYED	SIGNING OF MAYFLOWER COMPACT
1517	1526	1534	1536	1558	1585	1588	1607	1620	1624
TYNDALE'S ENGLISH NEW TESTAMENT	CALVIN'S *INSTITUTES* PUBLISHED	FIRST ROANOAK SETTLEMENT	JAMESTOWN, VIRGINIA FOUNDED	DUTCH FOUND NEW NETHERLAND

Family Feuds

Maryland took a long time to grow because of its initial feudal system, in which only a few people owned land and the rest were merely peasants. When a man does not own the fields he works on, there is no incentive for him to exert himself to improve his holdings. Besides, the biblical model is for families to own their own property, not for a man to become someone else's serf.

with the local Indians and, after finding a suitable site, purchased the land from them. A few days later, they laid out their first settlement, erected a stockade, planted gardens, and named their new city St. Mary's.

A Maryland shilling

Lord Baltimore was determined that his colony avoid a disaster like Virginia's starving time, so he ordered adequate provisions be stored up. Later, when Maryland colonists appeared to be devoting too much land to the cultivation of tobacco, he ordered all tobacco farmers to set aside two acres for corn.

Annapolis in colonial times (below)

City of Anne: The Nation's Capital

The city of Annapolis was originally called Providence by the Puritans who first settled it in 1649. It became Maryland's capital in 1694 and was renamed Annapolis after Princess Anne, who later became Queen of England. "Annapolis" means "City of Anne," from the Greek word *polis,* "city." From 1783 to 1784, the city served as the nation's capital. Today, it is still the capital of Maryland, as well as the home of the United States Naval Academy. The State House (above), built between 1772 and 1779, is the oldest capitol building still in use in the United States.

Tussles and Toleration

The Maryland colony weathered two major conflicts during its early years. The first one had to do with Lord Baltimore's right to initiate all the legislation for the colony. The colonists did not want to live under laws handed down to them by a foreign ruler and flatly refused to accept the group of laws sent over from England by the proprietor. The Maryland assembly insisted on the right to propose its own legislation. Governor Calvert, the proprietor's brother, denied that the assembly had this right, but then decided that the best way to avoid an ugly confrontation was to allow the formation of a committee to propose legislation. Shortly afterwards, Lord Baltimore sent word to Maryland that the assembly would be permitted to draw up a limited number of laws. The Marylanders had won their first battle in their struggle for self-government.

The other problem for Lord Baltimore was William Claiborne's trading post which was reaping profits in furs from the same area that the proprietor himself hoped to exploit. To make matters

Conflict on the Chesapeake

Though many Indian tribes lived in the Chesapeake Bay region, Maryland never experienced major uprisings like Virginia and New England did. Nevertheless, many individual settlers died at the hands of Indians, while many Indians died in retaliatory raids by settlers. Whiskey proved the most deadly source of trouble. Indians had little tolerance for alcohol and got drunk easily. Settlers took advantage of this and gave whiskey to the Indians when they wanted to entice them to sell their lands. This tactic enabled the settlers to get much cheap land, but it also resulted in many of them getting scalped by drunken Indians. By 1650, however, Indians ceased to be a major threat in Maryland. Most of them had died from smallpox and other European diseases for which they had no natural immunity.

Martin Luther's 95 Theses	Henry viii Splits from Rome	Reign of Queen Elizabeth i Begins	Spanish Armada Destroyed	Signing of Mayflower Compact
1517	1526	1534	1536	1558	1585	1588	1607	1620	1624
Tyndale's English New Testament	Calvin's *Institutes* Published	First Roanoak Settlement	Jamestown, Virginia Founded	Dutch Found New Netherland

worse for Baltimore, Claiborne began promoting an anti-Catholic and anti-Maryland attitude among the Indians with whom he traded. In 1637, while Claiborne was in England, Maryland governor Leonard Calvert took advantage of Claiborne's absence by invading Kent Island, which he easily captured. Soon afterwards, the Maryland assembly officially took away all of Claiborne's property within the colony. Claiborne retaliated by seizing St. Mary's City which he held from 1644 to 1646.

Meanwhile, the authorities of Virginia began to enforce colony-wide religious conformity to the Anglican Church, a policy which eventually had a profound effect on Maryland. In 1643, Virginia passed laws strengthening the Anglican Church in that colony by requiring all ministers to conform to the practices of the Church of England. All **"nonconformists"** were to "be compelled to depart the colony with all convenience" because the authorities feared that people who were not loyal to the official church might not be loyal to the colony either. The conflict entered Maryland when a group of Puritans, who had left Boston and settled in Virginia, were forced to move out because they were thought to be dangerous to the stability and well-being of that Anglican colony. These Puritans settled in Maryland where they struggled with the Catholics over the management of the colony. Inspired by the English Civil War between the Puritan-dominated Parliament and King Charles i, the Puritans of Maryland seized control of that colony, forcing Governor Leonard Calvert to flee temporarily to Virginia.

Lord Baltimore did not get personally involved in this religious battle, but he managed to keep his colony's charter with the help of powerful friends in England, some of whom

Claiborne's trading post on Kent Island

C H A P T E R   T H I R T Y   O N E

MASSACHUSETTS BAY FOUNDED		RHODE ISLAND FOUNDED		KING PHILIP'S WAR		GLORIOUS REVOLUTION		GEORGIA FOUNDED	
1629	1634	1636	1649	1675-6	1681	1688	1692	1733	1740-43
	MARYLAND FOUNDED		CHARLES I OF ENGLAND BEHEADED		PENNSYLVANIA FOUNDED		SALEM WITCH TRIALS		GREAT AWAKENING

were Puritans. He aided his cause in Maryland by appointing a Protestant, William Stone, as governor in 1648, and told Stone to welcome the Puritans who were being driven out of Virginia. Most importantly, he sent over his "Act concerning Religion," sometimes called the **Toleration Act.** This Act has become one of the most important documents in shaping the attitude of Americans toward government and religion.

The Toleration Act stated that no one professing belief in Jesus Christ should be persecuted or bothered by the state for his religious beliefs. Lord Baltimore firmly believed that all Christians of different denominations should be able to live together in peace. However, the Toleration Act did not separate religion from civil government. The Act declared that the state was to punish by death anyone cursing God, and that a Christian calling another Christian an offensive name like "heretic" or "antinomian" was to be fined and imprisoned.

Governor Calvert's invasion of Kent Island

Martin Luther's 95 Theses	Henry VIII Splits from Rome	Reign of Queen Elizabeth I Begins	Spanish Armada Destroyed	Signing of Mayflower Compact
1517	1526	1534	1536	1558	1585	1588	1607	1620	1624
Tyndale's English New Testament	Calvin's *Institutes* Published	First Roanoak Settlement	Jamestown, Virginia Founded	Dutch Found New Netherland

The Monumental City

Baltimore, named after the Lords Baltimore, is Maryland's largest city and one of the greatest seaports in America. It is sometimes called the "Monumental City" because of its many historic monuments. In fact, the nation's first major memorial to George Washington stands in Mount Vernon Place in Baltimore. Baltimore even served as the nation's capital after Philadelphia was captured by the British in 1776 during the Revolutionary War. During the War of 1812, Francis Scott Key wrote the national anthem while viewing the British bombardment of Baltimore's Fort McHenry.

Kicking out King and Calvert

The Glorious Revolution of 1688 bloodlessly forced the unpopular English King James II to relinquish his throne. Word of this revolution electrified the colonies and touched off a wave of Protestant unrest. Maryland, like New England and New York, saw its own shake-up in the wake of the Glorious Revolution. Anxious to proclaim William and Mary their lawful rulers, Protestant Marylanders formed the Protestant Association naming **John Coode**, a former Anglican minister, as leader of the Association. In July 1689, Coode (pronounced "Code") led about 250 men into Maryland's capital of St. Mary's and forced the governor and his council to turn the government of the colony over to the Association. The "rebels" convened a new legislature which immediately proclaimed Maryland's loyalty to William and Mary and begged them to assume control over the colony. For the next few years, Coode governed the colony fairly and moderately. Coode asked the king and queen to make Maryland a royal colony. The crown agreed to his plea and in 1692 sent Sir Lionel Copley to Maryland as its first royal governor. This meant that Lord Baltimore was no longer absolute lord of Maryland; however, he still retained his title to the land and still earned revenue from the colony.

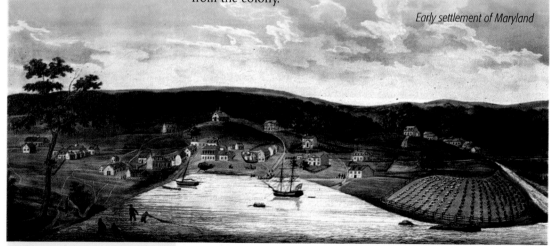

Early settlement of Maryland

The Last Proprietary Colony

Maryland remained a royal colony for nearly a quarter century. Then Benedict Calvert, the fourth Lord Baltimore, converted to the Protestant faith. With the support of the king, he regained control over the colony in 1715. Three years later, he deprived the Catholics of the right to vote, although they were not persecuted for their faith.

Maryland remained the property of the Calvert family until the colonies declared their independence from England in 1776. By this time, Maryland was the only remaining proprietary colony, having belonged to seven generations of Calverts.

Frederick Calvert (1732–1771), Sixth Lord Baltimore

An original boundary stone on Mason and Dixon's line, showing the coat of arms of the Calverts. The other side, facing north, bears the coat of arms of the Penns.

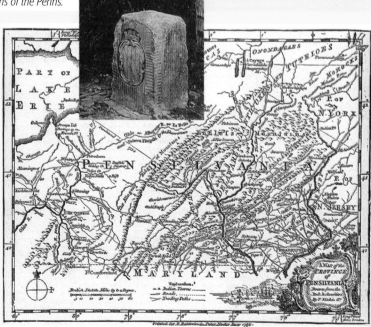

Drawing the Line

Throughout the 1700s, Pennsylvania and Maryland quarreled over their boundary. Finally in 1763, Charles Mason and Jeremiah Dixon of England were commissioned to survey the territory. They finished the task in 1767, laying out a boundary which became known as Mason and Dixon's Line. For many years to come, the **Mason-Dixon Line** would be considered the unofficial dividing line between North and South.

| MARTIN LUTHER'S 95 THESES | HENRY VIII SPLITS FROM ROME | REIGN OF QUEEN ELIZABETH I BEGINS | SPANISH ARMADA DESTROYED | SIGNING OF MAYFLOWER COMPACT |

| 1517 | 1526 | 1534 | 1536 | 1558 | 1585 | 1588 | 1607 | 1620 | 1624 |

| TYNDALE'S ENGLISH NEW TESTAMENT | CALVIN'S *INSTITUTES* PUBLISHED | FIRST ROANOAK SETTLEMENT | JAMESTOWN, VIRGINIA FOUNDED | DUTCH FOUND NEW NETHERLAND |

FOR STUDY

CHAPTER 31:

A Place of Refuge: Building Maryland

Terms

Chesapeake Bay

Ark and Dove

manor

royalties

nonconformists

Toleration Act

Mason-Dixon Line

People

William Claiborne

George Calvert

Cecilius Calvert

Leonard Calvert

John Coode

The Calvert family established Maryland as a haven for persecuted Roman Catholics. From the beginning, they faced conflicts with previous settlers, an unfriendly neighboring colony, Indians, and the colony's own Protestant majority. But the Calverts had learned from the mistakes of their neighbors and had initiated wise policies which avoided the starving times of other colonies. They also left a lasting legacy in fostering an attitude of toleration between Christians of differing beliefs.

Discussion Questions

1. What measures did the Calverts take to avoid the problems of the Virginia colony?
2. What was the origin of the Mason-Dixon Line? What did the term later come to mean?

Optional Enrichment Projects

1. Research the text and history of the "Act Concerning Religion," or the Toleration Act. Would this Act be considered tolerant today? Why or why not?
2. Look up definitions for "tolerate," "toleration," or "tolerance" in several dictionaries including an historical one such as the Oxford Dictionary of the English Language. How does "tolerance" relate to the idea of "truth"?

C H A P T E R

VIRGINIA:
Created in England's Image

The character of the Virginia colony differed from that of the other colonial settlements in a number of ways. Massachusetts was settled by Pilgrims and Puritans who sought to establish a godly community. Rhode Island was established by people who were disgruntled with Puritan "restrictions." Quakers in Pennsylvania were dissenters who hoped to establish a refuge for their unique brand of religious expression. Maryland was founded by Roman Catholics who sought freedom to express their particular religious views.

Virginia was unique in that while it harbored religious dissenters and those seeking relief from religious persecution, it also included English gentlemen who took advantage of the abundance of land open to all who had the means and the ability to develop it. Their hope was to climb the ladder of financial success and social position. As a result, English traditions as well as the established Church of England were planted firmly in the soil and soul of Virginia.

Virginia, named by Sir Walter Raleigh after Queen Elizabeth, the "Virgin Queen," was the tenth colony to ratify the Constitution and enter the Union on June 25, 1788. Virginia's motto: "Thus always to tyrants."

VIRGINIA: CREATED IN ENGLAND'S IMAGE

MARTIN LUTHER'S 95 THESES		HENRY VIII SPLITS FROM ROME		REIGN OF QUEEN ELIZABETH I BEGINS		SPANISH ARMADA DESTROYED		SIGNING OF MAYFLOWER COMPACT	

1517   1526   1534   1536   1558   1585   1588   1607   1620   1624

TYNDALE'S ENGLISH NEW TESTAMENT   CALVIN'S *INSTITUTES* PUBLISHED   FIRST ROANOAK SETTLEMENT   JAMESTOWN, VIRGINIA FOUNDED   DUTCH FOUND NEW NETHERLAND

William Fitzhugh (1651–1701) was an English gentleman who arrived in Virginia in 1673 and founded a family dynasty.

Virginia Gentlemen

Virginia's government developed in terms of one main factor, property. The goal of what we would call the "middle class" in England was to acquire a manor and to live the life of a "gentleman." With a landed estate usually came political position, anything from a justice of the peace to a member of Parliament, possibly even a seat in the House of Lords. Land in England was at a premium and very expensive. On the other hand, Virginia had much undeveloped land and no established gentry class.

Initially, voting for members of the House of Burgesses—the Virginia legislature—was open to "every free white man," whether or not he owned property. It was not long, however, before the legislature established a property qualification for voting. After 1699, a man could not vote unless he owned land outright: one hundred unsettled acres or 25 acres with a house

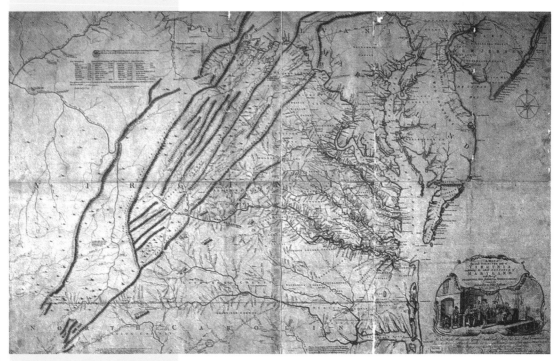

On March 22, 1622, Indian warriors struck the Jamestown settlement without warning

No Peace-Pipes in Virginia

Chief Powhatan, the father of Pocahontas, had lived in peace with the Virginia settlers. When he died, his brother, Opechancanough, became chief. Opechancanough feared and hated the English and in 1622 led a sudden uprising which killed about 350 of the settlers. War continued intermittently for a number of years. Then in 1644, Opechancanough led another bloody uprising against the settlers which resulted in as many as 500 deaths. The uprising ended as quickly as it began. Governor Berkeley sent a large force to drive the Indians out of Virginia or kill them. One band of soldiers captured Opechancanough, who by then was nearly one hundred years old, and led him in triumph into Jamestown. Shortly after the aged chief was placed in confinement, one of his guards shot him in the back, delivering a wound which soon proved to be fatal.

Death of Opechancanough

What's In a Nickname?

Every state has a nickname. For example, Pennsylvania is the "Keystone State" and New York is the "Empire State." Virginia is called **Old Dominion** because after Charles II regained the English throne in 1660, he made it known that the colony was under his "dominion" like England, Ireland, and Scotland, and Virginia remained loyal to the English royalty.

MARTIN LUTHER'S 95 THESES		HENRY VIII SPLITS FROM ROME		REIGN OF QUEEN ELIZABETH I BEGINS		SPANISH ARMADA DESTROYED		SIGNING OF MAYFLOWER COMPACT	
1517	1526	1534	1536	1558	1585	1588	1607	1620	1624
	TYNDALE'S ENGLISH NEW TESTAMENT		CALVIN'S *INSTITUTES* PUBLISHED		FIRST ROANOAK SETTLEMENT		JAMESTOWN, VIRGINIA FOUNDED		DUTCH FOUND NEW NETHERLAND

Giving Puritans the Boot

In the 1640s, Virginia began to mirror the struggles taking place in England between the largely Puritan Parliament and King Charles I. In this officially Anglican colony, Puritans had at first been viewed merely as religious dissenters. When the English struggle erupted into civil war, Virginia's royal governor, who was loyal to the king, began to view the growing numbers of Puritans as dangerous political dissenters as well. He ordered their meetings broken up and drove many of them into neighboring Maryland where they soon clashed with the Roman Catholic leaders of that colony.

and a developed plantation. The idea behind this qualification was quite reasonable: those who owned land had greater interest in the welfare of the colony. By 1700, vast land fortunes had been secured in Virginia. Established families often intermarried, combining their land holdings and thereby creating a new aristocratic class with strong political power. The result was that Virginia started looking more and more like England.

Politics in Virginia was serious business. Voting was compulsory for those who had the privilege. A landowner could vote in every county where he owned land. Moreover, he could choose to run for a seat in any district where he owned land and believed he had the best chance of winning. Attendance at the opening of the first session of the House of Burgesses was also compulsory. A member could be fined, even arrested, if he failed to attend.

Breaking up a Puritan meeting

*It was during the reign of Charles II that **John Bunyan** (1628–1688) spent nearly twelve years in prison for refusing to give up his preaching. During his imprisonment, he wrote the Christian classic* Pilgrim's Progress.

On With the Show

The crowning of Charles II returned the Stuart line to power and marked the beginning of the **Restoration.** The era was called a "restoration" because it *restored* the Stuarts to the throne. Under Oliver Cromwell, theaters had been closed because of their immoral content. Charles reopened the playhouses. This began a new era for drama, marked by frivolity and loose morality inspired by Charles himself.

Bishops Need Not Apply

Not only did Virginians adopt English social and political traditions, but they also embraced English religious traditions as well. The churches of New England were congregational; that is, local congregations governed themselves through congregational votes, and ministers were ordained by the congregation. Bishops were not needed or wanted.

Likewise, although the church in Virginia was basically Anglican in theology and church government, it had no resident bishop. In fact, the Virginia church did not acquire a bishop until 1783, after the colonial break from England. This freedom from English church hierarchy made the church governments of Puritan New England and Anglican Virginia more similar than different.

407

MARTIN LUTHER'S 95 THESES	HENRY VIII SPLITS FROM ROME	REIGN OF QUEEN ELIZABETH I BEGINS	SPANISH ARMADA DESTROYED	SIGNING OF MAYFLOWER COMPACT
1517 1526	1534 1536	1558 1585	1588 1607	1620 1624
TYNDALE'S ENGLISH NEW TESTAMENT	CALVIN'S *INSTITUTES* PUBLISHED	FIRST ROANOAK SETTLEMENT	JAMESTOWN, VIRGINIA FOUNDED	DUTCH FOUND NEW NETHERLAND

Parliament sends fleet to Virginia to demand the surrender of the colony

The Fall and Rise of Berkeley

Sir William Berkeley (right), the royal governor of Virginia since 1641, was completely loyal to Charles I in the English Civil War. After the forces of Parliament defeated the king, they sent a fleet to Virginia in 1652 to demand the surrender of that colony. Governor Berkeley put up a slight show of resistance, but he soon surrendered and was replaced by a Puritan governor. Berkeley was restored to power upon the restoration of Charles II in 1660.

A Head Start for Virginia

Another example of Virginia's allegiance to English traditions is that during the Puritan Revolution in England, Virginia remained loyal to the Stuart kings. When word reached Virginia that Cromwell's son, Richard, had resigned in 1659, Virginians were still unsure whether the monarchy would be restored by the crowning of Charles I's son or whether some other arrangements would be made. Since they did not have a king to claim, the colonial assembly declared itself to be the highest authority over Virginia until further word came from England. Sir **William Berkeley** (1607–1677) was governor of Virginia at the time, and he was re-elected with instructions to call a meeting of the assembly every two years.

Massachusetts Bay Founded	Rhode Island Founded	King Philip's War	Glorious Revolution	Georgia Founded	
1629	1634	1636	1649	1675-6	1681	1688	1692	1733	1740-43
	Maryland Founded		Charles I of England Beheaded	Pennsylvania Founded		Salem Witch Trials			Great Awakening

The Hazards of Ordination

To serve as a minister in Virginia, a man would have to be ordained. But only a bishop could ordain a prospective Anglican minister. Since the colonies had no resident bishop, every candidate for the Anglican clergy had to go to England for ordination. The expense and hazards of such a trip were great. In 1767, of the fifty-two candidates who went to England for ordination, only forty-two returned safely.

Lifestyles of the Rich and Highfalutin

The English Civil War is often called the war between the Cavaliers (supporters of the king) and the Roundheads (supporters of Parliament). Roundheads were named for their short haircuts, as opposed to the fashionable hairstyle of the day which was rather long and flowing. Cavalier is a term meaning "knight" or "courtly gentleman." Although many Cavaliers were financially ruined by the Civil War, many emigrated to Virginia where they could enjoy the fashionable lifestyle they were used to.

Berkeley Goes Berserkly

When word came that Prince Charles had been crowned as King Charles II, Virginia quickly recognized him as its lawful ruler. Governor Berkeley carried out his duties, and all seemed to be going well. But Berkeley had begun to enjoy the taste of power. First, he pushed through a law which took away the right to vote (**franchise**) from the less wealthy. Understandably, the disenfranchised did not like this turn of events. In addition, they were irritated that Berkeley had a permanent annual salary from the fur trade and from high rent payments on land. Berkeley's independent source of wealth meant that he did not have to depend on the colonial assembly for his pay.

Besides dipping into the public purse for his personal gain, Berkeley also began to assume more power. From 1660 to 1674, he did not call new elections but kept the same House of Burgesses which "rubber-stamped" any laws he wanted. Many people, especially those in the fast-growing Virginia frontier, were denied representation simply because no new elections were held. Berkeley also chose the justices of the peace and sheriffs, thereby controlling the county courts as well as the legislature.

Cavaliers wined and dined in Virginia by a family loyal to the king

| MARTIN LUTHER'S 95 THESES | HENRY VIII SPLITS FROM ROME | REIGN OF QUEEN ELIZABETH I BEGINS | SPANISH ARMADA DESTROYED | SIGNING OF MAYFLOWER COMPACT |

1517   1526   1534   1536   1558   1585   1588   1607   1620   1624

| TYNDALE'S ENGLISH NEW TESTAMENT | CALVIN'S *INSTITUTES* PUBLISHED | FIRST ROANOAK SETTLEMENT | JAMESTOWN, VIRGINIA FOUNDED | DUTCH FOUND NEW NETHERLAND |

Let's Play Royal Ball

The state of Virginia is still proud of its royalist traditions. The University of Virginia even named its football team the "The Cavaliers."

Nathaniel Bacon confronting Governor Berkeley

Taxes and Plagues and Indians—Oh My!

The people of Virginia were growing more and more unhappy. Not only was their governor acting like a tyrant, but they were paying a high price for his oppression. Taxation was high. In addition, Virginians who had settled on the frontier complained bitterly that Berkeley had done nothing to protect them from the Indians. The governor had promised to build forts on each of the colony's rivers and had even raised taxes for that purpose. The forts were never built. When a group of Susquehanna Indians killed thirty-six frontiersmen in January of 1676, the protest increased. But Berkeley said he could do nothing until the assembly met. By the time it convened, over three hundred settlers had been killed. The legislature officially declared war on the Indians, but no troops were provided.

MASSACHUSETTS BAY FOUNDED	RHODE ISLAND FOUNDED		KING PHILIP'S WAR		GLORIOUS REVOLUTION		GEORGIA FOUNDED	
1629	1634	1636	1649	1675-6	1681	1688	1692	1733	1740-43
	MARYLAND FOUNDED	CHARLES I OF ENGLAND BEHEADED		PENNSYLVANIA FOUNDED			SALEM WITCH TRIALS		GREAT AWAKENING

*Landing of first
African "servants"*

Contract for indentured servitude

I Owe, I Owe,
It's Off to Work I Go

The majority of laborers throughout the seven-teenth century were white indentured servants. **Indentured servitude** means working off a debt a person can not repay. In 1640, there were very few African slaves, only about 250. By 1670, their numbers had risen to two thousand out of a population of some forty thousand. Farmers actu-ally preferred English-speaking indentured ser-vants because it was easier to supervise them than Africans who spoke a strange language. Not until the end of the seventeenth century did slave labor begin to increase in Virginia. Plantations were larger, following years of clearing the forests. In time, a growing number of American-born slaves learned to speak English, making them more desirable as laborers.

411

MARTIN LUTHER'S 95 THESES	HENRY VIII SPLITS FROM ROME	REIGN OF QUEEN ELIZABETH I BEGINS	SPANISH ARMADA DESTROYED	SIGNING OF MAYFLOWER COMPACT
1517	1526	1534	1536	1558	1585	1588	1607	1620	1624
TYNDALE'S ENGLISH NEW TESTAMENT	CALVIN'S *INSTITUTES* PUBLISHED	FIRST ROANOAK SETTLEMENT	JAMESTOWN, VIRGINIA FOUNDED	DUTCH FOUND NEW NETHERLAND

Superstar or Rabble-Rouser?

There is a great deal of debate about Nathaniel Bacon. Some think he was a great American hero, but others criticize him as a malcontent anarchist. There is probably some truth in each view. Bacon did have the good intention of challenging an oppressive ruler, but it seems he became a little over-zealous. On one occasion, he accidentally fought the wrong people—the Indians he battled were part of a friendly tribe.

Berkeley Gets Egged by Bacon

All these matters made an explosive mixture which touched off an uprising led by **Nathaniel Bacon** (1647–1676) called **Bacon's Rebellion.** In 1676, Bacon, a member of the upper house of Virginia's legislature, decided that it was time someone did something to protect the colony, so he led a force of three hundred men to fight the hostile Indians. Bacon's army successfully forced back the Indians, but Berkeley was not pleased. He immediately labeled Bacon an outlaw and removed him from office.

Berkeley did not anticipate the level of support that Bacon inspired. There was so much disruption within the legislature that Berkeley was forced to call new elections. This turned out to be a bad move for Berkeley. The new House of Burgesses extended the franchise, restored Bacon to office, and authorized him to raise a force of one thousand men to fight the Indians on the frontier. Berkeley was even forced to sign an order making Bacon commander of the Virginia militia.

The governor was obviously upset. Less than a week after the elections, he issued another official condemnation of Bacon as a rebel and called on two county militia forces to fight him. They refused. In fact, Bacon's followers in the House took an oath to support him and declared legal all the actions he had taken to that point. Going further, they declared Governor Berkeley's actions to be illegal and vowed they would fight anyone who opposed them—even English soldiers.

Nathaniel Bacon

412

MASSACHUSETTS BAY FOUNDED		RHODE ISLAND FOUNDED		KING PHILIP'S WAR		GLORIOUS REVOLUTION		GEORGIA FOUNDED	
1629	1634	1636	1649	1675-6	1681	1688	1692	1733	1740-43
	MARYLAND FOUNDED		CHARLES I OF ENGLAND BEHEADED		PENNSYLVANIA FOUNDED		SALEM WITCH TRIALS		GREAT AWAKENING

Hats Off to England!

England tried to promote its own economic well-being, often at the expense of its colonies, by passing a series of **Navigation Acts** beginning in 1651. The first act stated that no merchandise could be carried to England or its colonies except in English vessels built and manned by English subjects. A second act, passed in 1660, prohibited sugar and tobacco from being shipped from English colonies to anywhere but England or other English colonies. Later, the Woolen Act, the Hat Act, and the Iron Act prohibited colonial-made goods from being shipped from America to England, because they would compete with English-made goods. The goal of these acts was to make the colonies suppliers of cheap raw materials and to make the colonists the consumers of more costly finished products manufactured in England. Colonists resented these unfair laws and considered them one of the causes of the American Revolution.

LEX, REX

The Law Is King

Samuel Rutherford (1600–1661), whose works were known both in England and in the colonies, wrote a book in 1644 called *Lex, Rex, Or the Law and the Prince*. In it he argued that even the king must be ruled by set laws. In addition, he maintained that the Bible provided the proper way to resist a civil government which overstepped its bounds. Rutherford, following principles set forth by John Calvin, said that a lesser magistrate could resist a greater magistrate if he broke covenant with the people he governed. As a member of Governor Berkeley's advisory council, Nathaniel Bacon was a lesser magistrate and therefore arguably justified in his rebellion.

Samuel Rutherford

413

VIRGINIA: CREATED IN ENGLAND'S IMAGE

MARTIN LUTHER'S 95 THESES	HENRY VIII SPLITS FROM ROME	REIGN OF QUEEN ELIZABETH I BEGINS	SPANISH ARMADA DESTROYED	SIGNING OF MAYFLOWER COMPACT
1517	1526	1534	1536	1558	1585	1588	1607	1620	1624
	TYNDALE'S ENGLISH NEW TESTAMENT	CALVIN'S INSTITUTES PUBLISHED	FIRST ROANOAK SETTLEMENT	JAMESTOWN, VIRGINIA FOUNDED	DUTCH FOUND NEW NETHERLAND

Stamping out the Fires of Rebellion

Bacon's Rebellion ended quickly when Bacon suddenly died of dysentery. Without a leader, the uprising fizzled out a month later. Governor Berkeley promptly vetoed the laws which had extended the franchise and executed twenty-three followers of Bacon.

King Charles II responded to news of Bacon's uprising by dispatching to Virginia a thousand soldiers commanded by Colonel Herbert Jeffreys. The king commissioned Jeffreys to replace Berkeley as lieutenant governor, restore order, and pardon the rebels. Charles also sent two special representatives to investigate the whole matter. Back-woods Virginians told them that the quarrel was due to poor defense of the frontier against Indian attacks. On the other hand, the Tidewater colonists (those living along the coast) blamed the tension on high taxes and corrupt colonial officials—from the governor to the local justices of the peace. The investigators reported back to the king that the colony was not in a rebellious mood and that the laws extending the franchise were reasonable.

Charles II dispatched a thousand soldiers in response to Bacon's uprising

A Royal Opportunist

Francis Lord Howard (1643–1695) served as governor of Virginia from 1683 to 1692, although he returned to England in 1689. He had been appointed primarily because he was an impoverished nobleman who needed money and had friends in high places, and because he was thoroughly loyal to the king. He came to Virginia knowing almost nothing of the colony. His goal was to make great profits there. At the same time, he planned to make the colonists more submissive to the king and to their royal governor, which placed him in almost constant conflict with the House of Burgesses. He was only moderately successful in imposing his will on the unwilling Virginians during his stormy governorship.

Francis Lord Howard

MASSACHUSETTS BAY FOUNDED	RHODE ISLAND FOUNDED	KING PHILIP'S WAR	GLORIOUS REVOLUTION	GEORGIA FOUNDED	
1629	1634	1636	1649	1675-6	1681	1688	1692	1733	1740-43
MARYLAND FOUNDED	CHARLES I OF ENGLAND BEHEADED	PENNSYLVANIA FOUNDED	SALEM WITCH TRIALS	GREAT AWAKENING

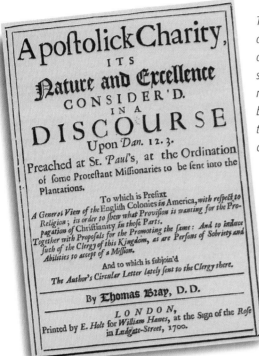

Title page (left) of an ordination sermon for missionaries being sent to the American colonies

College of William and Mary

In 1628, the governor of Virginia was directed to establish a college "for the training up of the children of those infidels in true religion, moral virtue, and civility, and for other godly uses." Plans for the college languished for more than forty years when the House of Burgesses enacted a new law providing for a college "for the advancement of learning, education of youth, supply of the ministry, and promotion of piety." Finally, in 1693, Virginia got her college, named William and Mary in honor of England's reigning monarchs. Its original charter states that the college's founders had as their goals "that the Church of Virginia may be furnished with a Seminary of Ministers of the Gospel, and that the Youth may be piously educated in good Letters and Manners, and that the Christian Faith may be propagated among the Western Indians, to the Glory of Almighty God."

Absolute Power Corrupts, Absolutely!

The amount of power Berkeley had seized, even briefly, must have looked attractive to other officials, because governors who came after Berkeley tried to assume similar power. Fortunately, they found tyranny impossible to maintain because Virginians had learned a valuable lesson in resisting overbearing rule.

Bacon's Rebellion is a very important incident in American history. It is a good example of the frontier conflict with the Indians as well as of the tension between frontiersmen and the Tidewater planters who ruled the colony. Furthermore, this episode shows that the colonists were gravely concerned about unfair taxation and tyrannical rule. In many respects, Bacon's Rebellion was a preview of the American Revolution which would occur almost exactly a century later.

MARTIN LUTHER'S 95 THESES	HENRY VIII SPLITS FROM ROME	REIGN OF QUEEN ELIZABETH I BEGINS	SPANISH ARMADA DESTROYED	SIGNING OF MAYFLOWER COMPACT
1517	1526	1534	1536	1558	1585	1588	1607	1620	1624
	TYNDALE'S ENGLISH NEW TESTAMENT	CALVIN'S *INSTITUTES* PUBLISHED	FIRST ROANOAK SETTLEMENT	JAMESTOWN, VIRGINIA FOUNDED	DUTCH FOUND NEW NETHERLAND

FOR STUDY

CHAPTER 32:
Virginia: Created in England's Image

After a stormy beginning, Virginia experienced a stormy period of growth. Indian uprisings, tyrannical governors, religious strife, English civil war, and divisions among the colonists all marked the development of this key colony. Once established, Virginia bore a distinct resemblance to England in its aristocratic class and Anglicanism. Even so, the colonists demonstrated a strong independent spirit when Virginia magistrates briefly overthrew a tyrannical colonial governor.

Terms

Old Dominion
Pilgrim's Progress
Restoration
franchise
indentured servitude
Bacon's Rebellion
Navigation Acts

People

John Bunyan
William Berkeley
Nathaniel Bacon
Samuel Rutherford
Francis Lord Howard

Discussion Questions

1. What factors in the development of the Virginia colony caused it to identify so strongly with English culture and royalist politics?
2. Describe the principal concerns of the two different cultures of colonial Virginia—the established aristocratic families of the Tidewater and the newer settlers on the frontier.
3. What common problems did Virginians face in the 1670s?
4. What events led to Bacon's Rebellion? What were the immediate and long-term consequences of the rebellion?

Optional Enrichment Projects

1. Research what modern writers, politicians, and ministers are saying about the complex issue of the relationship between the church and the state.
2. Explain what John Calvin and Samuel Rutherford concluded about the biblical basis for civil disobedience and rebellion.
3. Discuss the "pros" and "cons" of a political franchise based on ownership of land.
4. Probe deeper into the issues and persons involved in Bacon's Rebellion. What reasons do modern historians give for the many colonial rebellions like Bacon's, Coode's (Chapter 31), Leisler's (Chapter 29), and the overthrow of Andros (Chapter 28)?

MASSACHUSETTS BAY FOUNDED		RHODE ISLAND FOUNDED		KING PHILIP'S WAR		GLORIOUS REVOLUTION		GEORGIA FOUNDED	
1629	1634	1636	1649	1675-6	1681	1688	1692	1733	1740-43
	MARYLAND FOUNDED		CHARLES I OF ENGLAND BEHEADED		PENNSYLVANIA FOUNDED		SALEM WITCH TRIALS		GREAT AWAKENING

C H A P T E R

CAROLINA:
the Land of Charles

Giovanni da Verrazano

A Slow Start

In the 1620s, Lord Baltimore petitioned King Charles I for a grant of land south of Virginia. Instead, the king gave him the territory which lay to the north, present-day Maryland, because the land south of Virginia had already been granted to Sir Robert Heath, the king's attorney general. "Carolana," as the area was called at that time, was the entire English claim south of Virginia. It included present-day North and South Carolina and Georgia. The territory extended, at least on paper, to the Pacific Ocean. Heath's plan to colonize Carolina never got beyond the planning stage, and a decade later he gave the land to the Duke of Norfolk, who also failed to establish a settlement.

In 1650, Edward Bland published a tract entitled *The Discovery of New Britain.* Bland described the Carolina territory as nothing less than a Garden of Eden. This description enticed settlers to migrate from neighboring Virginia and as far away as New England hoping to reap the fruits of the region's rich soil and mild climate.

First Failures of Carolina

The first Europeans to explore the Carolina coast were Spaniards led by Francisco Gordillo who came from Santo Domingo in 1521. Three years later, Giovanni da Verrazano, who sailed for King Francis I of France, visited the Cape Fear area. He sent home glowing reports of the territory, but the king showed no interest in following up by planting a colony. Spaniards under Lucas Vasquez de Ayllon founded the first settlement there in 1526, but disease and starvation killed so many of his people that the colony was abandoned after several months.

417

C A R O L I N A :   T H E   L A N D   O F   C H A R L E S

Martin Luther's 95 Theses	Henry VIII Splits from Rome	Reign of Queen Elizabeth I Begins	Spanish Armada Destroyed	Signing of Mayflower Compact
1517 1526 1534 1536 1558 1585 1588 1607 1620 1624				
Tyndale's English New Testament	Calvin's *Institutes* Published	First Roanoke Settlement	Jamestown, Virginia Founded	Dutch Found New Netherland

Charles II

Ready, Set, Grow!

The charter which King Charles II granted to the Carolina proprietors was in many ways similar to the charter that his father had granted to Lord Baltimore in 1632. The eight proprietors were given the power to legislate "by and with the advice, assent and approbation of the freemen." However, this charter also contained two new provisions: to encourage settlement by granting colonists the right to worship as they pleased, only requiring that they participate in some form of *Christian* worship, and to encourage them to grow a number of subtropical products that could not be grown in England. Settlers were granted exemptions on English customs duties on those products for seven years after experimental tests had ended.

A Foundation is Laid

By 1660, Charles II was restored to the English throne after the death of Oliver Cromwell and the collapse of the Puritan Commonwealth. At that time, some of the king's most influential advisors, including **Sir Anthony Ashley Cooper** (1621–1683), Sir George Carteret, and Virginia Governor Sir William Berkeley, promoted the colonization of the Carolina region. These men

Oliver Cromwell

and their friends were leaders in shaping or administering England's colonial policy, and they had all worked for the restoration of Charles to the throne. Thus, when they asked for approval to colonize Carolina, the king could not easily refuse them. In 1663, Charles granted the first colonial charter of his reign to eight Carolina proprietors.

The proprietors decided not to encourage residents of England

Sir Anthony Ashley Cooper

to make the long and costly voyage to America where many of them would likely die from diseases. Instead, they encouraged settlers from other colonies to relocate to the Carolinas. To entice these settlers to come to Carolina, the proprietors issued in 1663 "A Declaration and Proposals to All That Will Plant in Carolina," promising settlers generous land grants and religious and political freedom.

418

Lured by these incentives and by glowing reports of the soil and climate of Carolina, a group of settlers from the West Indian island of Barbados planted a community in the **Cape Fear** region the following year. Within two years, the Cape Fear plantations had a population of 800.

In 1665, a fleet of three ships left Barbados to establish a colony at Port Royal, the site of a French colony which had failed a century earlier. Unfortunately, the flagship of the fleet sank, carrying to the bottom most of the supplies headed for the new colony. The Port Royal colony was never born. Worse, the seemingly successful Cape Fear settlement collapsed soon afterwards when many colonists left the Carolinas for Virginia, New England, and Barbados. The proprietors abandoned hope of realizing any profit from their Carolina colony. Only Sir Anthony Ashley Cooper, Earl of Shaftesbury, continued to work to keep the Carolina venture alive.

Keeping the Lord's Day Holy

A South Carolina law of 1691 which called for a better observance of the Lord's Day began by pointing out that "…there is nothing more acceptable to Almighty God than the true sincere performance of and obedience to the most divine service and worship…."

John Locke

Order in the Wilderness

The Earl of Shaftesbury's friend and physician was the famous English philosopher **John Locke** (1632–1704). With Locke's help, Shaftesbury drew up the Fundamental Constitutions for Carolina in 1669. The purpose of this document was to create a pattern for the orderly settlement of the Carolinas. It called for the land to be divided into squares of 12,000 acres each. Forty of these squares would become a county. Within each county, eight squares would be set aside as "seignories" of the proprietors, while eight would become "baronies" for an American hereditary nobility. The remaining twenty-four squares were called "colonies" and were open to settlement by ordinary farmers, although provision was made for the establishment of a few manor houses within the colonies.

CAROLINA: THE LAND OF CHARLES

| MARTIN LUTHER'S 95 THESES | | HENRY VIII SPLITS FROM ROME | | REIGN OF QUEEN ELIZABETH I BEGINS | | SPANISH ARMADA DESTROYED | | SIGNING OF MAYFLOWER COMPACT | |
1517 1526 1534 1536 1558 1585 1588 1607 1620 1624
| TYNDALE'S ENGLISH NEW TESTAMENT | | CALVIN'S *INSTITUTES* PUBLISHED | | FIRST ROANOAK SETTLEMENT | | JAMESTOWN, VIRGINIA FOUNDED | | DUTCH FOUND NEW NETHERLAND | |

A New Foundation is Laid

In 1669, Lord Shaftesbury persuaded his fellow proprietors to pledge £500 each toward a new colonization effort and to contribute £200 pounds a year for the next four years. With this investment money in hand, Shaftesbury sent out a fleet of three ships loaded with settlers and supplies. This expedition stopped off first at Barbados to pick up various kinds of seeds to try out in their new home. Agricultural experimentation would be the main enterprise in Carolina for the next several years, and, in order to help encourage this industry, Shaftesbury offered to buy all their crops at London prices, which meant an economic loss for him but a great help to the colonists.

Colonial Charleston

420

MASSACHUSETTS BAY FOUNDED		RHODE ISLAND FOUNDED		KING PHILIP'S WAR		GLORIOUS REVOLUTION		GEORGIA FOUNDED	
1629	1634	1636	1649	1675-6	1681	1688	1692	1733	1740-43
	MARYLAND FOUNDED		CHARLES I OF ENGLAND BEHEADED		PENNSYLVANIA FOUNDED		SALEM WITCH TRIALS		GREAT AWAKENING

Amber Waves of ... Rice

One of the first crops that Carolinians tried to raise was rice. Their first crops failed, but in 1690 they tried again with improved seed from Madagascar and the East Indies. This time they met with success. Rice quickly became one of the main exports of colonial South Carolina, which shipped large amounts to Northern Germany, the Netherlands, and Belgium.

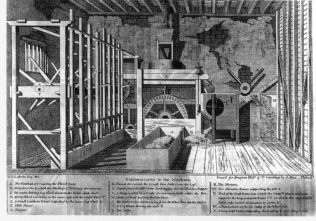

The low swampland near the coast of South Carolina proved ideal for rice cultivation. Since rice is grown in flooded fields, plantation owners quickly learned to use the rise and fall of the ocean tides to flood and drain the rice fields.

Machine for removing rice husks

Although cutting and threshing the rice was not particularly hard work, the process of removing the inner husk by pounding the grain in large wooden mortars proved to be backbreaking. To ease the burden of preparing the rice for market, the colonists built elaborate machines and also began to import thousands of African slaves. Eventually, these slaves began to outnumber everyone else in the state.

Carolina rice plantation

421

Shaftesbury's efforts at re-establishing a Carolina colony eventually paid off. In the spring of 1670, following an eight-month voyage, his fleet arrived at Port Royal. The colonists soon moved their settlement north, where they built a fort on the Ashley River. Their arrival alarmed the Spanish in neighboring Florida who, fearing the presence of a potential enemy so close by, sent a naval force to evict the English. Providentially, a storm swept away the Spanish attack force. The Carolina colony was firmly established, although it would face many hardships such as food shortages and rebellion.

Shaftesbury believed that a nobility was "the very life and soul" of society, but because of his biblical understanding of human nature he knew that when nobility was allowed to rule without any form of restraint, it became "the utter bane and destruction" of society. Thus, when he gave his colony a written constitution, he incorporated a system of **checks and balances,** where one branch of

Plagues and Paradise

A popular saying went that South Carolina was "a hospital" in the fall and "a paradise" in the spring. It resembled a hospital at times because of the diseases settlers caught from animals that inhabited the area. Alligators in the swampland rarely attacked people, but they did pose a threat to livestock. Rattlesnakes and water moccasins were a more deadly threat to people. Tiny mosquitoes, however, were the deadliest threat of all, because they transmitted both yellow fever and malaria which killed thousands.

However, South Carolina was also "a paradise." Beautiful flowers abounded, while colorful birds entertained settlers with their cheerful melodies. Wildlife was so abundant that most people believed it would flourish forever. One exception to this view was the opinion of Johann Martin Bolzius, a German minister who had come to South Carolina in the middle 1700s. Concerned about over-grazing of the canebrakes and the reckless slaughter of the deer, he declared, "Oh, how good it would be for the present and future world if the abuse of freedom in this land would be limited a little."

government serves to restrain another branch of government. In
practice, the government of the Carolinas resembled that of early
Virginia and Massachusetts. Proprietors, nobles, and the representatives of landowning freemen sat together in a one-house
assembly called the **Parliament.** The proprietors or their deputies
made up the **Grand Council** which prepared all bills or laws.
Parliament merely approved or disapproved the bills. The constitution required that representatives to Parliament must reside in
the districts they represented. By contrast, members of the
English Parliament often lived outside the districts they represented.

In 1680, English colonists founded the settlement of **Charles
Town** at the junction of the Ashley and Cooper Rivers, both
rivers named for Lord Shaftesbury whose given name was
Anthony Ashley Cooper. Charles Town, which in 1783 became
Charleston, followed Shaftesbury's plan for orderly settlement
with its streets laid out in checkerboard fashion. But Charleston
was the only settlement that
followed this plan. Other
settlers in Carolina ignored the
proprietor's neat system of
squares and moved inland into
the wilderness following the
courses of the colony's rivers
and streams. These waterways
allowed settlers to fill up the
backcountry more easily than
settlers could in the other
colonies. They also made it
easier for those on the frontier
to send their crops to market.
These rivers, plus an excellent
harbor at Charleston, brought
rapid prosperity to the colony.

*Plan of Charleston,
South Carolina*

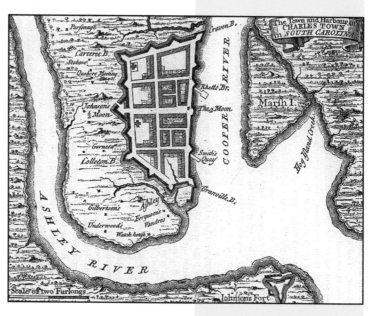

423

C A R O L I N A :   T H E   L A N D   O F   C H A R L E S

MARTIN LUTHER'S 95 THESES		HENRY VIII SPLITS FROM ROME		REIGN OF QUEEN ELIZABETH I BEGINS		SPANISH ARMADA DESTROYED		SIGNING OF MAYFLOWER COMPACT	
1517	1526	1534	1536	1558	1585	1588	1607	1620	1624
	TYNDALE'S ENGLISH NEW TESTAMENT		CALVIN'S *INSTITUTES* PUBLISHED		FIRST ROANOAK SETTLEMENT		JAMESTOWN, VIRGINIA FOUNDED		DUTCH FOUND NEW NETHERLAND

Cracks in the Foundation

Not everyone was pleased with the rule of the proprietors. The first Carolinians had come from Virginia. They were angry when the region came under the control of the original eight proprietors because they believed that the proprietors and their appointed governors were more interested in making money than in governing wisely. By 1677, these colonists had had enough. That year they overthrew their governor in a revolt known as **Culpeper's Rebellion.** The rebels took over their colonial government and ran it for a year, appointing **John Culpeper** as their governor. Culpeper ruled the settlement for about fourteen years until 1691 when the king stepped in and appointed the first governor over the entire Carolina colony. Charles also assigned a deputy governor to head the North Carolina region until it became a separate colony in 1712.

South Carolina Settlement

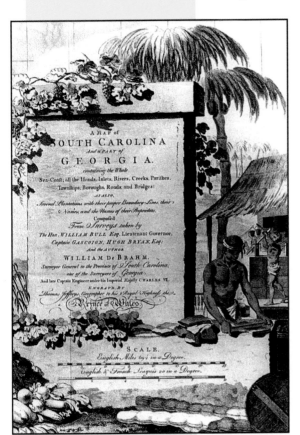

Sir Nathaniel Johnson *(right) had once been a member of Parliament and governor of the Leeward Islands in the West Indies. After the Glorious Revolution in England, Johnson had refused to take the oath of allegiance to William and Mary and instead emigrated to South Carolina, where he lived several years before being appointed governor in 1702. Under Johnson's governorship, the Anglican Church became the established church in South Carolina. After Johnson died, his son Robert served as governor for several years until he was overthrown in 1719 and replaced by the popularly elected head of the militia.*

424

Queen Anne of England

Indians, Pirates, and Spaniards Attack

In 1710, German and Swiss settlers came to North Carolina and founded the settlement of **New Bern** in territory controlled by the **Tuscarora Indians.** The colony prospered briefly until one fall morning in 1711 when the Tuscaroras attacked. Within two hours, they had massacred hundreds of settlers and burned most of the settlements. The **Tuscarora War** was the worst war in the colony's history and did not end until the Indians were defeated in 1713.

Indians were not the only threat to the Carolinians. Pirates like the infamous **Edward Teach,** who was better known as **Blackbeard,** preyed on merchant ships and raided coastal settlements. Many pirates were captured and publicly hanged from the gallows on Execution Dock at Charleston. But it was not until 1718, when Blackbeard was killed, that Carolinians began to free themselves from the scourge of piracy.

The First and Greatest Commandment

A South Carolina law of 1704 calling for the establishment of religious worship according to the Church of England and for the erecting of church buildings for public worship began by stating that "in a well grounded Christian commonwealth matters concerning religion and the honor of God ought in the first place to be taken into consideration and honest endeavors to attain to such good ends countenanced and encouraged, as being not only most acceptable to God, but the best way and means to obtain his mercy and a blessing upon a people and country."

425

MARTIN LUTHER'S 95 THESES		HENRY VIII SPLITS FROM ROME		REIGN OF QUEEN ELIZABETH I BEGINS		SPANISH ARMADA DESTROYED		SIGNING OF MAYFLOWER COMPACT	
1517	1526	1534	1536	1558	1585	1588	1607	1620	1624
	TYNDALE'S ENGLISH NEW TESTAMENT		CALVIN'S *INSTITUTES* PUBLISHED		FIRST ROANOAK SETTLEMENT		JAMESTOWN, VIRGINIA FOUNDED		DUTCH FOUND NEW NETHERLAND

"It Is a Glorious Thing to Be a Pirate King"

The appearance of Blackbeard the pirate was terrifying. He got his name from the "large quantity of hair, which, like a frightful meteor, covered his whole face." He carried six pistols, and in battle he clenched a sword between his teeth and twisted lighted matches into locks of his hair.

Blackbeard, whose real name was Edward Teach (or Thatch), began as a privateer, a sort of semi-official pirate, during Queen Anne's War (1702–1713). After the war ended, he went on to full-fledged piracy. He captured a large French merchant ship, renamed her *Queen Anne's Revenge,* armed her with forty cannons, and began to ravage ships across the Atlantic.

Blackbeard spent his winters in an inlet on the North Carolina coast, where he bribed the colony's governor to leave him alone by sharing some of his spoils. In November 1718, the governor of Virginia sent two British warships to North Carolina to deal with him. After a sharp fight, the British commander boarded Blackbeard's ship and personally shot the pirate dead.

The notorious Blackbeard

During these desperate times, the proprietors had done almost nothing to aid the colonists in repelling Indian and pirate raids. They also left the colony open to French and Spanish attacks during **Queen Anne's War** (1702–1713). In addition, the proprietors forced the establishment of the Church of England upon the Carolinians, and they repeatedly rejected laws requested by the colonists. Finally, in 1719, the colonists rebelled. However, England could not afford to alienate Carolina. South Carolina, which included the future colony of Georgia, was

426

vital to England's southern line of defense against Spanish attack. To keep the peace in the colony and prevent the Spanish from taking advantage of any unrest, King George I purchased South Carolina from the proprietors and made it a royal colony. Although the Crown now directly controlled South Carolina, the colonists were allowed a great deal of self-government.

In 1729, the proprietors sold their remaining North Carolina territory back to the Crown. The following year, the king divided the Carolina region into the two royal provinces of North Carolina and South Carolina and appointed a royal governor to administer each of them. In 1732, the southern part of South Carolina split off from the colony and became the colony of Georgia. The Carolina colonies prospered after the end of proprietary rule.

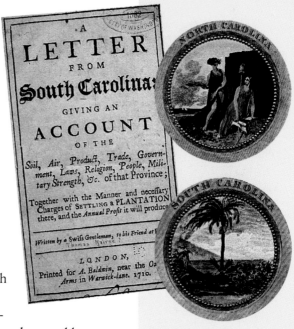

Charleston's seaport was a major cause of South Carolina's prosperity

The Carolinas

The "province of Carolana," which includes present-day **North** and **South Carolina,** was named after King Charles II. North Carolina was the twelfth colony to ratify the United States Constitution on November 21, 1789. State motto: *Esse Quam Videri,* "To Be Rather Than to Seem."

South Carolina was the eighth colony to ratify the Constitution on May 23, 1788. State mottoes: Animis Opibusque Parati, "Prepared in mind and resources" and Dum Spiro Spero, "While I breathe, I hope."

427

MARTIN LUTHER'S 95 THESES	HENRY VIII SPLITS FROM ROME	REIGN OF QUEEN ELIZABETH I BEGINS	SPANISH ARMADA DESTROYED	SIGNING OF MAYFLOWER COMPACT	
1517	1526	1534	1536	1558	1585	1588	1607	1620	1624

| TYNDALE'S ENGLISH NEW TESTAMENT | CALVIN'S *INSTITUTES* PUBLISHED | FIRST ROANOAK SETTLEMENT | JAMESTOWN, VIRGINIA FOUNDED | DUTCH FOUND NEW NETHERLAND |

FOR STUDY

CHAPTER 33:
Carolina:
The Land of Charles

Terms

Cape Fear
checks and balances
Parliament
Grand Council
Charles Town
Culpeper's Rebellion
New Bern
Tuscarora Indians
Tuscarora War
Queen Anne's War

People

Sir Anthony Ashley Cooper,
Earl of Shaftesbury
John Locke
John Culpeper
Edward Teach ("Blackbeard")

As the British colonists moved south, they discovered new opportunities and new hazards. In addition to disease and Indians which continued to take their toll, colonists in Carolina also faced threats from pirates and Spaniards in nearby Florida. As in so many other colonies, these settlers resisted their proprietors and revolted against their appointed governor. Because of Carolina's strategic importance, the king took measures to keep the peace and eventually turned one proprietary colony into two royal colonies.

Discussion Questions

1. Why were the climate and geography of Carolina both a blessing and a bane to the colony?
2. In what ways did Lord Shaftesbury try to insure the success of his colony?
3. Why did the Carolina colonists prefer that their colony become a royal colony rather than a proprietary one?

Optional Enrichment Projects

1. Colonial dissatisfaction with proprietors and their governors arose once again in Culpeper's Rebellion. Research this rebellion and compare and contrast it to others studied earlier.
2. Edward Teach was one of many pirates who terrorized the colonial coastline. Who were these pirates, where did they come from, and what did they do to earn so much fear?
3. Shaftesbury's friend, John Locke, had a profound influence on America. Research the life and ideas of this influential philosopher, especially as they relate to the cause of American independence.

MASSACHUSETTS BAY FOUNDED		RHODE ISLAND FOUNDED		KING PHILIP'S WAR		GLORIOUS REVOLUTION		GEORGIA FOUNDED	
1629	1634	1636	1649	1675-6	1681	1688	1692	1733	1740-43
	MARYLAND FOUNDED		CHARLES I OF ENGLAND BEHEADED		PENNSYLVANIA FOUNDED		SALEM WITCH TRIALS		GREAT AWAKENING

CHAPTER 34

GEORGIA:
the Last Colony

No Man's Land

For nearly two centuries, the region now known as Georgia was "no man's land" because it was claimed by several countries. The French, Spanish, and English had all explored and settled parts of the region, and its boundaries were vague. The Spanish believed the area was part of their Florida colony, while the English viewed it as part of Carolina. However, the English avoided planting colonies there for many years because they feared Spanish naval power.

Georgia served as a buffer between English settlers and the Spanish in Florida

A Land In Between

Britain's destruction of the Spanish Armada in 1588 was a turning point for England. A major military threat had been removed, giving the English more confidence to explore and colonize the east coast of North America. Despite existing Spanish claims to Georgia, King Charles I included the area in his 1629 grant of Carolina to Sir Robert Heath. For nearly a century, however, the English did nothing with the land. Finally in 1721, an English fort was built on the Altamaha River but was abandoned six years later following a fire. Three years later, the **Board of Trade,** which advised the king on matters of colonial policy, recommended that the "debated" land between Carolina and Florida be settled by "the poor persons of London." This suggestion piqued the interest of **General James Edward Oglethorpe** (1696–1785).

Georgia was named after King George II and was the fourth colony to ratify the Constitution on January 2, 1788. Georgia's motto: "Wisdom, Justice, and Moderation."

Georgia was named after George II

Poor Man's Land

Oglethorpe was born in London in 1696 to a wealthy and influential family. He was well educated and had served in a war against Spain. In 1722, he entered Parliament as a member of the House of Commons. Most importantly, he was a professing Christian who believed in the importance of doing good works. Because of this emphasis, Oglethorpe was a natural choice to be put on a Parliamentary committee studying prisons.

Dr. Thomas Bray, a prominent English clergyman and humanitarian, had proposed that a colony be founded to help provide work for freed prisoners and the jobless. After Bray died, Oglethorpe and twenty others borrowed Bray's ideas and proposed a similar plan to provide a fresh start for "unfortunate but worthy individuals." In the summer of 1730, these men asked **King George II** (1727–1760) for land on the "southwest of Carolina for settling poor persons of London." They knew that, although the king was not particularly interested in the plight of

MASSACHUSETTS BAY FOUNDED		RHODE ISLAND FOUNDED		KING PHILIP'S WAR			GLORIOUS REVOLUTION		GEORGIA FOUNDED	
1629	1634	1636	1649	1675-6	1681	1688	1692	1733	1740-43
	MARYLAND FOUNDED		CHARLES I OF ENGLAND BEHEADED		PENNSYLVANIA FOUNDED		SALEM WITCH TRIALS		GREAT AWAKENING

the poor, he *was* interested in defending his empire. Therefore, they proposed a way for England to defend her colonies from the Spanish in Florida and from the French who were pushing east from the Mississippi River. The key was the speedy settlement of Georgia. Oglethorpe and his peers also pointed out the economic and religious advantages of such a settlement. The colonists would no doubt share in trade with the Indians. In addition, they could produce silk, cotton dyes, and wine, products which England had to import from France and Spain at great cost.

Because of Georgia's warm climate and long growing season, the colonists could grow spices and semi-tropical fruit. Furthermore, they could offer religious freedom to Protestants mistreated by the Roman Catholics in Europe. All in all, Oglethorpe's group argued that a Georgia colony would guarantee more land and power for England and more prestige for its king.

In 1732, George II gave a charter to the twenty-one trustees to establish Georgia and manage it for twenty-one years. Because of Oglethorpe's plan to use part of this colony to help the poor and needy, Georgia immediately became the concern of Christians throughout England. Churches across the nation gave £18,000 in support of the colony. Even the Bank of England pledged its financial support. For the first time in history, Parliament contributed funds to help maintain a colony by appropriating £136,608 for the Georgia experiment.

A "Horrid Crime"

General Oglethorpe (above) had strong feelings on the matter of slavery: "The name of slavery is here unheard, and every inhabitant is free from unchosen masters and oppression….Slavery is against the gospel as well as the fundamental law of England. We refused, as trustees, to make a law permitting such a horrid crime."

Representatives of the Yamacraw Indians traveled from Georgia to England to request that the king and the Georgia trustees send them Christian preachers.

431

| MARTIN LUTHER'S 95 THESES | | HENRY VIII SPLITS FROM ROME | | REIGN OF QUEEN ELIZABETH I BEGINS | | SPANISH ARMADA DESTROYED | | SIGNING OF MAYFLOWER COMPACT |

1517   1526   1534   1536   1558   1585   1588   1607   1620   1624

TYNDALE'S *ENGLISH NEW TESTAMENT*   CALVIN'S *INSTITUTES* PUBLISHED   FIRST ROANOAK SETTLEMENT   JAMESTOWN, VIRGINIA FOUNDED   DUTCH FOUND NEW NETHERLAND

Cruel and Unbiblical Punishment

In the early 1700s, it was a common English practice to imprison people who could not pay their debts. This was an unbiblical punishment because the Bible requires debtors to repay their debts or to work them off if they have no financial means. However, advocates of prison sentences hoped that friends and relatives would pay the financial liabilities of debtors to keep them out of prison. Unfortunately, many people wasted away years of their lives locked up and were no closer to paying off their debts than when they were first thrown in prison. One such debtor was the architect Robert Castell, a friend of General Oglethorpe. He died tragically of smallpox in debtors' prison at the very time Oglethorpe was serving on the Parliamentary committee to study prison reform.

Making Friends

In November, the ship *Anne* left London with over a hundred settlers and their sheep, hogs, ducks, geese, and several dogs. In February of the next year, the ship landed near the mouth of the Savannah River. Before establishing the colony, General Oglethorpe made friends with the Yamacraw Indians who lived in the region. The Yamacraw chief **Tomochichi** gave his permission to the colonists to settle **Savannah,** and he became Oglethorpe's lifelong friend.

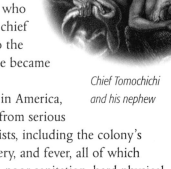

Chief Tomochichi and his nephew

Like many of the earlier settlers in America, the colonists of Savannah suffered from serious disease. In its first year, forty colonists, including the colony's only doctor, died of scurvy, dysentery, and fever, all of which were probably caused by poor diet, poor sanitation, hard physical labor, and changes in the climate. At the peak of the illness in

Savannah in the early 1700s

C H A P T E R   T H I R T Y   F O U R

Massachusetts Bay Founded	Rhode Island Founded		King Philip's War		Glorious Revolution		Georgia Founded	
1629	1634	1636	1649	1675-6	1681	1688	1692	1733	1740-43
	Maryland Founded		Charles I of England Beheaded		Pennsylvania Founded		Salem Witch Trials		Great Awakening

July of 1733, a ship carrying forty-two Jews docked in Savannah and asked Oglethorpe if they might settle there. At any other time, non-Christians would probably have been discouraged from settling. But Oglethorpe needed more able-bodied men in the militia, and since the only people the Georgia charter specifically forbade were Catholics, he agreed to let them stay. Besides, one of the Jews, **Dr. Samuel Nunis,** was a physician, and his skills were desperately needed.

A Colonial Fighting Force

The Georgia trustees had a moral problem with slavery, but there was another, more practical, reason for Georgia to forbid slavery. Slavery, it was reasoned, would lead to the development of large plantations which would then scatter the population. Since one main reason for the colony's existence was to serve as a military outpost against the Spanish to the south, it was necessary for settlements to be compact so the soldier-settlers could be gathered together quickly in the event of an attack or invasion.

*Persecuted Lutherans
from Salzburg*

The Salt of Salzburg

In 1734, a band of German-speaking Protestants fleeing Roman Catholic-controlled Salzburg arrived in Georgia seeking refuge. Oglethorpe directed these **Salzburgers** and their pastor, John Martin Bolzius (right), to a site twenty-five miles from Savannah. There they established Georgia's second town, **Ebenezer,** which in Hebrew means "Rock of Help." They later relocated to a site more suitable for farming which they dubbed *New* Ebenezer. These energetic immigrants were not afraid of hard physical labor in Georgia's sultry heat. They believed that slave labor was unnecessary and wrong. In fact, the Salzburgers continued to support the trustees' anti-slavery policy even when most other Georgians were clamoring for slave labor.

433

Martin Luther's 95 Theses	Henry VIII Splits from Rome	Reign of Queen Elizabeth I Begins	Spanish Armada Destroyed	Signing of Mayflower Compact
1517	1526	1534	1536	1558	1585	1588	1607	1620	1624
Tyndale's English New Testament	Calvin's *Institutes* Published	First Roanoak Settlement	Jamestown, Virginia Founded	Dutch Found New Netherland

Great Scot, More Settlers!

While Oglethorpe was in England in 1735, the third major settlement in Georgia was established south of Savannah. **Darien** was founded by a group of Scottish Highlanders. These Scottish laborers were seeking to better their lives in the New World. They also opposed slavery: "It is shocking to human nature, that any race of human kind, and their posterity, should be sentenced to perpetual slavery."

George Whitefield preaching

A Mission Land

Before long, Oglethorpe returned to England, taking with him Chief Tomochichi and eight other Indians who all became instant celebrities in London society. There they were presented to King George II and the Archbishop of Canterbury. Chief Tomochichi requested that his English hosts send a Christian preacher to serve his people. So when Oglethorpe returned to Georgia in early 1736, with him came three hundred new colonists, many of whom were seeking religious refuge, as well as two young ministers who had volunteered to serve the Indians: **John Wesley** (1703–1791) and his brother **Charles Wesley** (1707–1788). The Wesley brothers would later found the **Methodist Church.** John Wesley preached to the Indians and the colonists for a year and every Sunday conducted Bible study classes for the children. Those classes were probably the first "Sunday School" classes held in America. Charles Wesley assisted his brother in the missionary work and also served as Oglethorpe's secretary.

In 1738, one of the most dynamic preachers in history, **George Whitefield** (1714–1770), came to Georgia to establish an orphanage. His preaching was so powerful that it sparked a great spiritual awakening which ultimately affected every colony and almost every denomination. Just as the Wesley brothers are best known as the founders of Methodism, so George Whitefield is best known as the greatest evangelist of the **Great Awakening.**

John Wesley

434

| MASSACHUSETTS BAY FOUNDED | | RHODE ISLAND FOUNDED | | KING PHILIP'S WAR | | GLORIOUS REVOLUTION | | GEORGIA FOUNDED | |

1629   1634   1636   1649   1675-6   1681   1688   1692   1733   1740-43

MARYLAND FOUNDED   CHARLES I OF ENGLAND BEHEADED   PENNSYLVANIA FOUNDED   SALEM WITCH TRIALS   GREAT AWAKENING

An Unhappy Land

When Oglethorpe returned to Georgia, he returned to a failing colony. One of the major industries the Georgia settlers had attempted was the production of silk. The founders of the colony had heard that silkworms feast upon the leaves of mulberry trees, which Georgia had in

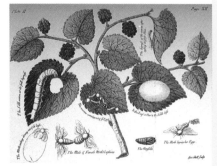

Life cycle of silkworms

abundance. However, they discovered too late that the kind of trees that grew in Georgia were *black* mulberry trees, and the silkworms only ate the leaves of the *white* mulberry tree. Furthermore, colonists also failed to make profits growing indigo, flax, hemp, and grapes for producing wine for export. Neighboring South Carolina, on the other hand, was prospering in the production of rice, cotton, and tobacco. The difference between that colony and Georgia was that South Carolina, unlike Georgia, did not limit settlers in the size of their farms. However, the greatest difference between the colonies was that South Carolina allowed settlers to own slaves.

Georgians became restless. They wanted more land, they wanted the prohibition against alcohol consumption in the colony lifted, and they especially wanted slave labor.

Christian Motivation for the Founding of Georgia

Georgia was the last of the English colonies to be founded. Its charter of June 9, 1732, declared "that forever hereafter, there shall be a liberty of conscience allowed in the worship of God, to all persons inhabiting, or which shall inhabit or be resident within our said province, and that all such persons, except papists, shall have a free exercise of their religion, so they be contented with the quiet and peaceable enjoyment of the same, not giving offence or scandal to the government."

Feeding leaves to silkworms

435

| MARTIN LUTHER'S 95 THESES | HENRY VIII SPLITS FROM ROME | REIGN OF QUEEN ELIZABETH I BEGINS | SPANISH ARMADA DESTROYED | SIGNING OF MAYFLOWER COMPACT |

1517   1526   1534   1536   1558   1585   1588   1607   1620   1624

TYNDALE'S ENGLISH NEW TESTAMENT   CALVIN'S *INSTITUTES* PUBLISHED   FIRST ROANOAK SETTLEMENT   JAMESTOWN, VIRGINIA FOUNDED   DUTCH FOUND NEW NETHERLAND

A Christian Culture, By Design

In 1733, General Oglethorpe (above) explained the proprietors' purpose for establishing the colony of Georgia and stated quite explicitly that they were interested in more than just meeting physical needs: "Christianity will be extended by the execution of this design, since the good discipline established by the society will reform the manners of those miserable objects who shall be by them subsisted, and the example of a whole colony, who shall behave in a just, moral, and religious manner, will contribute greatly towards the conversion of the Indians and taking off the prejudices received from the profligate lives of such who have scarce anything of Christianity but the name."

The Diversions of War

Georgia faced serious civil unrest until war between England and Spain erupted in 1739. Oglethorpe welcomed this war not only because a common enemy helped ease tensions within Georgia, but also because he hoped to expand England's control in America by pushing back the Spanish. Oglethorpe quickly organized a force of about two thousand Indians and settlers from Georgia and South Carolina to invade the Spanish-held territory of Florida. However, in 1740, a Spanish force surprised him and sent the English forces fleeing. For the next two years, both sides attacked and counterattacked. Finally, in the summer of 1742, Oglethorpe saw his opportunity. With 650 men, he set off to ambush a Spanish invading force of several thousand troops. After lying in wait in dense woods along the marshes on St. Simons Island, Oglethorpe's men completely surprised the Spanish in the **Battle of Bloody Marsh.** This clash was little more than a skirmish, and it was not very bloody, but it did send the Spanish fleeing for Florida and gave the Georgians a secure southern frontier for the first time.

MASSACHUSETTS BAY FOUNDED		RHODE ISLAND FOUNDED		KING PHILIP'S WAR		GLORIOUS REVOLUTION		GEORGIA FOUNDED	
1629	1634	1636	1649	1675-6	1681	1688	1692	1733	1740-43
	MARYLAND FOUNDED		CHARLES I OF ENGLAND BEHEADED		PENNSYLVANIA FOUNDED		SALEM WITCH TRIALS		GREAT AWAKENING

The following year, Oglethorpe was recalled to England to answer charges for his defeat in his 1740 attempt to invade Florida. He was cleared of all charges, but he never returned to Georgia. Instead, he married a young heiress, commanded British troops during the Jacobite Rebellion in Scotland, and spent his last years supporting charitable causes in England. When John Adams arrived in London as the first United States Ambassador to Great Britain following the American Revolution, the first person to call on him was 88-year-old James Oglethorpe.

In Oglethorpe's absence, Georgians pressed for changes. Even before Oglethorpe's recall, the authorities had given up their attempt to prohibit the sale of rum. By 1750, Georgians succeeded in obtaining the rights to own as much land as they wanted and to own slaves. Soon afterwards, many of the settlers who had left for other colonies returned. In 1752, one year before the Georgia charter was to expire, the trustees turned Georgia over to King George II to become a royal colony.

Battle of Bloody Marsh

No Drunks, No Slaves, and Especially No Lawyers!

The trustees of Georgia maintained strict control over the colony by issuing one regulation after another. They made it clear that Georgia was not open to everyone. Georgia's regulations would not admit liquor dealers, "papists" (Roman Catholics), Africans, or lawyers. The reason why the trustees banned "rum, brandies, spirits or strong waters" was that they feared that settlers would not work if strong drink were available. Roman Catholics were excluded because of the long history of religious hatred and persecution suffered by Protestants at their hands. The importation of Africans was forbidden because the trustees did not want slavery to take root. Lastly, they banned lawyers because they wanted to encourage colonists to settle their differences out of court instead of being tied up in one lawsuit after another.

MARTIN LUTHER'S 95 THESES	HENRY VIII SPLITS FROM ROME	REIGN OF QUEEN ELIZABETH I BEGINS	SPANISH ARMADA DESTROYED	SIGNING OF MAYFLOWER COMPACT
1517	1526	1534	1536	1558	1585	1588	1607	1620	1624
TYNDALE'S ENGLISH NEW TESTAMENT	CALVIN'S *INSTITUTES* PUBLISHED	FIRST ROANOAK SETTLEMENT	JAMESTOWN, VIRGINIA FOUNDED	DUTCH FOUND NEW NETHERLAND

The Wright Way to Govern

Sir James Wright (above) was Georgia's third royal governor, holding office from 1761 to 1782. He was an able administrator who believed in dealing justly with the many Indians living in Georgia. Wright saw that much of the colony's trouble with Indians was the result of unscrupulous Indian traders, who were often the "worst & most abandoned Set of Men." To preserve the peace between Indians and colonists, Governor Wright enacted tight controls over the Indian trade. He also signed an important treaty in which the Creek Indians gave a sizeable portion of land to Georgia.

Salvaging the Colony

The noble vision the trustees held for Georgia was never realized. Few debtors ever settled in Georgia. The colony was an economic failure. The trustees could not keep out either rum or slaves. Indeed, by the time the colony was turned over to the king, nearly a third of the three thousand colonists were slaves.

However, Georgia was not a complete failure. The colony did become a haven for Europe's Protestants to practice their faith without fear of persecution. In addition, Georgia colonists maintained good relations with the Indians. Georgia also succeeded in becoming a buffer against Spanish invasion. The other English colonies could breathe easier because of the protection Georgia gave them.

The greatest success of Oglethorpe's Georgia, however, is one which historians cannot measure because it is spiritual in nature. The colony was founded upon Oglethorpe's *Christian* ideals, and his *Christian* practices established a firm friendship with the Indians. This foundation led to the invitation which brought the Wesley brothers to Georgia, which in turn brought the Gospel to hundreds of colonists and Indians alike. In addition, the Christian goals of Georgia's founders encouraged George Whitefield to establish an orphanage in Georgia and therefore brought the celebrated evangelist to America to begin the first of many missions. Whitefield's powerful preaching changed countless lives and reached thousands with the Gospel message.

James Oglethorpe

MASSACHUSETTS BAY FOUNDED		RHODE ISLAND FOUNDED		KING PHILIP'S WAR		GLORIOUS REVOLUTION		GEORGIA FOUNDED	
1629	1634	1636	1649	1675-6	1681	1688	1692	1733	1740-43
	MARYLAND FOUNDED		CHARLES I OF ENGLAND BEHEADED		PENNSYLVANIA FOUNDED		SALEM WITCH TRIALS		GREAT AWAKENING

FOR STUDY

CHAPTER 34:
Georgia:
The Last Colony

Terms

Board of Trade
Savannah
Salzburgers
Ebenezer
Darien
Methodist Church
Great Awakening
Battle of Bloody Marsh

People

General James Oglethorpe
King George II
Tomochichi
Dr. Samuel Nunis
John Wesley
Charles Wesley
George Whitefield

With the birth of Georgia, British colonization of North America came to a close. Georgia had begun with the noble goal of providing a second chance for worthy debtors of England, but few such debtors ever reached the colony. Disease ravaged Georgia's first settlers, early agricultural experiments failed, nearby Spanish Florida threatened the colony's existence, and the colonists themselves threatened rebellion over the prohibition of alcohol and slavery. Yet God, in His providence, preserved Georgia, and from there launched the greatest spiritual revival in American history.

Discussion Questions

1. General Oglethorpe gave various reasons why England should plant a colony in Georgia. Which reasons were realistic and successful? Which proved impractical? Why did they fail?
2. What were the restrictions the Georgia trustees established for the colony? (Read all the main text and sidebars.) Which of these governing policies were rooted in Christian convictions? Which of these policies clashed with the desires of the colonists? Which policies do you think were right, based upon biblical reasoning?
3. Georgia proved to be a disappointment in many ways. However, explain how Georgia had a *positive* impact upon America.
4. Discuss the spiritual and practical objections to slavery stated by Georgia's founder.

Optional Enrichment Projects

1. Read a good biography of General James Oglethorpe. Identify the Christian influences in his early life and the various ways in which his faith influenced his public and private actions.
2. Research the role of Georgia as a buffer against the Spanish in Florida. Read an account of the Battle of Bloody Marsh and Georgia's actions in King George's War.

439

| MARTIN LUTHER'S 95 THESES | HENRY VIII SPLITS FROM ROME | REIGN OF QUEEN ELIZABETH I BEGINS | SPANISH ARMADA DESTROYED | SIGNING OF MAYFLOWER COMPACT |

1517   1526   1534   1536   1558   1585   1588   1607   1620   1624

| TYNDALE'S ENGLISH NEW TESTAMENT | CALVIN'S *INSTITUTES* PUBLISHED | FIRST ROANOAK SETTLEMENT | JAMESTOWN, VIRGINIA FOUNDED | DUTCH FOUND NEW NETHERLAND |

Perspectives

This afternoon someone led us to the Indians who live in this neighborhood. We found them in circumstances which made our hearts bleed. The members of our congregation had been there shortly before, and the pitiful sight had filled them likewise with compassion and sorrow.

In this sad mood we assembled for prayers, and God led us to the verse: FOR GOD SO LOVED THE WORLD, etc., John 3:16. We were aroused to thankfulness toward God for the Holy Gospel, especially since we had seen among the Indians what a great pity it is not to have it. At the same time we gained hope that God will continue to show clearly that He loved the world, and still loves it. We were strengthened in the high hope of the 72nd Psalm, which followed in order, that God would show mercy to these poor heathens as He had done to others. We shall pray for them diligently. The counsel of man is very dear in this case, and it will not be easy to help them because their language is said to be extremely difficult to learn....

Mr. Oglethorpe is a man of exceptionally fine qualities. Since it means a great deal to him to bring true knowledge of God to the poor Indians as well, he urged us today to learn their language which has only about one thousand primitive words. Our Saltzburgers have been cautioned very much to refrain from drinking a certain sweet-tasting brandy…because this drink has already brought death to many. Intelligent people who have visited them these days were favorably impressed with their devotion and general deportment. Consequently they predict much good for the land.

— Rev. Samuel Urlsperger

ACKNOWLEDGMENTS

CHAPTER 17
163 TOP: GP (4:178)
BOTTOM: BH (1:340)
164 HR (156)
165 TOP: GP (6:122–23)
BOTTOM: PP (24)
166 AVC
167 HROCH AND SKYBOVÁ, *ECCLESIA MILITANS*
(NY: DORSETT PRESS, 1988), 195
168 LEFT: HR (FRONTPIECE)
RIGHT: AKG
169 TOP: GP (1:88–89)
MIDDLE: GUSTAV KÖNIG, *THE LIFE OF MARTIN LUTHER*
BOTTOM: GP (1:34–35)
170 TOP: HROCH AND SKYBOVÁ, *ECCLESIA MILITANS*
(NY: DORSETT PRESS, 1988), 42
170–171 BOTTOM: HR (48)
171 PP (26)
172 LEFT: LC
RIGHT: AKG
173 GM (5:126)
174 LEFT: BG
RIGHT: BRIDGEMAN ART LIBRARY, LONDON
BOTTOM: BG
175 BG
176 THE TOLEDO MUSEUM OF ART
177 TOP: PP (33)
BOTTOM: ROLAND H. BAINTON,
ERASMUS OF CHRISTENDOM
(NY: CHARLES SCRIBNER'S SONS, 1969), 157
178–179 HR (208–209)
180 TOP: HR (264)
BOTTOM: HR (481)
CHAPTER 18
183 BACKGROUND: HR (220)
FOREGROUND: SWISS NATIONAL MUSEUM, ZÜRICH,
DEPOSITUM OF THE CENTRAL LIBRARY OF ZÜRICH
184 LEFT: HR (341)
RIGHT: GP (2:56)
185 PP (67)
186 RS (115)
187 TR (145)
188 BG
189 LC
190 TR (240)
191 LC
19 J.A. WYLIE, *HISTORY OF PROTESTANTISM*, 2 VOLS.
(LONDON, PARIS, AND NEW YORK: CASSELL, PETER, AND
GALPIN, N.D., 19TH CENTURY), 1:433
193 TOP: RS (130)
BOTTOM: RS (131)
194 TOP: TR (256)
BOTTOM: PP (83)
195 TOP: WYLIE, *HISTORY OF PROTESTANTISM*, 1:438
BOTTOM: AVC

CHAPTER 19
197 BIBLIOTHÈQUE PUBLIQUE ET UNIVERSITAIRE, GENEVA
198 TOP: GM (3:47)
MIDDLE: GM (3:63)
BOTTOM: AVC
199 HR (404)
200 PP (74)
201 TOP: SH (2:646)
BOTTOM: GP (6:55)
202 PP (73)
203 BRIDGEMAN ART LIBRARY, LONDON
204 HR (200)
205 AVC
206 PP (73)
207 BG
208 TOP: PP (238)
208–209 BOTTOM: PP (75)
210 AVC
211 LC
212 TOP: AVC
BOTTOM: INHP
CHAPTER 20
215 AVC
216 HE (2:129)
217 TOP: FOX PHOTOS LIMITED, LONDON: HAMPTON COURT
BOTTOM: GP (2:73)
218 TOP: BG
BOTTOM: AVC
219 HR
220 NPG
221 LEFT: AVC
RIGHT: LC
222 TOP: NPG
BOTTOM: BG
223 GILBERT BURNET, *THE HISTORY OF THE REFORMATION OF
THE CHURCH OF ENGLAND*
(LONDON: RICHARD CHIFWELL, 1679), 1:TITLE PAGE
224 AVC
225 BG
226 NPG
227 TOP: AVC
BOTTOM: HE (2:321)
228 LEFT: AVC
RIGHT: LC
MIDDLE: BG
LOWER, RIGHT: BG
229 TOP: NPG
BOTTOM: BG
230 NATIONAL GALLERY OF SCOTLAND
231 TOP: HE (3:129)
BOTTOM: AVC

LEGEND
AP: *DICTIONARY OF AMERICAN PORTRAITS*
(NY: DOVER, 1967)
AKG: ARTS AND HISTORY PICTURE LIBRARY, LONDON
AVC: AMERICAN VISION COLLECTION
BA: GEORGE BANCROFT, *HISTORY OF THE UNITED
STATES FROM THE DISCOVERY OF THE AMERICAN
CONTINENT*, 10 VOLS. (BOSTON: LITTLE, BROWN,
AND CO., 1856)
BG: BILLY GRAHAM CENTER MUSEUM
BH: WILLIAM CULLEN BRYANT, *A POPULAR HISTORY
OF THE UNITED STATES*, 2 VOLS. (NEW YORK:
CHARLES SCRIBNER'S SONS, 1883)
BK: *BOOK OF KNOWLEDGE*, 20 VOLS. (NY: GROLLIER
SOCIETY, 1927)
CSL: CHARLES CARLETON COFFIN, *THE STORY OF
LIBERTY* (GAINESVILLE, FL: MARANATHA
PUBLICATIONS, 1987)
FB: JOHN FISKE, *THE BEGINNINGS OF NEW
ENGLAND* (BOSTON AND NEW YORK:
HOUGHTON MIFFLIN CO., 1930)
GM: *GREAT MEN AND FAMOUS WOMEN*, 8 VOLS.
(NY: SELMAR HESS, 1894)
GP: CHARLES KNIGHT, *THE GALLERY OF PORTRAITS
WITH MEMOIRS*, 7 VOLS. (LONDON: PALL-MALL
EAST, 1833)
HE: CHARLES KNIGHT, *HISTORY OF ENGLAND*, 8
VOLS. (LONDON: BRADBURY AND EVANS, 1857)
HM: VERNON HEATON, *THE MAYFLOWER* (NEW YORK:
MAYFLOWER BOOKS, 1980)
HR: J.H. MERLE D'AUBIGNÉ, *HISTORY OF THE
REFORMATION IN THE SIXTEENTH CENTURY*
(GLASGOW, EDINBURGH, AND LONDON:
WILLIAM COLLINS, SONS, AND COMPANY, 1871)
INHP: INDEPENDENCE NATIONAL HISTORICAL PARK
LC: LIBRARY OF CONGRESS
ME: MARY EVANS PORTRAIT GALLERY, LONDON
OWW: *OUR WONDER WORLD*, 11 VOLS. (CHICAGO:
GEORGE SHUMAN AND CO., 1923)
NPG: NATIONAL PORTRAIT GALLERY, LONDON
NYPL/
RBMD: RARE BOOKS AND MANUSCRIPTS DIVISION, THE
NEW YORK PUBLIC LIBRARY, ASTOR, LENOX AND
TILDEN FOUNDATIONS
NYPL/
SC: I.N. PHELPS STOKES COLLECTION, MIRIAM AND
IRA D. WALLACH DIVISION OF ART, PRINTS AND
PHOTOGRAPHS, THE NEW YORK PUBLIC LIBRARY,
ASTOR, LENOX AND TILDEN FOUNDATIONS
PE: COURTESY: PEABODY ESSEX MUSEUM, SALEM,
MASS.
PHP: DAGOBERT RUNES, *PICTORIAL HISTORY OF
PHILOSOPHY* (NY: BRAMHALL HOUSE, 1959)
PP: VERGILIUS FERM, *PICTORIAL HISTORY OF
PROTESTANTISM* (NY: PHILOSOPHICAL LIBRARY,
1957)
RIHS: RHODE ISLAND HISTORICAL SOCIETY
RS: A.G. DICKENS, *REFORMATION AND SOCIETY IN
SIXTEENTH-CENTURY EUROPE* (NY: HARCOURT
BRACE JOVANOVICH, INC., 1979)
SGN: EDWARD S. ELLIS AND CHARLES F. HORNE, *THE
STORY OF THE GREATEST NATIONS*, 9 VOLS.
(NEW YORK: FRANCIS R. NIGLUTSCH, 1906)
SH: JOHN RICHARD GREEN, *A SHORT HISTORY OF
THE ENGLISH PEOPLE*, 4 VOLS. (LONDON:
MACMILLAN, 1893)
TR: HANS J. HILLERBRAND, *THE REFORMATION* (NY:
HARPER & ROW, PUBLISHERS, 1964)
USC: UNITED STATES CAPITOL
WH: JUSTIN WINSOR, *NARRATIVE AND CRITICAL
HISTORY OF AMERICA*, 8 VOLS. (BOSTON AND
NY: HOUGHTON, MIFFLIN AND COMPANY, 1884)

LEGEND

AP: *Dictionary of American Portraits* (NY: Dover, 1967)

AKG: Arts and History Picture Library, London

AVC: American Vision Collection

BA: George Bancroft, *History of the United States from the Discovery of the American Continent*, 10 vols. (Boston: Little, Brown, and Co., 1856)

BG: Billy Graham Center Museum

BH: William Cullen Bryant, *A Popular History of the United States*, 2 vols. (New York: Charles Scribner's Sons, 1883)

BK: *Book of Knowledge*, 20 vols. (NY: Grollier Society, 1927)

CSL: Charles Carleton Coffin, *The Story of Liberty* (Gainesville, FL: Maranatha Publications, 1987)

FB: John Fiske, *The Beginnings of New England* (Boston and New York: Houghton Mifflin Co., 1930)

GM: *Great Men and Famous Women*, 8 vols. (NY: Selmar Hess, 1894)

GP: Charles Knight, *The Gallery of Portraits with Memoirs*, 7 vols. (London: Pall-Mall East, 1833)

HE: Charles Knight, *History of England*, 8 vols. (London: Bradbury and Evans, 1857)

HM: Vernon Heaton, *The Mayflower* (New York: Mayflower Books, 1980)

HR: J.H. Merle D'Aubigné, *History of the Reformation in the Sixteenth Century* (Glasgow, Edinburgh, and London: William Collins, Sons, and Company, 1871)

INHP: Independence National Historical Park

LC: Library of Congress

ME: Mary Evans Portrait Gallery, London

OWW: *Our Wonder World*, 11 vols. (Chicago: George Shuman and Co., 1923)

NPG: National Portrait Gallery, London

NYPL/
RBMD: Rare Books and Manuscripts Division, The New York Public Library, Astor, Lenox and Tilden Foundations

NYPL/
SC: I.N. Phelps Stokes Collection, Miriam and Ira D. Wallach Division of Art, Prints and Photographs, The New York Public Library, Astor, Lenox and Tilden Foundations

PE: Courtesy: Peabody Essex Museum, Salem, Mass.

PHP: Dagobert Runes, *Pictorial History of Philosophy* (NY: Bramhall House, 1959)

PP: Vergilius Ferm, *Pictorial History of Protestantism* (NY: Philosophical Library, 1957)

RIHS: Rhode Island Historical Society

RS: A.G. Dickens, *Reformation and Society in Sixteenth-Century Europe* (NY: Harcourt Brace Jovanovich, Inc., 1979)

SGN: Edward S. Ellis and Charles F. Horne, *The Story of the Greatest Nations*, 9 vols. (New York: Francis R. Niglutsch, 1906)

SH: John Richard Green, *A Short History of the English People*, 4 vols. (London: Macmillan, 1893)

TR: Hans J. Hillerbrand, *The Reformation* (NY: Harper & Row, Publishers, 1964)

USC: United States Capitol

WH: Justin Winsor, *Narrative and Critical History of America*, 8 vols. (Boston and NY: Houghton, Mifflin and Company, 1884)

Chapter 25
295 Courtesy: Le Louvre
296 Left: LC
Right: NPG
Bottom: SH (3:1316)
297 SH (3:1116)
298 Top: SH (3:1118)
Bottom: SH (3:1152)
299 SH (3:1325)
300 Top: BH (1:525)
Bottom: Massachusetts State Archives
301 Top: Massachusetts State House Art Collection
Bottom: American Antiquarian Society
302–303 BG
303 Robert G. Athearn, *The American Heritage New Illustrated History of the United States* (New York: Dell Publishing Co., Inc., 1963), 96
304 Clarence P. Hornung, *Handbook of Early Advertising Art* (New York: Dover Publications, Inc., 1956), 200
305 Middle: USC
Bottom: LC
306 BH (1:542)
307 Top: LC
Bottom: FB (141)
308 Top: Courtesy: Dover Publications, Inc., New York, NY
Bottom: Courtesy: Dover Publications, Inc., New York, NY
309 Edgar Newgass, *An Outline of Anglo-American Bible History* (London: B.T. Batsford Ltd, 1958), 15
310 BH (1:535)
311 Edward S. Ellis, *The Story of the Greatest Nations*, 8 vols. (NY: Francis R. Niglutsch, 1901), 8:1531

Chapter 26
313 LC
314 Top: RIHS
Bottom: LC
315 Left: AP
Right: GP (7:15)
316 Top: FB (123)
Bottom: Brandt Aymar and Edward Sagarin, *A Pictorial History of the World's Great Trials* (New York: Crown Publishers, Inc., 1967), 71
317 Courtesy: Museum of Art, Rhode Island School of Design
318 BG
319 Top: WH (4:26)
Bottom: LC
320 Left: HE (3:320–21)
Right: Edward S. Willis, *The Story of the Greatest Nations*, 8 vols. (New York: Francis R. Niglutsch, 1901), 8:1533
321 BH (1:100)
322 BH (1:555)
323 Top: SH (3:1230)
Bottom: BH (1:457)
324 Top: RIHS
Bottom: BH (2:97)
325 Top: AVC
Bottom: RIHS
326 Inset: LC
Bottom: RIHS

Chapter 27
329 Top: BH (2:454)
Bottom: AVC
330 Top: Francis Hill, *A Delusion of Satan* (New York: Doubleday, 1995), 142
Bottom: PE
331 Top: BH (2:457)
Bottom: PE
332 PE
333 Top: Jeffrey B. Russel, *A History of Witchcraft* (London: Thames and Hudson Ltd., 1980), 101
Bottom: LC
334 Top: WH (5:125)
Bottom: LC
335 Top: Massachusetts Historical Society
Bottom: LC
336 Top: LC
Bottom: AP (559)
337 Top: Courtesy, American Antiquarian Society
Bottom: Brandt Aymar and Edward Sagarin, *A Pictorial History of the World's Great Trials* (New York: Crown Publishers, Inc., 1967), 94
338 BH (2:459)

Chapter 28
341 Right: LC
Bottom: WH (3:342)
342 Inset: LC
Bottom: LC
343 Top: SH (3:1204)
Bottom: LC
344 Top: BA (2:Frontpiece)
Middle: LC
Bottom: Wilbur F. Gordy, *A History of the United States* (New York: Charles Scribner's Sons, 1911), 50–51
345 HE (3:386)
346 Top: WH (3:332)
Left: LC
Bottom: BH (2:28–29)
347 NYPL/SC
348 Top: LC
348–349 Bottom: LC
349 BA (2:109)
350 Top: FB (260)
351 Top: Courtesy of Massachusetts State Archives
Inset: BH (2:392)
352 Left: HE (3:320)
Bottom: BH (2:394)
353 HE (4:442)
354 Left: FB (231)
Right: The Henry E. Huntington Library and Art Gallery
355 BA (2:72–73)
356 Left: LC
Right: BG
357 BG

Legend
AP: *Dictionary of American Portraits* (NY: Dover, 1967)
AKG: Arts and History Picture Library, London
AVC: American Vision Collection
BA: George Bancroft, *History of the United States from the Discovery of the American Continent,* 10 vols. (Boston: Little, Brown, and Co., 1856)
BG: Billy Graham Center Museum
BH: William Cullen Bryant, *A Popular History of the United States,* 2 vols. (New York: Charles Scribner's Sons, 1883)
BK: *Book of Knowledge,* 20 vols. (NY: Grollier Society, 1927)
CSL: Charles Carleton Coffin, *The Story of Liberty* (Gainesville, FL: Maranatha Publications, 1987)
FB: John Fiske, *The Beginnings of New England* (Boston and New York: Houghton Mifflin Co., 1930)
GM: *Great Men and Famous Women,* 8 vols. (NY: Selmar Hess, 1894)
GP: Charles Knight, *The Gallery of Portraits with Memoirs,* 7 vols. (London: Pall-Mall East, 1833)
HE: Charles Knight, *History of England,* 8 vols. (London: Bradbury and Evans, 1857)
HM: Vernon Heaton, *The Mayflower* (New York: Mayflower Books, 1980)
HR: J.H. Merle D'Aubigné, *History of the Reformation in the Sixteenth Century* (Glasgow, Edinburgh, and London: William Collins, Sons, and Company, 1871)
INHP: Independence National Historical Park
LC: Library of Congress
ME: Mary Evans Portrait Gallery, London
OWW: *Our Wonder World,* 11 vols. (Chicago: George Shuman and Co., 1923)
NPG: National Portrait Gallery, London
NYPL/
RBMD: Rare Books and Manuscripts Division, The New York Public Library, Astor, Lenox and Tilden Foundations
NYPL/
SC: I.N. Phelps Stokes Collection, Miriam and Ira D. Wallach Division of Art, Prints and Photographs, The New York Public Library, Astor, Lenox and Tilden Foundations
PE: Courtesy: Peabody Essex Museum, Salem, Mass.
PHP: Dagobert Runes, *Pictorial History of Philosophy* (NY: Bramhall House, 1959)
PP: Vergilius Ferm, *Pictorial History of Protestantism* (NY: Philosophical Library, 1957)
RIHS: Rhode Island Historical Society
RS: A.G. Dickens, *Reformation and Society in Sixteenth-Century Europe* (NY: Harcourt Brace Jovanovich, Inc., 1979)
SGN: Edward S. Ellis and Charles F. Horne, *The Story of the Greatest Nations,* 9 vols. (New York: Francis R. Niglutsch, 1906)
SH: John Richard Green, *A Short History of the English People,* 4 vols. (London: Macmillan, 1893)
TR: Hans J. Hillerbrand, *The Reformation* (NY: Harper & Row, Publishers, 1964)
USC: United States Capitol
WH: Justin Winsor, *Narrative and Critical History of America,* 8 vols. (Boston and NY: Houghton, Mifflin and Company, 1884)

LEGEND
AP: *Dictionary of American Portraits* (NY: Dover, 1967)
AKG: Arts and History Picture Library, London
AVC: American Vision Collection
BA: George Bancroft, *History of the United States from the Discovery of the American Continent*, 10 vols. (Boston: Little, Brown, and Co., 1856)
BG: Billy Graham Center Museum
BH: William Cullen Bryant, *A Popular History of the United States*, 2 vols. (New York: Charles Scribner's Sons, 1883)
BK: *Book of Knowledge*, 20 vols. (NY: Grollier Society, 1927)
CSL: Charles Carleton Coffin, *The Story of Liberty* (Gainesville, FL: Maranatha Publications, 1987)
FB: John Fiske, *The Beginnings of New England* (Boston and New York: Houghton Mifflin Co., 1930)
GM: *Great Men and Famous Women*, 8 vols. (NY: Selmar Hess, 1894)
GP: Charles Knight, *The Gallery of Portraits with Memoirs*, 7 vols. (London: Pall-Mall East, 1833)
HE: Charles Knight, *History of England*, 8 vols. (London: Bradbury and Evans, 1857)
HM: Vernon Heaton, *The Mayflower* (New York: Mayflower Books, 1980)
HR: J.H. Merle D'Aubigné, *History of the Reformation in the Sixteenth Century* (Glasgow, Edinburgh, and London: William Collins, Sons, and Company, 1871)
INHP: Independence National Historical Park
LC: Library of Congress
ME: Mary Evans Portrait Gallery, London
OWW: *Our Wonder World*, 11 vols. (Chicago: George Shuman and Co., 1923)
NPG: National Portrait Gallery, London
NYPL/
RBMD: Rare Books and Manuscripts Division, The New York Public Library, Astor, Lenox and Tilden Foundations
NYPL/
SC: I.N. Phelps Stokes Collection, Miriam and Ira D. Wallach Division of Art, Prints and Photographs, The New York Public Library, Astor, Lenox and Tilden Foundations
PE: Courtesy: Peabody Essex Museum, Salem, Mass.
PHP: Dagobert Runes, *Pictorial History of Philosophy* (NY: Bramhall House, 1959)
PP: Vergilius Ferm, *Pictorial History of Protestantism* (NY: Philosophical Library, 1957)
RIHS: Rhode Island Historical Society
RS: A.G. Dickens, *Reformation and Society in Sixteenth-Century Europe* (NY: Harcourt Brace Jovanovich, Inc., 1979)
SGN: Edward S. Ellis and Charles F. Horne, *The Story of the Greatest Nations*, 9 vols. (New York: Francis R. Niglutsch, 1906)
SH: John Richard Green, *A Short History of the English People*, 4 vols. (London: Macmillan, 1893)
TR: Hans J. Hillerbrand, *The Reformation* (NY: Harper & Row, Publishers, 1964)
USC: United States Capitol
WH: Justin Winsor, *Narrative and Critical History of America*, 8 vols. (Boston and NY: Houghton, Mifflin and Company, 1884)

CHAPTER 29
359 LC
360 Top: USC
Bottom: Tate Gallery, London/Art Resource, New York
361 Top: LC
Bottom: LC
362 Top: NYPD/SC
Left: BH (2:267)
Bottom: 362–63: LC
363 Museum of the City of New York
364 LC
365 NYPL/SC
366 Middle: BH (2:Frontpiece)
Bottom: LC
367 Top: BH (2:267–268)
Bottom: Wilbur F. Gordy, *A History of the United States* (New York: Charles Scribner's Sons, 1911), 69
368 Top: AVC
Middle, Left: Gabriel Sivan, *The Bible and Civilization* (New York: Quadrangle/New York Times Book Co., 1973), 237
Middle, Right: Columbia University
Bottom: LC
369 New York Historical Society
371 Left: U.S. Department of State
Right: John Fiske, *A History of the United States* (Boston, New York, and Chicago: Houghton Mifflin Company, 1907), 131
372 Middle: BH (2:321)
Bottom: BH (2:230–31)
373 Left: Henry W. Elson, *United States, Its Past and Present* (New York: American Book Company, 1931), 69
Right: BH (2:476)
Bottom: LC

CHAPTER 30
375 BH (2:486–87)
376 Top: AVC
Bottom, Left: LC
Bottom, Right: BH (2:186–87)
377 LC
378 Ruth West and Willis Mason West, *The Story of Our Country* (NY: Allyn and Bacon, 1926), 106
379 Top: LC
Bottom: Pennsylvania Academy of the Fine Arts, Philadelphia
380 INHP
381 AVC
382 NYPL/SC
383 Top: LC
Bottom: Reproduced Courtesy of the Franklin Collection, Yale University Library
384 INHP
385 Top: WH (3:511)
Bottom: LC
386 Top: AP (686)
Bottom: INHP
387 LC
388 Top: LC
388–389 Bottom: NYPL/SC
389 LC

CHAPTER 31
391 Top: BH (1:487)
Bottom: LC
392 BH (1:262)
393 Top: BH (1:484–85)
Bottom: MHS
394 Top: MHS
Bottom: Enoch Pratt Free Library, Baltimore
395 Top: SH (3:1049)
Bottom: BH (1:493)
396 Top: BH (1:499)
Inset: MHS
Bottom: Maryland State Archives
397 BH (1:509)
398 BH (1:500)
399 BH (1:502)
400 MHS
401 Top: WH (5:262)
Inset: U.S. Geological Survey Photographic Library
Bottom: WH (5:239)

CHAPTER 32
403 LC
404 Top: Virginia Historical Society
Bottom: LC
405 Top: LC
Bottom: BH (2:205)
406 BH (2:203)
407 SH (3:1343)
408 Top: AVC
Bottom: Courtesy, Winterthur Museum
409 Top: AVC
Bottom: BH (2:209)
410 Colonial National Historical Park
411 Left: The Library of Virginia, Richmond
Right: The Library of Virginia, Richmond
412 AVC
413 Marcus L. Loane, *Makers of Religious Freedom in the Seventeenth Century* (Grand Rapids, MI: Wm. B. Eerdmans Publishing Co., 1961), 57
414 Top: SH (3:1352)
Bottom: Virginia Historical Society
415 Left: WH (5:785)
Right: WH (5:279)

CHAPTER 33
417 TOP: NORTH CAROLINA COLLECTION,
UNIVERSITY OF NORTH CAROLINA AT CHAPEL HILL
MIDDLE: BH (2:289)
418 LEFT: NPG
RIGHT: GP (4:11)
BOTTOM: SH (3:1330)
419 GP (5:53)
420 THE SOUTH CAROLINIANA LIBRARY,
UNIVERSITY OF SOUTH CAROLINA
421 TOP: THE EDWARD E. AYER COLLECTION,
THE NEWBERRY LIBRARY
BOTTOM: GIBBES MUSEUM OF ART, CHARLESTON, SC
422 LC
423 WH (5:330)
424 LEFT: THE SOUTH CAROLINIANA LIBRARY,
UNIVERSITY OF SOUTH CAROLINA
RIGHT: GIBBES MUSEUM OF ART, CHARLESTON, SC
425 TOP: HE (5:FRONTPIECE)
BOTTOM: EDGAR E. AYER COLLECTION,
THE NEWBERRY LIBRARY
426 TOP: NORTH CAROLINA COLLECTION,
UNIVERSITY OF NORTH CAROLINA AT CHAPEL HILL
426–427 BOTTOM: NYPL/SC
427 TOP THREE: LC
CHAPTER 34
429 BH (1:206–67)
430 TOP, LEFT: GHS
TOP, RIGHT: LC
BOTTOM: HE (5:328–29)
431 TOP: OGLETHORPE UNIVERSITY
BOTTOM: COURTESY,
THE HENRY FRANCIS DU PONT WINTERTHUR MUSEUM
432 TOP: GHS
BOTTOM: METHODIST ARCHIVE CENTER, MADISON, NJ,
PHOTOGRAPHER:GEORGE GOODWIN
433 LEFT: NYPL/RBMD
RIGHT GHS
434 TOP: NPG
BOTTOM: NPG
435 TOP: GHS
BOTTOM: GHS
436 TOP: LC
436–37 BOTTOM: COPYRIGHT 1996 JACKSON WALKER
438 TOP: COURTESY, GEORGIA DEPARTMENT OF
ARCHIVES AND HISTORY
BOTTOM: BH (3:448–49)

EVERY EFFORT HAS BEEN MADE TO CONTACT THE HOLDERS OF
COPYRIGHT MATERIAL, BUT IF ANY HAVE BEEN INADVERTENTLY
OVERLOOKED, THE PUBLISHERS WILL BE PLEASED TO MAKE ANY
NECESSARY AMENDMENTS.

LEGEND
AP: DICTIONARY OF AMERICAN PORTRAITS
(NY: DOVER, 1967)
AKG: ARTS AND HISTORY PICTURE LIBRARY, LONDON
AVC: AMERICAN VISION COLLECTION
BA: GEORGE BANCROFT, HISTORY OF THE UNITED
STATES FROM THE DISCOVERY OF THE AMERICAN
CONTINENT, 10 VOLS. (BOSTON: LITTLE, BROWN,
AND CO., 1856)
BG: BILLY GRAHAM CENTER MUSEUM
BH: WILLIAM CULLEN BRYANT, A POPULAR HISTORY
OF THE UNITED STATES, 2 VOLS. (NEW YORK:
CHARLES SCRIBNER'S SONS, 1883)
BK: BOOK OF KNOWLEDGE, 20 VOLS. (NY: GROLLIER
SOCIETY, 1927)
CSL: CHARLES CARLETON COFFIN, THE STORY OF
LIBERTY (GAINESVILLE, FL: MARANATHA
PUBLICATIONS, 1987)
FB: JOHN FISKE, THE BEGINNINGS OF NEW
ENGLAND (BOSTON AND NEW YORK:
HOUGHTON MIFFLIN CO., 1930)
GM: GREAT MEN AND FAMOUS WOMEN, 8 VOLS.
(NY: SELMAR HESS, 1894)
GP: CHARLES KNIGHT, THE GALLERY OF PORTRAITS
WITH MEMOIRS, 7 VOLS. (LONDON: PALL-MALL
EAST, 1833)
HE: CHARLES KNIGHT, HISTORY OF ENGLAND, 8
VOLS. (LONDON: BRADBURY AND EVANS, 1857)
HM: VERNON HEATON, THE MAYFLOWER (NEW YORK:
MAYFLOWER BOOKS, 1980)
HR: J.H. MERLE D'AUBIGNÉ, HISTORY OF THE
REFORMATION IN THE SIXTEENTH CENTURY
(GLASGOW, EDINBURGH, AND LONDON:
WILLIAM COLLINS, SONS, AND COMPANY, 1871)
INHP: INDEPENDENCE NATIONAL HISTORICAL PARK
LC: LIBRARY OF CONGRESS
ME: MARY EVANS PORTRAIT GALLERY, LONDON
OWW: OUR WONDER WORLD, 11 VOLS. (CHICAGO:
GEORGE SHUMAN AND CO., 1923)
NPG: NATIONAL PORTRAIT GALLERY, LONDON
NYPL/
RBMD: RARE BOOKS AND MANUSCRIPTS DIVISION, THE
NEW YORK PUBLIC LIBRARY, ASTOR, LENOX AND
TILDEN FOUNDATIONS
NYPL/
SC: I.N. PHELPS STOKES COLLECTION, MIRIAM AND
IRA D. WALLACH DIVISION OF ART, PRINTS AND
PHOTOGRAPHS, THE NEW YORK PUBLIC LIBRARY,
ASTOR, LENOX AND TILDEN FOUNDATIONS
PE: COURTESY: PEABODY ESSEX MUSEUM, SALEM,
MASS.
PHP: DAGOBERT RUNES, PICTORIAL HISTORY OF
PHILOSOPHY (NY: BRAMHALL HOUSE, 1959)
PP: VERGILIUS FERM, PICTORIAL HISTORY OF
PROTESTANTISM (NY: PHILOSOPHICAL LIBRARY,
1957)
RIHS: RHODE ISLAND HISTORICAL SOCIETY
RS: A.G. DICKENS, REFORMATION AND SOCIETY IN
SIXTEENTH-CENTURY EUROPE (NY: HARCOURT
BRACE JOVANOVICH, INC., 1979)
SGN: EDWARD S. ELLIS AND CHARLES F. HORNE, THE
STORY OF THE GREATEST NATIONS, 9 VOLS.
(NEW YORK: FRANCIS R. NIGLUTSCH, 1906)
SH: JOHN RICHARD GREEN, A SHORT HISTORY OF
THE ENGLISH PEOPLE, 4 VOLS. (LONDON:
MACMILLAN, 1893)
TR: HANS J. HILLERBRAND, THE REFORMATION (NY:
HARPER & ROW, PUBLISHERS, 1964)
USC: UNITED STATES CAPITOL
WH: JUSTIN WINSOR, NARRATIVE AND CRITICAL
HISTORY OF AMERICA, 8 VOLS. (BOSTON AND
NY: HOUGHTON, MIFFLIN AND COMPANY, 1884)

GLOSSARY

allegiance: loyalty to a sovereign, nation, or cause

altar: any elevated structure upon which sacrifices may be offered

Anabaptism: a radical movement that maintained that the Reformation did not go far enough; rejected the idea that children were included in God's covenant promises and called for the *rebaptism* of adults baptized as infants; shunned all politics, refused to bear arms, and did not wish to reform the church but to restore it to the days of the New Testament

anarchist: a person who advocates anarchy, that is, who seeks to overturn by violence all legitimate forms and institutions of society and government, with no purpose of establishing any other system of order in the place of what is destroyed

anarchy: absence of any political authority; political disorder

Anglicanism: of the Anglican Church (the Church of England, or the Protestant Episcopalian Church)

annul: to declare void or invalid

antichrist: someone who denies that Jesus has come in the flesh (1 JOHN 4:3); an adversary of Christ (Protestant theologians of several centuries believed this adversary to be the pope)

antinomianism: the idea that, under the gospel, the law of God is of no use or obligation, and that good works and a virtuous life are no longer necessary

apparition: a ghost

arbitrary: determined by whim or impulse, not by reason or law

archbishop: a bishop of the highest rank

Archbishop of Canterbury: the highest church official of the Anglican Church

aristocracy: a hereditary privileged ruling class or nobility

artisan: a person skilled in making a particular product; a craftsman

authoritarian: requiring absolute obedience to authority

barony: the domain of a baron

barrister: a lawyer

Bay Psalm Book: a collection of Psalms written in verse for congregational singing published in Puritan Massachusetts

Book of Common Prayer: the book which the Anglican Church uses as its order of worship

burgess: a representative in the popular branch of the colonial legislature of Virginia or Maryland

Calvinism: the beliefs and practices taught by John Calvin, who emphasized the trinity, the sovereignty of God, the authority of the Scriptures, the total depravity of fallen man, justification by free and irresistible grace, predestination, perseverance of the saints, Presbyterian church government, and strict church discipline

canton: a small territorial unit, especially one of the states of the Swiss confederation

cardinal: in the Roman Catholic Church, a church official whose authority is just below the pope

cartography: map-making

catechism: book of religious instruction written in question-and-answer format

catholic: universal

Cavaliers: courtly gentlemen; supporters of King Charles I of England

centralization: concentration of power in a central government

charter: an official document granting certain rights and privileges

chattel slavery: a type of slavery whereby the slave becomes the master's personal property

checks and balances: the system of government whereby one branch of government serves to restrain another

clergy: the body of people ordained for religious service; ministers

common law: the system of laws developed in England and derived from common usage and custom

commonwealth: a nation or state founded on law and united by compact or tacit agreement of the people for the common good; a state in which the supreme authority is vested in the people; a republic

commune: a small community whose members have common interests and in which property is shared or owned jointly

communism: a social system in which production and goods are commonly owned and controlled by the state

common school: public school

compact: an agreement or covenant

compulsory: mandatory; required

confederation: a political alliance of persons, parties, or states

congregational: a kind of church government in which local churches have no formal, governing ties with one other (each church establishes its own government)

conquistador: a conqueror, especially a 16th century Spanish conqueror of Mexico and Peru

constitution: the fundamental laws of an institution or government

contraband: goods barred from import or export; smuggled goods

coronation: the crowning of a monarch

covenant: a binding agreement; a compact

democratic: pertaining to government by the people

depose: to remove from office

dialect: a regional form of a language

diplomacy: the practice or art of conducting negotiations

disenfranchise: to deprive of a legal right or privilege, especially of the right to vote

dispensation: (as in papal dispensation): an exemption or release from an obligation or rule granted by an authority

disputation: a debate, an argument

dissenter: one who disagrees; a religious nonconformist

doctrine: something that is taught; a body of principles

Dominion of New England: a union of New England and some Middle Atlantic colonies under the rule of a royal governor, Sir Edmund Andros, 1686-1689, forced upon the colonies by the English king

double jeopardy: trying a person twice for the same crime

dysentery: an infection of the lower intestines

ecclesiastical: of or relating to a church

ecclesiology: church government; church architecture or decoration

episcopal: a kind of church government where local churches are bound together by a top-down hierarchy headed by bishops; *examples:* the Anglican Church and the Roman Catholic Church

ethics: a system of moral values

excommunication: a formal church censure that deprives a person of the right of church membership

executive: the branch of government responsible for putting political laws into effect

exhume: to remove from a grave

expedient: serving to promote a person's interest

feudalism: a medieval political and economic system based on the relation of lord to vassal held on condition of homage and service

flax: a plant with seeds that yield linseed oil and slender stems from which a fine textile fiber is derived

freeman: a person who possesses land; a person who possesses all the rights and privileges of a citizen

gangrene: death and decay of tissue in a part of the body, usually a limb, due to failure of blood supply, injury, or disease

gentry: social rank of an individual born into a prominent family

girdling: making a ring around a tree by cutting through the bark, thus causing the tree to die

Glorious Revolution: the "bloodless revolution" of 1688 in which the Roman Catholic King James II of England was deposed and replaced by the Protestant monarchs William and Mary

Half-Way Covenant: the compromise made by many New England churches to allow people to become "half-way" members if they could not profess a conversion experience

hemp: a plant whose stems yield a fiber used to make rope

heresy: an opinion or doctrine in conflict with orthodox religious beliefs

heretic: a person under any religion, but especially the Christian religion, who holds and teaches opinions repugnant to the established faith; among Christians, a person who holds and avows religious opinions contrary to the doctrines of Scripture, the only rule of faith and practice

hierarchy: an authoritative body, especially of clergy, organized according to rank

hornbook: an early primer consisting of a single page protected by a transparent sheet of horn

House of Burgesses: the first legislative assembly of Virginia; the lower house of Virginia's legislature

House of Commons: the lower house of Parliament in England

House of Lords: the upper house of Parliament in England, made up of members of the nobility and high-ranking clergy

Huguenots: French Protestants

hull: the frame or body of a ship, excluding masts, sails, and rigging

humanitarian: a person who is devoted to the promotion of human welfare and social reforms

idealism: the practice of envisioning things in perfect form

immunity: not affected or responsive; resistance to a specific disease

incentive: something which incites a person to action or effort

incriminate: to charge with a crime or fault

indenture: a contract obligating one person to work for another for a specified period of time

indentured servant: a person who owes a debt but, since he cannot pay it back with money, must work for a specific time in order to pay off his obligation

indigo: a blue dye obtained from a plant

indulgence: in the Roman Catholic Church, remission of the punishment due to sins, granted by the pope or church, and supposed to save the sinner from purgatory; absolution from the censures of the church and from all transgressions

infallible: incapable of error

infidel: one who disbelieves or opposes Christianity

Islam: a religion based upon the teachings of Mohammed, believing in one god called Allah, and believing in the body of literature put forth in the Koran (Qur'an) and the Sunna; the followers of Islam are called Moslems

isthmus: a narrow strip of land connecting two larger land masses

joint stock company: an investment company in which members buy shares

judicial: of or relating to courts of law or the administration of justice

jurisdiction: the right or power to interpret and apply the law

justification: the condition of being freed from the guilt and penalty of sin

legislative: having the power to create laws

legislature: an officially selected body of persons with the power and responsibility to make and change laws

libertine: a member of a religious sect that emphasized reliance on the Holy Spirit while ignoring God's law; a morally unrestrained person

Lollards: a group of English Reformers who were followers of John Wycliffe

Lutheranism: of or relating to Martin Luther or his religious teachings and especially to the doctrine of justification by faith alone

magistrate: a civil officer with power to administer and enforce law

magnum opus: a great work, especially a literary or artistic masterpiece

malcontent: unhappy with existing circumstances

manor: the estate of a medieval lord; the lord's residence

Mass: in Roman Catholic churches, the celebration of the sacrament of the Lord's Supper

maverick: a person who refuses to abide by the policies or views of a group; a dissenter

mediator: a person who resolves or settles differences by acting as an intermediary agent between two or more parties

medieval: pertaining to the Middle Ages (c. 500-1500)

Mennonites: members of an Anabaptist Christian sect opposed to taking oaths, holding public office, or performing military service; followers of 16th-century Reformer Menno Simons

mercenary: a professional soldier hired for service by a foreign country

militant: having an aggressive, combative character

militia: a citizen army as distinct from a body of professional soldiers

Moslem: a believer in Islam; a follower of Mohammed

monastery: the dwelling place of a community of persons under religious vows, especially monks

monopoly: exclusive control by one group of the means of producing or selling a commodity or service

mugwump: an Algonquian word for "chief"; a person who acts independently, especially in politics

Muslim: alternative spelling of Moslem

mutiny: v. to commit open rebellion against lawful authority

National Covenant: the document drafted by the Scottish government in 1638, asserting that Scotland's religious and civil rights were independent from England

nationalism: devotion to the interests or culture of a particular nation

natural law: laws believed to be "self-evident" from observing the natural world

nonconformist: a person who does not conform to the mode of worship of an established church

omission: something that is left out or neglected

orthodox: adhering to established or traditional beliefs, especially in religion

pacifism: opposition to war or violence

papacy: the jurisdiction and office of a pope

papist: a Roman Catholic (usually used disparagingly)

parliament: a representative legislature

parochial: relating to a church parish

pastorate: the office or jurisdiction of a pastor

patent: a grant made by a government to a person giving him possession of public lands

patroon: a landowner under Dutch colonial rule

patroonship: a large estate in the Netherlands or in New Netherland

peasant: an agricultural laborer or small farmer

penance: according to Roman Catholic doctrine, an act of self-humiliation to show sorrow for sin and receive forgiveness

pestilent: deadly, harmful

Pilgrims: that group of Separatists who left England and eventually traveled to Plymouth, Massachusetts, in 1620, to establish a Christian commonwealth

pillory: n. a wooden frame with holes, in which the head and hands were locked as public punishment; v. to expose to public ridicule

plantation: a transplant of whole households into a newly established settlement; an estate or farm which is tended by resident labor

polygamy: the state of having more than one wife or husband at one time

pope: the Bishop of Rome and head of the Roman Catholic Church

popery: the doctrines, practices, and rituals of the Roman Catholic Church (used in a hostile sense)

predestination: the act whereby God foreordained all things

presbyterian: a kind of church government in which local churches are ruled by elders who represent them at regional government meetings called presbyteries and at national meetings called general assemblies; presbyterian churches are most commonly associated with the Reformed faith

primer: a first reader

privateer: a privately owned ship commissioned during wartime to capture enemy ships

prohibit: to forbid by law

propagation: the act of increasing or spreading something such as a faith

proprietary: privately owned

proprietor: a person who has legal title to something; an owner

Protestant: a Christian who belongs to the part of the Church that broke from the Roman Catholic Church at the time of the Reformation

providence: God's care, guardianship, and control

purgatory: according to Roman Catholic doctrine, an intermediate state between heaven and hell in which the souls of those who have died must atone for their sins (be "purged") before going to heaven

Puritans: members of a 16th and 17th century Protestant group that opposed the elaborate ceremonies of the Church of England and embraced the Reformed (Calvinistic) faith

puritanical: marked by stern morality

Quakers: members of the Society of Friends who embraced pacifism and the belief that every person possessed an "Inner Light," the voice of God speaking directly to their spirits

recant: to make a formal denial of an earlier statement

radical Reformers: another name for Anabaptists

Reformation: the 16th-century European movement that resulted in the separation of the Protestant Church from the Roman Catholic Church

Reformed faith: the Protestant Christian religion taught by such theologians as Luther, Calvin, and Zwingli which emphasizes such doctrines as *sola fide* (salvation is obtained through faith in Christ alone) and *sola Scriptura* (the standard for faith and practice is Scripture alone)

relic: an object esteemed and venerated because of its association with a saint or martyr

Renaissance: that era of European history roughly from the 14th through the 16th centuries and which was marked by a return to classical literature, art, and philosophy

repudiate: to reject as invalid or untrue

Restoration: that era of English history which began with the return of Charles II to the English throne in 1660

retaliatory: intended to pay back evil for evil

Roman Catholic Church: the church whose headquarters is in Rome and which has a hierarchical structure of priests and bishops with the pope (the Bishop of Rome) at its head

Roundheads: supporters of the Puritan Parliament during the English Civil War (so named because of the close-cropped hair of the Puritans)

royalties: a payment to an inventor or proprietor for the right to use his invention or services

rubber-stamp: to endorse, vote for, or approve without question or deliberation

sacrament: a Christian ceremony, baptism or the Lord's Supper, instituted by God as a means of grace

scapegoat: a person bearing blame for others

scurvy: a disease caused by deficiency of vitamin C

sedition: behavior or language that brings about rebellion against established authority

seigniory: the domain, or feudal estate, of a lord

seizure: a sudden convulsion

Separatist: one who withdraws from an established church

Septuagint: a Greek translation of the Old Testament; also written as LXX

serf: a slave

sola Christo: Latin for "Christ alone"

sola Deo gloria: Latin for "all glory be to God"

sola fide: Latin for "faith alone"

sola gratia: Latin for "grace alone"

sola Scriptura: Latin for "the Bible alone"

Solemn League and Covenant: that document drafted by the Scottish government in 1643 which preserved Presbyterianism in Scotland and proposed to spread the Reformed faith throughout England and Ireland as well

sovereignty: supremacy of rule or authority

stadholder: the governor of the Netherlands

stockholder: a person who owns a share or shares of stock in a company

subsequent: following in time or order

supererogation: the performance of more than is required, demanded, or expected

tenet: an opinion, doctrine, or principle

Tidewater colonists: in Virginia, those colonists that lived along the coast

transubstantiation: according to Roman Catholicism, the doctrine that the bread and wine of the Lord's Supper are transformed into the literal body and blood of Christ

triangular trade: the three-way trade of rum, slaves and sugar that existed between New England, Africa, and the West Indies

tribute: tax

trustee: a member of a board that directs the funds and policy of an institution or territory

unconsecrated: according to Roman Catholicism, the elements of the Lord's Supper before transubstantiation

unregenerate: not renewed in heart; remaining at enmity with God

utopia: an ideally perfect place; an impractical concept for social reform

vocation: one's calling, employment, or occupation, from the Latin vocare, "to call"

Walloons: people who speak French dialect of southern Belgium and adjacent regions of France

West Indies: islands between southeast North America and northern South America, separating the Caribbean and the Atlantic

Westminster Catechism: the Larger and Shorter Catechisms published in 1648 by the Westminster Assembly of theologians. The catechisms, together with the Westminster Confession of Faith, were drafted in order to describe the tenets of the Reformed faith in all areas of faith and practice. The Shorter Catechism was intended to instruct children and people "of weaker capacity."

INDEX Side bar page references are shown in **bold face.**